Women
Twentieth-Century
Italy

Gender and History

Series editors: Amanda Capern and Louella McCarthy

Published

Ann Taylor Allen
WOMEN IN TWENTIETH-CENTURY EUROPE

Trev Lynn Broughton and Helen Rogers (eds)
GENDER AND FATHERHOOD IN THE NINETEENTH CENTURY

Shani D'Cruze and Louise A. Jackson
WOMEN, CRIME AND JUSTICE IN ENGLAND SINCE 1660

Rachel G. Fuchs and Victoria E. Thompson
WOMEN IN NINETEENTH-CENTURY EUROPE

Perry Willson
WOMEN IN TWENTIETH-CENTURY ITALY

Angela Woollacott
GENDER AND EMPIRE

Forthcoming

Paul Bailey
WOMEN AND GENDER IN TWENTIETH-CENTURY CHINA

William Foster
GENDER, MASTERY AND SLAVERY: FROM EUROPEANS TO ATLANTIC
WORLD FRONTIERS

Laurence Lux-Sterritt and Carmen Mangion (eds)
GENDER, CATHOLICISM AND SPIRITUALITY: WOMEN AND THE ROMAN
CATHOLIC CHURCH IN BRITAIN AND EUROPE, 1200–1900

Gender and History Series
Series Standing Order ISBN 978–14039–9374–8 hardback
ISBN 1–4039–9375–0 paperback
(Outside North America only)

You can receive future titles in this series as they are published by placing a standing order. Please contact your bookseller or, in case of difficulty, write to us at the address below with your name and address, the title of the series and the ISBN quoted above.

Customer Service Department, Macmillan Distribution Ltd
Houndmills, Basingstoke, Hampshire RG21 6XS, England

Women in Twentieth-Century Italy

Perry Willson

First published 2010 by
PALGRAVE MACMILLAN

Palgrave Macmillan in the UK is an imprint of Macmillan Publishers Limited,
registered in England, company number 785998, of Houndmills, Basingstoke,
Hampshire RG21 6XS.

Palgrave Macmillan in the US is a division of St Martin's Press LLC,
175 Fifth Avenue, New York, NY 10010.

Palgrave Macmillan is the global academic imprint of the above companies and has
companies and representatives throughout the world.

Palgrave® and Macmillan® are registered trademarks in the United States,
the United Kingdom, Europe and other countries

ISBN-13: 978–1–4039–9517–9   hardback
ISBN-13: 978–1–4039–9518–6   paperback

This book is printed on paper suitable for recycling and made from fully managed and
sustained forest sources. Logging, pulping and manufacturing processes are expected to
conform to the environmental regulations of the country of origin.

A catalogue record for this book is available from the British Library.

A catalog record for this book is available from the Library of Congress.

10   9   8   7   6   5   4   3   2   1
19 18 17 16 15 14 13 12 11 10

Printed and bound in China

Contents

List of Illustrations and Tables

Illustrations

Tables

Glossary

biennio rosso   red two years (1919–20)
bracciante/i   landless farm-labourer(s)
capoccia   male head of a peasant household
confino   internal exile
consultorio   health clinic
differenza sessuale   sexual difference
ginnasio   middle school
liceo   grammar school
madrine di guerra   war godmothers (women who corresponded with soldiers as a form of welfare)
maternage   mothering
patria   nation, motherland
patria potestas   father's authority over children
promessa   engagement (literally – promise)
reggitrice   most powerful female in a peasant household
repubblichini   supporters of the Republic of Salò, 1943–5
ruota   wheel (of foundlings' home)
sansepolcrista   person present at the founding meeting of the Fascist movement in 1919
sifilicomio   venereal disease clinic
squadrista   Fascist thug during the rise of Fascism
stafetta/e   Resistance courier(s)
udina/e   member(s) of UDI
uguaglianza   equality, sameness
ventennio   twenty years (of Fascist rule)

Acknowledgements

Invaluable in the completion of this book was the help of Lynn Abrams, Stefania Bartoloni, Maria Casalini, Paola Filippucci, Penny Morris, Maura Palazzi, Anna Rossi-Doria, Jane Slaughter and Simonetta Soldani, all of whom most generously read chapters for me and provided many stimulating comments. I am particularly indebted to Lynette McCafferty for her unfailing encouragement and for her helpful comments on the final draft. Thanks are also due to Laura Gasparini of the Biblioteca Panizzi in Reggio Emilia for her kind assistance with the illustrative material. I should also like to acknowledge the assistance of IASH at Edinburgh University and Nuffield College, Oxford, which both offered me study facilities; the staff of the Biblioteca Nazionale in Florence; and the Arts and Humanities Research Council, which funded some research leave during which much of this was written. Terka Acton, Sonya Barker and Felicity Noble at Palgrave Macmillan all provided speedy and helpful replies to my queries on many occasions. Finally, but far from least important, I would like to thank all my female friends in Italy (and a few males) for many interesting discussions over the years about gender relations both past and present, some of which have found their way into the pages of this book.

Chapter 5, 'Doing their Duty for Nation (or Church): Mass Mobilisation during the Fascist *Ventennio*', is partly based on an article by the author entitled 'Italy' which was first published in Kevin Passmore (ed.), *Women, Gender and Fascism in Europe, 1919–1945* (Manchester University Press and Rutgers University Press, 2003), pp. 11–32.

Introduction

The lives of Italian women were transformed over the course of the twentieth century. Gender disparities in both the public and private spheres diminished, family size grew smaller and female education improved dramatically. Feminist movements of various kinds were active, women voted for the first time and there were important legislative reforms. Women's dreams and aspirations were increasingly fuelled by the printed word and the spread of radio, film and television. Modes of dress and housework were transformed. All such trends, of course, were similarly evident in other European countries in this period but, in Italy, the pattern, timing and speed of gender change were also marked by aspects that were peculiarly Italian. Here, economic growth came later than in northern Europe and, when it did, its dramatic pace produced, in many ways, a society that was a particular mix of modernity and tradition. Moreover, this period of Italian history included two decades of Fascist rule that marked the nation deeply, creating a legacy that was hard to cast aside. The influence of the Catholic Church was matched in few other European countries. Another trend specific to Italy (albeit shared with other southern European nations) is the fact that, despite plummeting birth rates and the introduction of divorce, the institutions of both marriage and the family continued to be cornerstones of society right up to the very end of the century.

Gender and women's history are now well established in the English-speaking world. This process is taking a little longer in Italy. Only a few years ago it would have been possible to fairly quickly read the entire corpus of secondary work published on anything to do with Italian women's history of the last century. Today, however, this is no longer true and the wealth of scholarly works which appear in my endnotes demonstrates that this field of Italian historical endeavour is now thriving, although it remains somewhat uneven with clusters of publications on certain topics and little on others of great importance.[1] Despite the richness and dynamism of this recent crop of research, there have been only limited attempts at synthesis. Italian historians of women have mainly published on fairly narrowly defined topics. The recent upsurge in research, however, means that the time is now ripe for historians to step back a little and reflect on the broader picture. Moreover, what works of synthesis do exist, are all written in Italian, with the result that, in the English-speaking world, the history of modern Italian women has not received much attention. This history is, however, a truly fascinating one that deserves to be better known.

This collective biography of the female half of the Italian population explores how political, social, economic, legal and cultural changes shaped gender roles in Italy. It also looks at how women were affected by, and how they themselves helped mould, key events such as the rise of Fascism, the two world wars, the 'economic miracle', the cultural and political upheavals of the 1970s and so on. Of course, the cadences of gender history are often at odds with the periodisation that seems appropriate for other sorts of historical writing but I selected a (perhaps somewhat unfashionable) primarily chronological format after considerable deliberation. This was partly because the works of synthesis that do exist in this field have a thematic structure[2] and I preferred to do something different, in the hope of enriching and challenging what has been written, rather than covering similar ground. A chronological approach, moreover, can shed much light on continuities and change over time. I also chose this structure because, even though I consider myself primarily a social historian, I believe that, in this particular hundred years of women's history, politics did matter. As Simonetta Soldani, an authoritative voice in Italian women's history, recently argued, the thematic approach of most works of synthesis in modern Italian women's history has tended to obscure the importance of the political dimension.[3] For the twentieth century there is a strong argument for the usefulness of a chronological approach as this was, par excellence, 'the century of politics' (as the Italian Female Historians' Association entitled their annual summer school when they turned to this period for the first time, in 1995). In this hundred years, more than in earlier times, politics was an important force for change in gender relations (although, obviously, far from the only one). There were, for example, huge changes in family law, which were driven by political lobbying. This was also the century when women really moved into the political sphere for the first time, forming political organisations, acquiring suffrage rights and standing for political office. Women's political organisations, whether party-political or not, were instrumental in putting women's point of view forward (albeit with varying degrees of effectiveness).

Politics is, however, far from the whole story and I have also devoted a good deal of space to social, cultural and economic aspects. Indeed, in twentieth-century Italy, political change for women was as much a product of, as it was a shaper of other changes. This is partly due to the weaknesses of the Italian political system and of women's place in it but also due to the sheer dimension and pace of other types of change in this period. Thus, although these pages teem with political organisations, laws, elections and pioneering parliamentarians, there is much else too.

Unfortunately, the constraints of space in this relatively short volume have rendered it difficult to fully explore the great regional variations that existed in twentieth-century Italy. I have discussed this where possible, as many aspects of women's lives were shaped by the many cultural, economic, social and political peculiarities of Italy's different regions. Only a much bigger book, however, would be able to do true justice to this aspect.

The inherent difficulties in understanding, even less explaining, the history of gender relations in a society as complex and contradictory as that of Italy are hard to overestimate. The fact that I am a foreigner who does not live in Italy (but who has spent extensive periods of time there) may mean that I have failed to understand some things that an Italian would take for granted. I hope, nonetheless, that it has also given me insights that might not be obvious to Italians themselves.

1
Italian Women at the Dawn of the Twentieth Century

In his 1902 survey of the growing numbers of women graduates in Italy, Vittorio Ravà described them as, 'a strong and numerous phalanx . . . that is advancing and preparing to fight economic and social battles'.[1] Ravà was far from the only observer at the time to sense change in the air for Italian women. At the dawn of the twentieth century, education for girls was increasing and a few women were making their mark in the public sphere in professions like teaching, writing and medicine. Middle- and upper-class women were beginning to venture more beyond the home. A small, but determined and far from insignificant, feminist movement was campaigning for legal reform and attempting to challenge, or at least rethink, some of the prevailing ideas about the role of women in society.

This period was also one of broad changes which affected many women, including those beyond the educated elite. The final decade of the nineteenth century saw rapid industrial growth in parts of the North, which served to accelerate the rural–urban shift. The birth rate was beginning to fall in some areas. Life expectancy was on the rise as mortality rates fell steadily[2] and, despite the fact that Italy had Europe's highest emigration rate, the population was increasing (25 million in 1861, 33 million in 1901 and 37 million in 1921).[3] A new and vigorous, if divided and quarrelsome, socialist movement was active in many parts of both urban and rural Italy. The primacy of the Catholic Church in defining social and moral values was being challenged by a group of new social scientists.

Change, however, was uneven and, for millions of women, limited. Even Ravà's survey found only 224 women who had actually graduated from the universities of the unified state by 1900. Gender divisions were still wide and the sexes led very different and often separate existences. The legal, economic and social status of women was in many respects inferior to that of men. Excluded on the grounds of their sex from voting or holding public office, and lacking, particularly if married, many legal rights accorded to men, Italian women were not yet active citizens.

Women's lives were shaped by the fact that Italy was still a very regionally-based society, with a weak sense of national identity and a poorly functioning and only partly democratic political system. Economic development varied greatly from region to region as did social customs and cultural beliefs. Everywhere there were great inequalities of wealth and yawning social divides. The peasantry, most of whom led lives characterised by extreme poverty, was the largest occupational group. Despite the antagonism between Church and state created by national unification, the Catholic Church continued to exert great influence on society, particularly on moral questions relating to the family, sexuality and gender roles.

A belief in the inferiority of women was widespread. Many thought of women as weak, emotional beings little suited to interaction with the harsh, outside world. There was much emphasis on women's sexual conduct. In southern Italy (but also, to an extent, in parts of the rural North), the concept of 'honour' was extremely important. In the 'honour code', the social prestige of a family, particularly the male members of the family, could be damaged by the 'sexual immorality' of their female relatives. This moral code condoned the killing, by fathers, husbands and brothers, of women who had transgressed sexually. An unmarried woman who was known to have lost her virginity was seen as evidence of the weakness of her male relatives, proof of their inability to protect or control her properly. In this system, 'reparatory marriage' could restore a family's honour and this potentially might include forcing a woman to marry her rapist. Although the honour code placed great emphasis on the virginity of unmarried women and the fidelity of wives, and essentially saw female sexuality as bad, it differed from Catholic morality. As Margherita Pelaia has noted, the difference lay, 'above all in the emphasis on the external dimension of reputation rather than the internal one of conscience, and in the violence of the sexual double standard, the huge gulf between the male prerogative of sexual conquest and women's obligation to remain chaste and pure'.[4] The Catholic Church, instead, saw all sexual pleasure, for either sex, as potentially sinful. There was, moreover, no room in the honour code for the cleansing effects of repentance and pardon.

Virtually all Italians were at least nominally Catholic and, for the vast majority, religious belief and religious practice were important aspects of everyday life. Despite the intense dispute between Church and state that had followed unification and the rise of the (mostly anti-religious) socialist movement, the Church was still a powerful force in society. The influence of the clergy, through sermons and the confessional, was, moreover, greatly enhanced by high levels of illiteracy which gave them a near monopoly on information for some sections of the population, particularly women and the peasantry.

The Church vehemently opposed divorce, saw men as inherently superior and believed that gender inequality in marriage was essential for it to work on a day-to-day basis. It saw women's primary role as motherhood and opposed female emancipation and extra-domestic employment. The most comprehensive spelling out of the Vatican's views on marriage and the family came with the Papal Encyclical *Casti Connubi* in 1930 but such ideas can also be found in various other late nineteenth-century papal pronouncements. According to *Casti Connubi*, married couples were meant to love each other but only in the context of accepting a clear gender hierarchy in the family. The encyclical spoke of the 'primacy of the husband with regard to the wife and children and the ready subjection of the wife and her willing obedience'. Female emancipation was dismissed as 'false liberty and unnatural equality with the husband'.[5]

It would be wrong, of course, to simply see the Church's attitude as timeless and immutable, for even the Church itself was changing. The cult of maternity, particularly the virginal maternity of the Marian cult, was especially strong at this time and increasing numbers of female saints were being created, such as Rita da Cascia, canonised by Leo XIII in 1900. All this had the potential to enhance the appeal of Catholicism among women. Moreover, by the end of the century, Catholic discourse which depicted the ideal mother as a long-suffering, self-sacrificing, silent creature, popular in the mid-nineteenth century, was giving way to a more active model.[6] Catholic mothers were assigned the task of stemming the tide of secularisation unleashed by the French Revolution and the advance of atheist socialism. Mothers were urged to play an active role in the religious education of their children and to be constantly vigilant about the corrupting influences of modern society on their offspring.

The Liberal state did little to challenge the Church's influence in matters relating to gender relations and the private sphere. Campaigns for the legalisation of divorce, for example, fell on stony ground in the late nineteenth century.[7] Sexuality was subject to little state regulation (apart from prostitution – see below) and mainly left to be policed by priests. Acts of 'indecency' were prosecuted if they sullied the public domain, but otherwise little was done. Unlike some other European countries, Italy did not make homosexuality explicitly illegal at this time, although homosexuals could be prosecuted under indecency laws.

A more serious challenge to Church authority came from a different direction, with the rise of the new social science. Criminologists, demographers, sexologists and others in this period began to actively investigate all sorts of matters that had previously been deemed largely private, moral issues. This academic movement had important implications for women since, unlike the clergy, who invoked God's will and simple tradition, these commentators believed that they spoke with the authority of science and 'modernity'. Many of their ideas were, however, essentially just prejudice posturing as science. Criminologist Cesare Lombroso (easily the best known of these academics), for example, attempted to 'scientifically demonstrate' the inferiority of women. According to Lombroso, it was evolution that had shaped women into creatures with 'smaller and softer muscles and lesser intelligence'.[8] Similarly, doctors often pathologised female behaviours which deviated from what they saw as 'natural' (the norm of the bourgeois wife, devoted to maternity) as 'diseases' like hysteria. The rise of one particular branch of this new social science – demography, with its interest in statistics that calculated women's reproductive output – was eventually to have important implications for gender relations, in the shape of the Fascist demographic campaign.

The Civil Code

Like women elsewhere in Europe at this time, Italian women were legally sub-ordinate to men in many respects. In 1900, women's legal position was still largely determined by the Pisanelli Code, the civil code introduced by the new-born Liberal State in 1865.[9] Despite various campaigns by feminists and other reformers, much of this code remained on the statute books until the 1970s (albeit with some modifications in 1919). Based on the Code Napoléon, it allotted women a subordinate position in the family. Its introduction meant that some women, from certain northern regions, lost rights they had previously enjoyed.[10]

Admittedly, the code's clauses did include provisions for gender equality. Girls and boys both enjoyed the same legal rights and, as sons and daughters, they could inherit equally. Unmarried adult women could own property, make a will, engage in commerce, and so on. Although dowries continued to have a legal status, they were not compulsory.

Despite these positive features, the Pisanelli Code contained many inequalities. An assumption of male superiority and the need to assert men's authority was inherent in many of its clauses. Women were denied suffrage rights and were banned from holding any kind of public office. Men's authority within the family and over their wives was bolstered in many ways. If a man hurt his wife whilst 'disciplining' her for what he considered disobedient or malicious behaviour, for example, he was punished quite leniently. The 'defence of honour' was accepted as an extenuating circumstance in murder cases. There was also inequality in the grounds for marital separation since male and female adultery were treated differently. Adultery was a serious matter in this period, a crime that could lead to imprisonment. Men were deemed guilty of it only if they flagrantly kept a concubine either in the marital home or elsewhere. If a husband had casual sex it was deemed irrelevant, whereas if a wife had extra-marital sex even once (either during or prior to marriage), or simply if public opinion believed her to have done so, this was grounds for marital separation.

Both sexes were equal in terms of not being able to divorce, but this had very different implications for men and women since, upon marriage, women lost a whole raft of legal rights. As wives, women were compelled to adopt their husband's name and citizenship, and live where he decreed. Although married women could still own, inherit and bequeath property, any acts relating to the management of this property (such as selling it or taking out a mortgage) required a 'marital authorisation' (their husband's consent). Although both parents were supposed to play a role in taking important decisions about their children (such as who they could marry), if they disagreed, by law the husband's view prevailed. Women could exercise *patria potestas* (the power to decide alone for their children) only where husbands had deserted the family, emigrated or were in prison.

Another group of mothers with *patria potestas* were widows (an improvement compared with the Code Napoléon). Widows also enjoyed many of the legal rights of unmarried women. They did, however, face some restrictions. Deceased husbands could, for example, continue to exercise control (through their wills) over how children should be educated and over the administration of their property. Widows who remarried within ten months risked losing their entire inheritance.[11]

The Pisanelli Code also discriminated against those born out of wedlock. Illegitimate children who had been recognised by their parents, for example, enjoyed lesser inheritance rights than their legitimately-born siblings. The code was also harsh on unmarried mothers as paternity searches were not permitted.

The Family

The bourgeois model of the male breadwinner and a full-time domestic and maternal role for women was increasingly influential in this period and this was, indeed, the reality for most upper middle-class (and some lower middle-class) married women. The middle-class home was seen as a haven from the harsh realities of the outside world, a nest of love and restorative domesticity for the husband after his day toiling in the public sphere. It was a place where women could devote themselves to being good wives and mothers. For millions of Italian women, however, this notion was to remain an unachievable fantasy until at least the 1950s. Most poor homes were overcrowded workplaces. Few men earned a 'family wage'.

A range of different family forms existed depending on class, region and whether they were urban or rural.[12] Families could be large or small, extended or nuclear. The largest households were found in northern and central rural areas, where certain types of peasants (generally those who were resident on the land they tilled), such as small landowners, small tenants and sharecroppers, tended to live in extended families. The exact size and composition of peasant households depended on many factors (particularly the size of the landholding). At one extreme were the enormous households of sharecropping families, particularly prevalent in central Italy, where up to 40 people lived and worked together as one unit. In the South, in contrast, households were often small because most peasants lived not on the land, but in towns and villages. Most urban Italians, of whatever class, lived in nuclear families, as did some of the *braccianti* (landless farm-labourers), who were numerous in the Po Valley. Nonetheless, extended families of various types could be found in all these groups in this period. Among urban small shopkeepers, traders and artisans, for example, family size and structure was fluid and changed according to business needs.[13] Even nuclear families, moreover, often relied on kin networks for material or emotional support.

In urban areas, most men became heads of household upon marriage, since newlyweds normally moved to an independent home. In rural households, many men had to await their father's death to gain this status. Some younger sons never achieved it. In most households, whether extended or nuclear, the male head of household was in charge (although the extent of his power varied in different types of families). Women only became heads of family in the absence of a suitable male.

In many poorer families (particularly peasant, extended families), relations tended to be formal. Forms of address emphasised hierarchy and deference.

Children often addressed their parents with *voi* (the polite form of 'you'). Many peasant men used the informal *tu* to address their wives, whereas the wives had to reply with a respectful *voi*. Female subordination was further underscored at mealtimes. Many peasant women suffered the indignity of eating on the porch or stairs. Only men ate at the table, lording over the household while women served them.

Virtually all middle- and upper-class couples and most urban working-class couples used *tu*. This was indicative of the fact that, around the beginning of the nineteenth century, a more intimate form of the family had begun to emerge among the middle classes. Their marriages, particularly for white-collar workers and professionals, were increasingly 'companionate', with an emphasis on bonds of love and affection. Not all men embraced this idea willingly. Some resisted it, threatened by the idea that a man should prefer the company of a mere woman to that of his male friends. Even in these new types of marriage, moreover, women were still subordinate, socially, economically and legally, to their husbands.

In contrast to the new bourgeois model of marriage was the situation in large peasant households. These were headed by a lead couple, the *capoccia* (usually the eldest male), and the *reggitrice* (usually the eldest female and often the *capoccia*'s wife).[14] Typically they ruled over a household composed of their sons, their unmarried daughters and their daughters-in-law. The *capoccia* had overall power in the family (only he, for example, dealt with the landowner) whilst the work done by women was governed by the *reggitrice*. The junior members of the household were dependent on this ruling couple for many things and even had to ask them for clothes or other small necessities. Although such units could be supportive and harmonious, they were often wracked by bitter rivalries between the younger women as they jostled for position. The *reggitrice*, moreover, not infrequently behaved in an authoritarian manner as her power was constantly threatened by the younger women, one of which would eventually replace her. The only males over whom peasant women had influence were their own sons, although a woman could sometimes use this to undermine the power of her husband.

The rigidity of gender roles in peasant communities was enforced, where necessary, by local women themselves who would voice their disapproval of those who stepped out of line. Those who 'misbehaved' might also be subjected to *scampanate* (charivari rituals) of various kinds. This was how many communities policed gender transgressions such as wives who beat their husbands, adultery, homosexuality, marriages between persons of very different ages, or 'improper sexual behaviour'.

Marriage and courtship

Marriage in this period was central to women's existence but it was often primarily an economic affair in which love played a minor role, if at all. Parents had a guiding, and sometimes authoritarian, hand. Love matches did occur but the pressure on young women to marry quickly (preferably before the age of 25) to avoid ending up as spinsters, forced them to choose from offers available in a competitive market, rather than waiting for Cupid's arrow to strike. If a girl did fall in love with the 'wrong' boy, it was difficult to actually marry him given the need for her parents to provide a dowry. Although not compulsory, dowries (which ranged from bed-linen and cooking pots for the poor to large sums of money or even entire factories for the rich) remained common. In many families this was a daughter's share of the family wealth, thereby often excluding her from other inheritance, a far from equitable solution given that it was usually her husband who managed her dowry. A few outwitted parental authority by dramatic means. Consensual kidnappings, where the fiancé kidnapped his bride if the parents disapproved of the marriage, did occur, but this was a risky strategy which could end in disaster for the woman. Sometimes, however, couples from poor families eloped with parental approval in order to avoid the expense of wedding festivities.

For peasants, faced with the cruel economics of a harsh life, it was often a girl's work capacity and health rather than beauty that would net her a husband. In Montferrato in Piedmont, for example, the ideal wife was said to have, 'the legs of a hare, the stomach of an ant and a donkey's back'.[15] Wise peasant girls, too, judged a suitor by his means: marrying a poor man, however handsome or kind, meant a life of poverty and struggle. In some sharecropping areas, not just parents but also landowners determined who could marry and when, according to the needs of the farm.

Because of the many limitations on who unmarried girls could meet, moreover, marriage for love was not always possible.[16] Families expended a good deal of effort on safeguarding the virtue of unmarried daughters, which meant few opportunities to meet members of the opposite sex, apart from relatives. Engagement and courtship were hemmed in with restrictions. Etiquette manuals laid down courtship rules for the middle class. Custom defined it for the poor. Engaged couples normally only met in the parental home of the future bride: to visit her fiancé's home could damage her reputation (although this was more usual practice in urban areas and among richer people). It was not respectable for unmarried women under the age of 40 to go out alone, although, by the turn of the century, this was changing a little in northern Italy, where restrictions were relaxed for those in their thirties. Restrictions were greatest on middle-class girls. Poorer girls, particularly in urban areas, had considerably more opportunities to meet a future spouse, in the workplace or travelling to work, for example, but even they could rarely act freely without parental consent. There were, however, signs of change: some writers were beginning to advocate the novel idea that girls and boys should get to know each other better, including calling for co-education.

Despite the levels of surveillance of unmarried women, far from all brides were virgins. In the early twentieth century, a survey of six Italian cities (Bologna, Florence, Genoa, Messina, Milan and Palermo) found that 12–16 per cent of brides were pregnant.[17] As Margherita Pelaia has argued, this was probably not due to freer, more modern attitudes to sexuality, but to the fact that historically, in certain areas, the *promessa* (betrothal) had been the most important moment, to the extent that engaged couples could meet freely and sometimes even sleep together.[18] Under the law of the Liberal state the *promessa* was no longer legally enforceable and many abandoned this practice, but in certain areas custom adapted slowly to legal change.

Far from all areas had such customs and many brides hardly knew their grooms when they married them. Even so, for urban women, getting married could be experienced as a liberating moment, the time when they moved into their own home and shrugged off the restricted, guarded life of girlhood. Although marriage entailed a loss of legal rights, as wives, women generally had far more freedom to move around and more public authority. As Tommasina Guidi wrote in 1912: 'Married! Its a grand word, a wonderful thing! Above all it means freedom, amusement, satisfied pride and greater respect in the world.'[19]

For peasant women, things could not have been more different: many peasant brides moved into their husband's family home. Marriage frequently meant just exchanging a subordinate position in their own family for submission to the will of their husband's relatives, particularly his mother. Stories of peasant brides bullied by mothers-in-law were legion.[20] Francesca (born 1903 into a peasant family), for example, remembered that, the day her father's mother died, her mother said: 'Whoever wants to come in and cry should come in: as for me, she's already made me cry far too much. If you want you can say the rosary. I won't.'[21] Marriage for peasant women usually meant even more work than before, particularly once they had children.

Lone women

Not everyone married. For women, this was always considered a failure. Indeed, as Maura Palazzi has noted, the meaning of the word 'spinster' changed in the late nineteenth century. Although, 'in the past it had referred to women of any age who had never married and particularly young women awaiting marriage', now it began to have 'increasingly negative connotations'.[22] The single life was a difficult option given women's legal inferiority and their limited earning power. In practice, of course, few of the various categories of 'lone' women were really alone. In 1901, 13 per cent were heads of families and most of the rest lived in the families of others. Only 4.9 per cent of women actually lived by themselves. Many found themselves on the margins of family life, continuing to contribute to a household but without power or influence in it.

Nonetheless, there were considerable numbers of 'lone' women in Italy. According to the 1901 census, 47.7 per cent of women (compared with 28.7 per cent of men) over 50 years old were unmarried or widowed. Only tiny numbers (0.11 per cent of the female population in 1911)[23] were legally separated or divorced (the latter having divorced abroad) but a good number, 11.1 per cent of women (and 11.3 per cent of men), had never married.[24]

Even wives could be 'lone' women. Early twentieth-century Italy had many 'white widows', mainly in the South, whose husbands had emigrated in the huge rush overseas, often for years and sometimes definitively.[25] Their numbers peaked in the census of 1911 but, already in 1901, nearly 200,000 women had an absent husband. Many 'white widows' were young, since men often married just before departure in order to send remittances to their wives rather than to their parents. Sometimes marriages were not even consummated, to enable the husband to protect his 'honour' by ensuring his wife's fidelity could be ascertained following his absence.[26]

A few rejected marriage for the life of a nun (although this was not always a choice – for some it was a necessity if they could not find a husband). As a result of the religious revival of the end of the nineteenth century, nuns were increasingly numerous. Numbers rose from 28,000 in 1880, to 40,000 in 1900, 71,000 in 1921 and 129,000 in 1936. Most nuns worked actively in the community in some way, mainly as teachers or nurses or in welfare roles of various kinds such as running orphanages.

About another category of potentially 'lone' women – lesbians – we still know little. Only more research will tell us the extent to which there were women who managed to live as lesbians in this period. But it is improbable that many did so given the social and economic pressures to conform and the risk of incarceration in a mental hospital for displaying such tendencies. Sexologists and social scientists were becoming increasingly interested in lesbianism, essentially with the aim of condemning it or stamping it out. In 1898, for example, Obici and Marchesini published a 'scientific' study of the 'problem' of *fiamme* (crushes) between teenage schoolgirls.[27] Even Lombroso himself turned his attention to lesbianism, seeing it as linked to prostitution and branding it a form of 'organic atavism'. Lombroso's work included detailed descriptions of what he saw as the characteristics of 'born-lesbians' or 'criminal man-women' ranging from their masculine attire to their 'mania for writing letters'.[28]

Motherhood

The idea of the *mamma italiana*, a generous and powerful figure whose unconditional love spoils her sons and keeps them at home almost indefinitely, influences both Italians' image of themselves and foreigners' perceptions of Italian womanhood. As Anna Bravo has summarised, the stereotype is a woman who is:

> Incomparably loving, servant and owner of her children, often tearful but always on her feet holding the family together. . . . Adored, feared and caricatured, in discussions about the Italian family '*la mamma*' has become a glorious archetype . . . the enduringly popular image of the Italian mother is of a strong woman who dotes on her son and dedicates herself to him intensively. In exchange she gets the right to veto his choices, his constant attentions and an unrivalled emotional and symbolic dependency.[29]

In a recent book, Marina D'Amelia has argued that this notion, the idea that there is, and has been since time immemorial, a particularly strong relationship between Italian mothers and their sons, is, in fact, far from a universal, timeless feature of Italian society. Instead it is an 'invented tradition' forged just after the Second World War.[30] D'Amelia's interesting hypothesis still needs further investigation but even a cursory glance at motherhood at the beginning of the century shows many women behaving in not obviously maternal ways.

Although some northern Italian women were beginning to have fewer children at this time, there was a great emphasis on the maternal role. Many voices extolled motherhood as women's highest destiny. In this respect, of course, Italy was part of a wider trend: many other European countries saw an increase in maternalist discourse in this period. In late nineteenth-century Italy, a range of different texts, often inspired by foreign ideas, destined to be read by literate middle-class and elite women, extolled the virtues of motherhood. Some authors, such as Paolo Mantegazza in his best-selling *Fisiologia del piacere* (1853), argued that maternity was not just a woman's destiny but also her greatest pleasure and that she could endure a good deal for this glorious reward. 'What does it matter (he wrote) if she is stuck on a lower step with her master's insolent foot on her neck? For hers is the sublime joy of sacrifice, she can be a mother . . .'[31] This theme was echoed by many other writers who venerated maternal love, a mother's selflessness and her sentimental attachment to her children.

By the last decades of the nineteenth century, maternalist discourse was increasingly underpinned by 'science'. Positivist 'experts' of various kinds, including doctors, emphasised motherhood. They too were often lyrical about the beauty and importance of maternal instinct but they also saw an improved maternal role as a key to improving the nation's health in 'defence of the race'. Mothers were now seen as important in hygiene campaigns that aimed to reduce infant mortality and infectious diseases and this inspired a flood of literature offering them practical advice on how to carry out their maternal role in a more modern, scientific manner. Such advice, which professionalised motherhood, was often combined with exhortations to shun extra-domestic work in order to do their mothering job properly.

This 'modern' approach to motherhood set standards far beyond the reach of most Italian mothers. Many children were very poorly looked after. Millions of peasant women, forced to work almost inhuman hours, lacked the time to care properly for their offspring. Peasant babies and toddlers were often left with only slightly older siblings while their mothers did farm-work. They might even be sedated with opiates or left alone all day tied to a chair.[32] Peasant parents were usually strict with children and rarely indulged in open displays of affection (although affectionate behaviour was more common among the middle class). Similarly, many poor urban women, forced to work to survive, had little time for parenting. Even those who did have time, the rich, delegated some of their maternal role to others. Many upper-class Italian mothers who were biologically perfectly capable of breast-feeding, chose not to do so, instead hiring wetnurses.

Despite the prevailing maternalist discourse, the state did little to support mothers. No legislation protected mothers at work until 1902. Nor was there any state-sponsored maternity leave until the weak and ineffective provisions introduced in 1910 (see Chapter 2). The fact that paternity searches were not legal meant that unmarried mothers were unable to make men share financial or moral responsibility for the consequences of extramarital sex.

Going out/leisure

Women's role in the family and ideas about respectable behaviour shaped their access to leisure pursuits. At the turn of the century, many men and women, including many husbands and wives, had little to do with each other and tended to mix mainly with own-sex kin and friends. Married peasants, for example, rarely went out together socially as a couple. Anna, a peasant woman born in 1897 near Verona, remembered: 'Never, he never went out with me. Even when we went to the village by bicycle he wanted me to go first so that we didn't have to meet.'[33] The spatial separation of the sexes was greatest in the South, where any female extra-domestic activity was deemed risky for family honour, but all over Italy leisure pursuits were highly gendered. Most leisure pursuits were for men only. Men met each other, for example, in *osterie* (taverns), clubs and *circoli* (circles). They also socialised in brothels (divided, by law, into first, second and third class establishments so that rich and poor need not mingle).

Many poorer women had little leisure time *per se*, usually going out only to work or Mass. Working-class women in urban areas socialised mainly with relatives and female neighbours. Nonetheless, working-class housewives were far from isolated in the home as they had to use communal taps and laundries. For peasants, whose workloads were so heavy that virtually no time remained for recreation, leisure activities remained fairly traditional, far from the new commercial leisure pursuits appearing in urban areas. Younger peasant women in large households had very little interaction with the wider world. Only the *reggitrice* went to market. Peasant women's non-work activities were mainly confined to church-going, local festivals, weddings and religious processions. They would also attend *veglie*, social gatherings (particularly in winter) in barns or cowsheds where the main entertainment was story-telling. But even in the *veglie* women were not totally 'at leisure': they usually spun thread or mended clothes as they listened or chatted.

Richer women had considerably more leisure time but much of it was spent at home, doing things like sewing, reading, receiving guests and hosting family parties. The situation was, however, changing a little. Middle- and upper-class women who, fifty years earlier, would rarely have set foot outside the house, because of the danger to their reputation, were increasingly beginning to go out. Admittedly, Italian women were less advanced in this respect than women in some other countries: American women living in Italy were seen as almost surreally emancipated in their disregard for 'proper' behaviour. In 1886, Angelo De Gubernatis described foreign ladies visiting Florence as 'intrepid amazons with teeth like horses and feet like elephants'.[34] Nonetheless, things were changing for Italians. Apart from outings connected with philanthropic or fundraising activities, attending religious functions or public lectures, middle-class women now went out to shop, particularly in the new department stores, rather than having goods brought to their homes. They frequented tea rooms and public parks. Walking outdoors was increasingly acceptable for ladies, albeit only on certain streets and paying due attention to appropriate behaviour and attire. The theatre was another respectable public space, to the extent that married ladies could go alone if chaperoned there and back. As a result, theatres themselves became increasingly feminised spaces in the late nineteenth century, in terms of both their décor and the plays they put on.[35] Dancing, too, was a social activity that middle-class girls could participate in

Illustration 1   Walking in the park, *c.* 1900.
(Collezione Eredi Ramusani. Reproduced courtesy of Fototeca Panizzi, Reggio Emilia.)

from about the age of 18 (accompanied, of course, by their mothers). Restrictions were far greater in the South. In 1902, according to the (northern) novelist and historian Dora Melegari, in small towns near Naples, 'noblewomen are not allowed to go out on foot alone, whatever their age'.[36]

There was an increasing recognition that women needed exercise of some kind for their health and this led to some girls doing gymnastics at school.[37] Sporting activity for women, however, was extremely unusual. A few bold pioneers cycled (although many considered this a grave threat to respectability).[38] Some elite women took up activities like tennis, mountaineering and skiing, all sports that could be practised with family members. Queen Margherita, an enthusiastic hiker and cyclist, was an important role model.

Some women got the opportunity to travel. Honeymoons were increasingly fashionable for the elite and many wealthy families spent the summer in their country villas or holidaying in the new emerging seaside resorts. Whilst poorer women sometimes travelled alone for economic reasons, middle-class and upper-class women usually only did so to visit relatives, and with a chaperone. For girls, however, education was increasingly a reason to go out.

Education

The public education system in the Liberal state (founded with the Casati Law of 1859) provided elementary education for children of both sexes. Girls and boys followed roughly the same curriculum albeit with some differences such as domestic science for girls. This notion, the idea that girls as well as boys should learn to read, was considerably more advanced than the social reality of the time: many still thought that the best education for girls was none at all.

Nonetheless, the second half of the nineteenth century was a period of slow but gradual progress in female education.

Female illiteracy declined. According to official statistics, in 1861, 72 per cent of men and 84 per cent of women had been illiterate. By 1901, the numbers were 42.5 per cent and 54.4 per cent respectively. The continuing gender disparity was partly because girls were more likely to be denied schooling, as their 'need' for education was considered less important. Some parents, moreover, kept daughters at home because of fears for their morality. Military service was also a factor as conscripts (all males of course) were taught to read.

By the early twentieth century, the idea that women should be kept illiterate had gone as had most of the antagonism to female education *per se*. But hostility to both the 'dangers' of co-education and of 'over-education' for girls persisted. Such attitudes were reinforced by Italy's endemic problem with what Marzio Barbagli has dubbed 'intellectual unemployment'. This was caused by the 'open' nature of the education system, where each step on the educational 'ladder' gave access to the one above, thereby creating incentives for pupils to carry on in education and producing a surfeit of graduates from schools and universities.[39] As many men found it hard to find jobs befitting their educational level, fear of female competition was common.

In the Casati Law the question of whether girls could frequent *ginnasi* and *licei* (academic middle and grammar schools, which provided the route to university) was unclear, although they were not explicitly forbidden from doing so. In 1883 the position was clarified: thereafter girls were officially permitted to attend *ginnasi*, *licei*, technical institutes and technical schools, although the actual situation continued to vary locally. Due to prejudice against co-education, only a handful of girls with broad-minded parents took up this opportunity. Although *ginnasi* did create girls' sections, few *licei* did so. In 1888, for example, Cesare Lombroso's daughter Gina was the only girl in her local *liceo*. Gina later wrote that her classmates, 'were all very nice to me',[40] but few parents were prepared to expose their daughters to such situations. Some pupils, like Maria Balbacci who passed her school leaving certificate in Faenza in 1880, instead 'attended' as 'externals', entering school premises only for examinations. According to official statistics, by 1900 there were 287 girls enrolled at *licei*, 1,778 at *ginnasi*, 148 at technical institutes and 3,900 at technical schools.

A popular alternative (albeit with a less academic curriculum) was teacher training, an affordable form of single-sex education for lower middle-class girls which also provided a useful fall-back qualification in case they failed to marry. Teacher training colleges were rapidly feminised with, by 1899, 19,864 female (and 1,323 male) students.[41] Initially, there was a gap between elementary education (which ended at the age of twelve) and teacher training (which started at fifteen) but, by the turn of the century, this was bridged with extra classes so that girls did not have to stay at home forgetting their lessons. Male and female students had roughly the same curriculum although girls also learned needlework. This was because, according to a ministerial circular of 1890: 'Women teachers or young women learning to teach should never forget that they are destined to be mothers or educators of good mothers.'[42] Special institutes to train female teaching staff for these colleges were set up in Rome and Florence in 1882, as a kind of lesser, women's alternative to university.

For girls from the elite there were the prestigious, exclusive state-run but expensive *educandati*. There were also many private single-sex schools, mainly run by nuns. In 1900, a survey of girls' secondary schools revealed that, of the 1,429 establishments surveyed (which educated 48,677 boarders and 59,179 day pupils between them), a striking 1,114 were Church-run; 299 were run by charities or private individuals and only 86 were public institutions.[43] In general these schools, whether private or public, were far less academic than *licei*. They taught mainly 'accomplishments' like piano and sketching, and placed much emphasis on safeguarding their pupils' morality. Some girls were kept at home, either taught by a governess or receiving no real education at all from about the age of twelve. For them, adolescence could be a lonely, isolated time, a gap in their lives while they awaited marriage.

More exciting were the lives of the pioneers who attended university, something that was permitted by the unified state only from 1876. At first, a university education was far from the norm for girls from middle- or upper-class families and many of the early graduates were from foreign, Jewish or Protestant backgrounds. Ernestina Paper, the first woman to graduate in Liberal Italy, exemplifies this. Paper, who completed a degree in medicine (started elsewhere) at Florence University in 1877, had been born in Odessa to a Jewish family as Puritz Manasse.[44] A disproportionate number of the graduations were in northern universities. This trickle of graduates was, of course, not dissimilar to the situation elsewhere in Europe at the time.

The opposition of the Catholic Church to truly academic education for women was a big stumbling block (as it was in France, where many of the first female university students likewise came from religious minorities). Even such small numbers, however, did create an impetus for change. Some prominent feminist activists came from this pioneering clutch of graduates. It also enabled a few women to move into those few graduate professions that were at least partially open to women, like teaching and medicine.

Employment

As far as official statistical indices are concerned, at the beginning of the twentieth century, female rates of employment were declining. According to the census of 1901, only 31.6 per cent of women worked, considerably less than the 40 per cent recorded in 1881. However, as Ornello Vitali has demonstrated, these figures should be treated with caution.[45] It is probable that a substantial number of those excluded from this percentage in 1901 did at least some form of work. Census figures are only a rough guide as apparent changes often reflect as much the prejudices of the compilers as any real shift in numbers. For example, in 1881 female part-timers were generally classified as workers, but by 1901 they were increasingly described as 'attendenti alle cure domestiche' (caring for the home) with their other activities deemed secondary and not recorded. In the 1901 census, people were asked to state what their main occupation was, as the enumerators tried to count only what they saw as 'real' workers, in a modern economy. Many women who would previously have been considered part of the 'economically active population' were excluded.[46] This reclassification helps explain at least some (although probably not all) of the apparent drop in women's work in this period. Numbers of female textile workers, for example, were recorded as falling from 1,351,454 in 1881 to 783,253 in 1901 partly because many who spun thread or wove cloth at home were now omitted.[47]

In practice, at least some form of employment was still the norm for poorer women. Although women's wages were low, they were still necessary: the male 'family wage' was not a reality for most working-class and peasant families. Millions of Italian women worked at the end of the nineteenth century in a whole range of occupations including as garment-makers, laundresses, craftswomen, landladies, midwives and wetnurses. They were also to be found (1,246,529 of them according to the 1901 census) in various kinds of manufacturing.

Some worked in factories. The economically important silk industry, for example, employed many female workers. In silk spinning-mills, the workforce, mainly girls from peasant families, plunged cocoons into steaming vats of near-boiling water then spun the floss. The state-owned tobacco-processing plants also employed a largely female workforce to cure the leaves and hand-roll cigars. Women and girls were employed in industry both because they were thought to be more docile than men and because their wages were low. There was also a supply factor, since, in many rural families, farm-work was still seen as more central to the survival of the family and thus men did it. Factory work was just an additional source of income. Because of the seasonal nature of some (although not all) such work, many factory workers continued to see themselves primarily as peasants.

Conditions for factory workers were, in Italy, as in most early industrialising nations, poor. Women did not necessarily endure worse conditions than men but their wages were lower and there was more anxiety about employing them. Moralists of various kinds voiced concern about the dangers to women's sexual morality as well as the potential effects on childbearing of factory work. Such worries were exacerbated by the fact that most female factory hands were young and unmarried. Only the tobacco-processing plants, where conditions were relatively better and work worth holding on to, employed substantial numbers of married women. Some employers tackled moral anxieties by providing dormitories run by nuns, where workers lived in an enclosed, all-female world, their leisure time filled with prayer and training to be future wives.[48] Factories that employed workers of both sexes often had spatial segregation to keep them apart.

By the turn of the century, however, factories increasingly employed men. The spurt of industrialisation of the 1890s brought to the fore new economic sectors, like engineering, with more year-round employment and a mainly male workforce. Although the new sectors did offer some jobs to women (they were found, for example, in the chemical, paper and pottery industries), overall women were mostly trapped in declining sectors like textiles.

By far the largest group of 'economically active' females were peasants. The 1901 census counted 3,200,302 of them, although real numbers were doubtless even higher. In peasant households tasks were divided up by gender but the specific type of work done by women varied according to region, crop, land tenure arrangements, the sex and age composition of the household, local custom and whether or not the home was located on the land tilled. Male farming roles were usually fairly rigid whereas women provided a flexible labour force ready to step in when required. Broadly speaking, most fieldwork was done by men whilst women looked after farmyard animals, grew vegetables, kept bees and raised silkworms. Women also did childcare and housework but the distinction between farm-work and housework was often blurred. Peasant women also did various forms of manufacturing, making items ranging from soap for direct consumption by the household, to goods for export. Some of the straw hats made in Tuscany and worn as far away as New York, for example, were plaited by peasant women. Far from being mere 'helpers' on the farm, women's ceaseless toil was essential to the rural economy and the survival of peasant households.

In some areas (mostly younger) women worked in the fields, at least at specific times of year. Olive-picking, for example, employed many women. The best known female field-hands were rice-weeders, a group with a reputation for assertive and militant behaviour. About 100,000 weeders, 90 per cent of them female, did this backbreaking work annually in the malarial paddy-fields of northern Italy, many of them migrants temporarily away from home. With their skirts hitched up to wade through the muddy water and working 'promiscuously' with male overseers, rice-weeders were the focus of much moral anxiety. Socialists, Catholics and then Fascists all tried to recruit or reform them.

Domestic service was another large employer of women, including many of peasant origin. In this period, in Italy as elsewhere in Europe, there was a chorus of complaints that industrialisation was creating a shortage of servants and inflating their wages. According to one commentator in 1907, 'half the worries of middle-class ladies' were about this 'servant crisis'.[49] Domestic service in Italy was, however, to persist long after this. It is difficult to be certain how many servants there were due to their high rate of turnover as well as changing definitions of exactly which occupations were defined as domestic service; 482,080 domestic servants, 83.2 per cent of them female, were recorded in 1901.

Another much discussed occupational group were the women who resorted to prostitution, either full-time or as something to turn to in hard times. Concern about prostitutes as deviant women, bearers of disease and a eugenic danger was high. Unlike other 'moral' issues (which the state tended to leave to the Church to deal with), the Liberal government closely regulated prostitution, seeing it as a public service and, as such, not part of the private sphere. It was deemed a 'deplorable necessity', an essential outlet for male desire, and even as beneficial for women, saving 'honest' women from being pestered or even raped.[50]

Nonetheless, prostitution was not considered something that could be openly exposed to public view. The policy followed (set down by the Cavour Law of 1860) was to enclose and regulate it. Prostitutes were forced to work in licensed brothels where standard prices were set for their services. They (but not their clients) had to undergo regular medical inspections for vene-real disease and obligatory treatment in *sifilicomi* (VD hospitals). They were also subject to a curfew: those found loitering at the wrong time could be arrested. The consequence of this policy was often to confirm their identity as prostitutes, making it difficult to leave the profession. As the feminist Anna Maria Mozzoni argued: 'Many clandestine prostitutes become honest women again, they get married or manage, in some way, to find a means of subsist-ence. Among registered prostitutes, this does not happen, and rehabilitation is virtually impossible.'[51]

There was some tinkering with this legislation, due partly to abolitionist campaigns. In 1888, regulation was relaxed somewhat. The *sifilicomi* were abolished: although VD examinations were still available, they were no longer compulsory. Forced registration was dropped although police surveillance of brothels continued and brothel managers had to supply lists of their employ-ees to the police. The Nicotera Regulation of 1891, however, eroded some of these meagre changes. It stipulated that brothels should be registered but not the individual women themselves, although lists continued to be supplied to the police. Even single women working alone were now deemed to consti-tute a 'brothel' and subject to registration. The humiliating compulsory health checks were in theory not reintroduced but health inspectors could carry out checks in brothels. Women refusing inspection were assumed to be infected and forcibly hospitalised.

Thus in 1900 Italy had 'neo-regulation' of prostitution. The control of the police had partly been replaced by the control of doctors but brothels were still seen as the proper place for sex to be sold. In practice, however, many women flouted the rules. By the first decade of the twentieth century there were between 5,500 and 6,500 registered prostitutes but some estimates said that twice or even ten times this number worked clandestinely. Clandestine prostitutes were far more likely to work part-time and combine this work with other occupations like dressmaking. Even some lower middle-class women, including housewives and teachers, sometimes resorted to it.

Unlike peasant and working-class women, aristocrats and the upper middle class rarely entered the labour market: their job was to be household managers. Lower middle-class women were more likely to seek paid employment although they, unlike poorer women, usually ceased working once married. Options available to middle-class women were limited. Women could not be state offi-cials, although some did get state employment. Some worked, for example, as post office telegraphers although, until 1899, they lost their jobs upon mar-riage. Even after that, married women needed their husband's permission to work. The marriage bar operated in other white-collar jobs too, such as teleph-ony, where it existed until 1908. Overall, compared with some other western countries where office work was becoming increasingly feminised, there was still relatively little 'white blouse' work in Italy by the early twentieth century. Nonetheless, by 1911 about 50,000 women were in this kind of employment. Larger numbers worked as shop assistants (144,405 in 1911).

The 'marital authorisation' was a big problem for women wanting to run a business, although some did manage to do so. In Milan in 1901, for example, a third of small shopkeepers and traders were female, albeit mainly clustered in less profitable enterprises such as street trading. Others worked with their husband in his business.[52] By 1908, 37,219 women were registered as running an industrial or commercial business in their own name.[53]

Women were poorly represented in the professions.[54] This was due to a number of factors including deeply entrenched ideas about women's intellectual inferiority and their maternal destiny, concern for their morality and respectability, the limitations of their education and fear of competition with men. Nonetheless, some women did manage to become professionals. There were even a few university lecturers, like the feminist Paolina Schiff (born in Mannheim in 1841), who taught German literature at Pavia University from 1890. Such pioneers had to face a good deal of prejudice and prove not only their capabilities but those of all women. One lecturer, Teresa Labriola, was unable to complete her inaugural lecture in 1901, which was interrupted by 'a great roar of shouting, hissing and groaning' from the students present.[55] Practising medicine aroused slightly less hostility but only if women confined themselves to gynaecology or paediatrics. By 1911, however, of 23,361 practising doctors, only 83 were female. Until 1919 they were not permitted to work in public hospitals.

The most entrenched opposition was faced by women wishing to practise law.[56] This issue became the focus of feminist campaigns and most of the women who tried to become lawyers in Liberal Italy were themselves feminists of various kinds. The fact that the Civil Code denied women the right to hold public office was used to exclude them from this profession, although the situation was ambiguous from a legal standpoint. The waters were further muddied by the fact that gradually women were allowed to work in various kinds of public employment such as in local government offices and libraries. As Simonetta Soldani argues, women's access to public employment tended to be decided on a case-by-case basis (given that the law gave no clear guidance), often with anomalous outcomes.[57] Only where women seemed to be getting close to power, were they rigidly denied entry.

The first woman to try to practise law in Liberal Italy was Lidia Poët, a young Protestant with a law degree. In 1883 she managed to register as a lawyer in Turin but, shortly after, her registration was overturned by the Court of Appeal and the Court of Cassation. A whole range of arguments emerged during the debate that preceded and followed this decision. Although she did garner some support, there was much opposition. Many argued that practising law was a form of public office and therefore closed to women. Some simply called the idea 'ridiculous' or 'strange' or raised the question of 'women's nature', their 'intellectual inferiority' and the 'needs of the family'. More extravagantly, some invoked women's 'strange and bizarre clothing' or warned that judges would be distracted from their work by attractive female lawyers.

The idea that women should practise law was, of course, problematic given their own legal inferiority. Nonetheless, a bill to allow them to do so, presented in parliament in 1899 by the Republican deputy Ettore Socci, was defeated by only a narrow margin. A second compromise bill, opening only certain legal professions to women, was passed in parliament in 1904 but never reached the statute books owing to the end of the legislature. Despite this, some women did attempt to become lawyers. The best known was Teresa Labriola. As a lecturer in the philosophy of law, in theory she could automatically register as a lawyer. Her attempt to do so in Rome in July 1912 was initially successful but subsequently overturned by the Court of Appeal. The judgement, however, suggested a new openness to change: it declared that ultimately parliament would have to decide the matter.

One profession open to women was writing. Because it took place in private it posed little danger to respectability. Moreover, there was less hostility to women here than in other professions as many men felt confident that women's writing would only ever be derivative and mimetic or, at best, sincere and emotional. This period saw a great increase in publishing aimed specifically at women as well as the rise of professional women writers and journalists.[58] Some of the new authors were aristocrats but many, in contrast to the previous period, were from the rising middle classes. Most wrote for publications aimed at women. Only exceptional figures like Matilde Serao, the prolific Neapolitan writer, whose works included novels, conduct books and newspaper articles, broke into the male world of 'general' journalism. Women, on the whole, needed to be careful what they wrote, indeed impose a degree of self-censorship and maintain an improving and educative tone. Much of their output, whether literary or not (many ranged over different genres, including journalism, fiction and conduct books), was at least partly, if not wholly, didactic in intent. Its primary aim, as well as to divert its audience, was to educate its readers on proper and moral behaviour.[59] Conduct books, aimed mainly at the middle class and emphasising the importance of domesticity, flourished and in part replaced devotional reading for women. Despite the restrictions on what female authors could write, this new outpouring of women's writing for a (relatively) mass public did bring discussion about women's role more into the public domain and, by the turn of the century, was offering space for many new themes to be discussed, including feminism. Far from all female writers, however, embraced the feminist cause. Serao, for example, ridiculed what she called, 'false emancipation, useless and harmful political rights'.[60]

The only mass female profession was teaching. Numbers of secondary school teachers, like numbers of journalists, doctors and so on, remained extremely small. Apart from in exceptional circumstances, they taught only girls and indeed from 1908 to 1920 they were officially banned from posts in mixed secondary schools. Much larger numbers did primary teaching. Training primary teachers was considered a priority by the Liberal state. They were seen as the front-line troops of the government's programme to forge national identity, bringing national culture and language to the masses. As in much of western Europe, Italian primary teaching quickly became feminised with, by 1901, 35,344 women teachers in the public sector alone. This represented 68 per cent of the total, a rapid increase on the 42 per cent of thirty years before. This rapid feminisation was largely due to the scarcity of alternative employment opportunities for lower middle-class women.

Primary teachers were poorly paid and often faced difficult conditions. Things were not so bad in urban schools but rural teachers might find themselves far from the nearest road, in primitive lodgings and with rudimentary premises. Carolina Gasparini, for example, who started work in the Appenine mountains in 1919, found that her remote school 'consisted of a little room made out of a converted cow-shed. It still had the beaten-earth floor of the cow-shed. . . . The manure heap was outside one window, with its stench and flies. . . . Teaching materials? Funding? Stationery? Nothing at all.'[61] Such teachers often had to contend with the frequent absences of pupils needed in the fields. Some even held classes outdoors to enable children guarding livestock to attend. Because of their miserable level of pay, they themselves were often not much richer than the peasantry they lived amongst, to the extent that festivities like wedding feasts were welcomed as opportunities to eat for free. Teachers were often important figures in rural communities, where they might be one of only a handful of educated people, and some became unofficial community secretaries. As anomalous women living alone away from home, they had to carefully safeguard their reputations. Many dressed modestly, in dark outfits, to give the right impression. One primary teacher, Itala Donati, committed suicide, aged only 23, in 1886 after she was falsely accused of being the mistress of the local mayor.[62]

Teaching was an acceptable job for women because it did not challenge the idea of their domestic destiny too much, being concerned with care of the young. Nonetheless, the army of primary teachers did represent a new type of female figure, a rather modern one, particularly in the case of those who lived away from family and parents. In some cases, teachers' work experiences opened their eyes to the social realities of the time and by the turn of the century some were becoming active in the new political movements of the time. For the late nineteenth century saw the rise of both socialism and a new movement which aimed to challenge some of the gender inequalities of the day and win rights for women: feminism.

2

The 'Tower of Babel': First-Wave Feminism[1]

The first Sunday in December 1880 was, according to Annarita Buttafuoco, a particularly important date in Italian history. She argued that: 'In a chronology that paid attention to gender as an integral part of national history, that date would be seen as one of the most significant for Italian women and men.'[2] The Sunday in question saw the foundation, by veteran feminist Anna Maria Mozzoni and the German-born university assistant Paolina Schiff, of the Lega Promotrice degli Interessi Femminili (League for the Promotion of Women's Interests), to campaign on issues like female suffrage, equal pay and paternity searches. Its Executive Committee included working-class women and even men and it was linked to the Unione delle Lavoranti (Female Workers' Union), a league of petty-bourgeois and working-class women. The significance of the foundation of this small organisation lay in the fact that it began a process that was to last for thirty years: it marked the moment when Italian feminism became a political movement rather than just an idea.

By the turn of the century a vibrant feminist movement was actively campaigning on a range of issues, including legal equality, paternity searches, equal pay and prostitution law reform. In pursuit of these objectives feminists lobbied politicians, organised conferences and published pamphlets, magazines and newspapers.[3] The movement was at its height in the first decade of the twentieth century in terms of its activities, political visibility and numbers involved.

Not by chance Mozzoni and Schiff's Lega was founded in Milan, Italy's most modern and industrial city, with a long tradition of philanthropy and mutualism. Milan was to become the heartland of the turn-of-the-century feminist movement but it never monopolised it. Groups and organisations emerged all over Italy, even in the South and in quite small provincial towns.

Although many of the feminists' campaigns appeared to be about gender equality, they tended to couch their demands in the language of gender difference and equivalence. Family law was to be reformed but the family itself was, in their view, still the proper place for women: they did not challenge the idea that women's primary role was to be wives and mothers. Indeed, few would have disagreed with the words of educationalist and feminist Maria Montessori when she wrote in 1902 that: 'The social victory of women will be a maternal victory.'[4] Feminists often spoke of the need for women themselves to change in order to forge a 'new woman' for the modern world.[5] This new woman, however, would not ape men: women had to be educated and 'elevated' but not made masculine. The terrain of many of their activities was welfare, particularly maternal welfare.

Many Italian feminist activists were middle or upper class, although they did campaign for the rights of working-class women. Some of them, particularly those connected to the socialist movement, were lower middle class, including many primary teachers, but most were very much part of the social elite. Largely urban, few had knowledge of, or interest in, the world of peasantry (although admittedly some of the legal reforms they proposed would have helped rural women too). The main exceptions were certain female socialist leaders, such as Argentina Altobelli, who fought to improve conditions for female field-hands.

In contrast to the feminism of the 1970s, this was not a youth movement or generational revolt. Many prominent activists were middle aged. In 1900, Anna Kuliscioff was 46, Paolina Schiff 59, Ersilia Majno 41 and Anna Maria Mozzoni 63. One exception was Adelaide Coari, born in 1881. Most turn-of-the-century feminists, moreover, were earnest types, who concentrated on 'doing good', working for all of society. There was none of the hedonistic exuberance of the 1970s, with its emphasis on pleasure and individual self-fulfilment.

Italian feminists were much influenced by foreign ideas. Anna Maria Mozzoni, for example, was inspired by, among others, the French communitarian Charles Fourier and the British liberal John Stuart Mill, socialist feminists by the German socialist August Bebel, and 'practical feminists' by social maternalist initiatives in Britain and elsewhere. Even 'Catholic feminists' gained confidence from foreign Catholic movements that advocated women's suffrage. Many feminists closely followed what was going on abroad, where women's movements had been making headway since the 1860s, and attended international conferences. News of foreign feminist movements frequently appeared in their press and the presence of many foreigners living in Italy helped the flow of ideas. Indeed, a noteworthy feature of the Italian movement was the prominent role of women of foreign birth or from religious minorities (Protestants and Jews), who were often better educated than their Catholic, Italian counterparts. This is not to say that there were no Italian influences that shaped the ideas of these activists and thinkers. Mazzini's democratic ideas, for example, were also important.

The Italian feminist movement can appear difficult to untangle as it was composed of a baffling maze of organisations and groupings, some of which were small, short-lived or not easily classifiable. As novelist Sibilla Aleramo commented: 'If anything resembles the tower of Babel, it is definitely the feminist question of today.'[6] There were indeed many different feminist voices, whose politics and analysis of gender issues varied greatly. Some devoted themselves wholeheartedly to the resolution of the 'woman question' and were active in autonomous groups, whilst others found their allegiances split between their feminist ideas and other politics and beliefs. Both Catholic and socialist feminists were in this difficult position. The different groupings also sometimes overlapped. Moreover, because many feminists were from the social elite, a web of social relations linked them: they frequently met not just in earnest committees but at elegant society events. Even socialists like Ersilia Majno and Anna Kuliscioff received guests in their own salons.[7] This meant that feminists also mingled with politicians and prominent intellectuals of the day.

Some broad trends can be identified. One was the shift from small uncoordinated groups in the 1890s to various attempts at forging unity in the early twentieth century. Another general trend is the fact that, in the 1890s, feminism was mainly dominated by activists who were radical or left-wing whereas, during the early twentieth century, the movement moved to the right. Most feminists, for example, opposed Italy's colonial ventures in the 1890s (indeed the Associazione per la Donna was dissolved in 1898 for adopting this position), whereas by 1911 some prominent feminists backed the invasion of Libya.

Early feminists

Only a few pioneering feminist voices had been raised in the first decades after unification. Women's mutual societies, which advocated women's improvement and education, did exist, but these were not really feminist organisations. Mid-century feminists were mainly aristocratic or upper middle-class writers and thinkers (although they did claim to be campaigning for all women), often from patriotic 'Risorgimental' families. Some were quite conservative; others sought radical change. The Mazzinians among them were 'maternal radicals' who called for equal rights to make women worthy mothers of good patriots.[8] Almost all, whether followers of Mazzini or not, tended to emphasise women's maternal role and most accepted the idea of different destinies for men and women, each in their own sphere. Their main concerns were the improvement of women's education and the reform of the civil code.[9] Some, although far from all, called for suffrage.

Many of these early feminists aired their views in the periodical *La donna*, founded by Gualberta Adelaide Beccari in 1868.[10] One of its contributors was Anna Maria Mozzoni (1837–1920),[11] the most theoretically coherent and radical of the early feminists. Arguably the most important feminist thinker of the late nineteenth century, she was Italy's foremost exponent of liberal/equal rights feminism. Indeed, despite her later interest in socialism, she was essentially a classic liberal feminist inspired by the Enlightenment idea that all humans have reason and therefore deserve equal civil rights. Mozzoni's rigorous adherence to this stance, followed by few others in Italy, was partly due to the fact that her views were much influenced by foreign ideas.

Mozzoni grew up in a 'Risorgimental' anti-Habsburg family in Lombardy, an area where women lost legal and civil rights after unification. In the 1860s she published various books setting out her ideas. Important topics for her were the inequalities of the new Civil Code and the need to improve female education. In 1870 she translated Mill's *The Subjection of Women* into Italian. Deeply committed to the idea that waged work was emancipatory, she argued against the double oppression of working-class women. She also campaigned on numerous other issues including the vote, against the sexual double standard, and for the reform of prostitution law. For a while a follower of Mazzini, she eventually embraced socialism, joining the Milanese Socialist League in 1889, although she later distanced herself from the PSI (Italian Socialist Party). Mozzoni is best known as a theoretician but she was also a political activist, authoring, for example, various petitions calling for female suffrage.

Feminism as a movement

Following in the footsteps of Mozzoni and Schiff's pioneering first organisation, the women's movement began to take off in the 1890s, with the emergence of various Leghe per la Tutela degli Interessi Femminili (Leagues for the Protection of Women's Interests). A magazine, *Vita femminile* (subtitled the 'organ of the Italian women's movement') helped link them together. They were often politically mixed (although many leaders were socialists), sometimes interclass and with many members who had previously been involved in mutual societies. The Milan Lega, for example, founded in 1893, included workers, clerks, primary teachers (like Linda Malnati), secondary teachers and a university lecturer (Paolina Schiff). It had a 'major programme' of legal reform that included suffrage, complete legal equality of the sexes and the abolition of the marital authorisation. It also had a 'minor programme' of immediate action: welfare initiatives to improve the lives of poorer women and a campaign for women to be admitted to the ruling bodies of various institutions.[12]

These Leagues were swept away during the *fatti di maggio* (the hurricane of repression against the Left and labour movement in 1898). Many did later regroup but they were quickly overshadowed by new national co-ordinating organisations. The first of these was the Associazione per la Donna (Women's Association). Founded in 1897 in Rome, then suppressed in 1898 only to reappear in 1900, it soon had branches in various Italian cities. By 1907 it became the Associazione Nazionale per la Donna. Other national organisations included the Unione Femminile Nazionale, the Comitato Nazionale Pro-Suffragio, and the Consiglio Nazionale delle Donne Italiane.

This period also saw the emergence of a rich panorama of feminist periodicals (around 30 different publications started to appear around the turn of the century) and the foundation of various associations that were not specifically feminist but which offered public spaces for women. One example was the Lyceum of Florence, founded in 1908, a cultural club to promote female interest in literature and the arts, inspired by foreign examples. Its members, as in the four other Lyceums that eventually emerged, tended to come from the social elite.

Political parties

Overall, few women joined political parties. This was doubtless at least in part because they lacked confidence in mixed organisations, preferring women-only groups, something that was understandable given the social mores of the time.[13] Moreover, Italy lacked a proper party system. Not even the ruling Liberals were organised as a party. There was, in any case, little support for feminism from them. More sympathetic were the Left – the Radicals, Republicans and Socialists. A number of feminists were close to the small, lay, democratic Radical Party, although, despite being allowed to do so, no women actually joined. A few were members of the Republican Party, which, in the early Liberal period, had been the main political supporter of women's issues, and a number of early feminists had rallied to it. By this time, however, the relationship had declined, despite the presence of pro-feminist Republican deputies like Roberto Mirabelli, as the Republicans were eclipsed by the rise of socialism.

By the turn of the century the PSI was the largest political grouping to give some sort of support to feminism. It was officially in favour of 'women's emancipation' and actively recruited women to its ranks. Indeed, it would have been strange had it ignored them, given that, when the party was founded in 1892, women constituted the majority of factory workers. The PSI's analysis of the 'woman question', however, like other European socialist parties, prioritised economics, ignoring the cultural aspects of women's oppression. The PSI, furthermore, proved a poor ally, providing, for example, only wavering support for female suffrage. For socialists, class was always more important than gender. Some opposed feminism even if they pretended to support it, or dismissed it as bourgeois and (often with reason) neglectful of the interests of working-class women. Moreover, many socialist men shared the ideological preconceptions of other males of their day about gender roles, such as the belief that inequality was necessary in marriage to avoid strife. New ideas were influential too including positivist arguments about women's supposedly smaller brains and biological inferiority. Some argued that it was the exploitative nature of capitalism that forced women to work, unnaturally, outside their rightful place in the home. The socialist press often depicted women as suffering victims of capitalism or lambasted them as too influenced by priests and lacking in class-consciousness. At heart, many socialists saw women's interests as peripheral. As Maria Casalini put this: 'man was the central reference point at the centre of the socialist universe, the star around which planet woman orbited'.[14]

Nonetheless, the PSI was still important to the women's movement and it undoubtedly inspired some feminists to pay more attention to the needs of working class women. Many feminists looked to the PSI for support on various issues and women were active in the party. Exactly how many actually joined is unclear: they probably numbered hundreds rather than thousands. A few did, however, rise to prominence in the PSI and labour movement, such as Argentina Altobelli and Angelica Balabanoff, who held seats on the party directorate. Many female socialist leaders were intellectuals, or at least primary teachers, rather than actual industrial workers. Some PSI members combined party activism with a role in feminist organisations, like the Unione Femminile. Indeed, some proved reluctant to leave these organisations when the PSI moved to a position of official disapproval of 'bourgeois feminism' after the split over the Libyan War (see below). A number of, mainly local, socialist women's periodicals appeared in the early years of the twentieth century but it was only with *La difesa delle lavoratrici* (founded 1911) that socialist women finally got a party-funded national newspaper. In 1912, a national socialist women's organisation (the Unione Nazionale delle Donne Socialiste) was set up at the women's conference held at the PSI national conference in Reggio Emilia.

Larger numbers of women joined socialist trade unions and women were often active in strikes. One major union, the Federterra (for farm-workers), had a female leader, Argentina Altobelli, who headed this important organisation from 1906 to 1925. She, however, was unusual. Although women's strikes had a reputation for being fiercely fought, undisciplined, short-lived and even violent, few female strikers were union members. Most women workers remained unorganised. In 1902, as far as can be told from the unreliable figures available, only 8.5 per cent of the membership of socialist industrial unions and 11.16 per cent of agricultural unions were female. Only 2 per cent of female textile workers were unionised.[15] There were many obstacles to women joining unions, including the dormitory system and the seasonal nature of much female employment. But lack-lustre support from union leaders was also a factor. Many male trade unionists, affected by middle-class discourse about the primacy of women's maternal role and worried about competition in the labour market, opposed female employment.

Catholic trade unions were more successful in recruiting women. In 1912, when only 15 per cent of the members of the socialist Chambers of Labour were female, women made up 40 per cent of the Catholic Leagues.[16] This was only partly due to greater female religiosity. Catholic unions targeted women specifically, had many female organisers, had lower membership fees and were more attentive to women's needs.

The most important socialist to take up the cause of the 'woman question' was the Russian émigrée Anna Kuliscioff (1854–1925). A prominent figure in Italian socialist politics, Kuliscioff already had a long experience of (mainly clandestine) left-wing politics by this time, in Russia, Switzerland and Italy. Intelligent, charismatic and beautiful, Kuliscioff was one of Italy's first female doctors. As early as 1880 she was already writing about the 'woman question' and, from the 1890s, frequently discussed it in the socialist press. Although she had much contact with feminists, she chose to work politically within the PSI. In contrast to many other socialist women, such as Linda Malnati,[17] she never joined a feminist organisation. This was not an easy position to be in since, unlike many socialists, she understood that women's subordination was more than just an economic question. In her best known intervention on the 'woman question', 'The Monopoly of Man', a speech (heavily influenced by Bebel) given in 1890, she spoke of the importance of employment for women, but also noted that: 'All men, of whatever class, see their sexual privilege as a natural phenomenon and defend it with a marvellous tenacity.' Such ideas were not popular with socialist men and Kuliscioff became increasingly isolated in the PSI.

Historians have debated whether Kuliscioff should be seen as a feminist. Franca Pieroni Bortolotti dismissed her commitment to feminism as limited, depicting her as someone who prioritised class issues over gender. This meant, for example, that she did not advocate divorce for fear of alienating grassroots socialists, and shelved it as a problem of 'bourgeois democracy'. Maria Casalini, in contrast, portrays her as valiant and interesting, someone who often spoke on feminist issues, like the iniquity of the adultery laws and the terms of the Civil Code, and who agitated tenaciously for women's suffrage despite the opposition of many male socialists. Casalini depicts Kuliscioff as in a contradictory position because her allegiances were split. It was difficult to be faithful to both socialism and feminism and as a result she often contradicted herself according to which audience she was addressing.[18] Other historians have similarly presented her as a feminist. Rosalia Colombo Ascari, for example, writes of her 'constant, genuine devotion to the emancipation of women'.[19] All agree she was caught between two stools.

Whilst Kuliscioff did side with feminists on many issues, her advocacy of protective legislation in the workplace was controversial. Italy's first protective employment legislation in 1886 affected only child labour but, in 1902, a new law was passed regulating women's work.[20] The primary motive for many of the deputies who voted for it was not social justice or a humanitarian desire to improve women's lives, but middle-class concerns, fanned by positivism, about the effects of female employment on the birth rate and racial fitness. Its target was factory and mineworkers: millions of women, including peasants, servants, outworkers and those in factories employing less than five women, were not covered by it. The 1902 legislation banned women from certain dirty jobs and night work, restricted them to a ten-hour working day and introduced (unpaid) maternity leave for 28 days after the birth (although this could sometimes be relaxed after 14 days).

In Italy, as elsewhere, there was considerable debate about protective legislation, a debate that divided both feminists and socialists. Generally male socialists and some (although not all) female socialists supported it. Some socialist men gave only half-hearted support or were enthusiastic primarily because they hoped to limit competition for jobs. Kuliscioff, however, believed it was needed to protect women from the worst excesses of capitalism.

Kuliscioff's advocacy of this legislation was fiercely contested by certain (both socialist and non-socialist) feminists. Mozzoni was extremely critical, arguing that it bracketed women with children and that it could be used to expel women from employment. It reinforced the idea that women's true place was in the home and that their working was simply something necessary but anomalous. Mozzoni's intransigence on this issue distanced her from the socialist movement. Other feminists, like Ersilia Majno, did not criticise the idea of protective legislation *per se*, only the limitations of this specific law.

'Practical feminism' and the Unione Femminile Nazionale

Ersilia Majno was the president of the 'practical feminist' organisation the Unione Femminile (Female Union), one of the most important of the panorama of feminist organisations of the early twentieth century.[21] Founded in 1899 in Milan, it soon spread to many other Italian cities and in 1905 became the Unione Femminile Nazionale (UFN). Many of those who had been involved in the Leagues of the 1890s joined it and it served as an umbrella organisation for numerous other women's associations. Its membership included many socialist-leaning feminists (Majno herself was married to a Socialist lawyer and parliamentarian), although it always remained autonomous, without formal links to the PSI. Although far from the only feminist group to display 'practical feminist' tendencies, it was arguably the most important to take this approach. 'Practical feminists' combined fighting for legal equality with a great deal of welfare activity.

Like a number of other feminist organisations, the UFN aimed to educate its own members. Indeed the idea of profound self-improvement, and helping other women to do so, was a core theme in its press. It ran libraries and organised seminars and talks.[22] But most UFN activities were aimed at helping others. Its welfare initiatives included numerous training courses (ranging from literacy to domestic science and childcare to professional development), employment agencies for servants, assistance to poor mothers and the Uffici Indicazioni e Assistenza (Information and Assistance Bureaux). The Uffici, modelled on the foreign settlement movement, advised the poor, particularly the female poor, on where to find welfare help as well as systematically gathering data about social conditions.[23] Before assistance was given, *delegate* (female volunteers) visited clients in their homes to assess need. The Uffici were popular: in 1910 alone, 7,552 people sought their help in Milan. Their work was undoubtedly useful although there were problems too. As in other, similar, initiatives abroad, the mainly, although not exclusively, middle-class *delegate* were sometimes inappropriately moralising to their clients.

Ultimately the UFN hoped that the state or local authorities would provide such welfare: their work was supposed only to lay the foundations. They also encouraged women to take up public positions. Since 1890, women had been allowed to be public administrators of charities. Many of the first women to do so, including Majno herself, took up their positions with UFN support and training. By 1907, about 1,500 women were directors or administrators of public charitable organisations (as well as 9,500 in private charities).[24]

Like social maternalists elsewhere in Europe, 'practical feminists' emphasised the 'social value of maternity' and women's right to motherhood. A central moment for them was the passing of protective legislation. Although many practical feminists supported the idea in principle, they were disillusioned by the actual legislation. Ersilia Majno, for example, had called for two months of maternity leave, an eight-hour day, equal pay for equal work and the extension of protection to other categories of women including peasants.

The UFN and other organisations campaigned for improvements to the legislation but they also offered their own remedies to the question of maternity pay. In various cities feminists set up, or co-operated in the setting up of, local funds to provide this.[25] Eventually, in 1910, partly as a result of feminist campaigns, the state stepped in with its own national Maternity Fund.

The story of women workers' response to protective legislation and this Fund demonstrates some of the complex problems facing feminists who aimed, 'to elevate and spread the idea of the social function of maternity in the interest of children and of society'.[26] Many women workers themselves, the supposed beneficiaries, objected both to the unpaid leave in the 1902 law (which meant losing wages) and to the paid leave introduced in 1910 (funded by contributions from the state, employers and female workers). Workers' hostility led to widespread evasion of the provisions (often in collusion with employers) and even strikes. Many were angry because all women of fertile age had to contribute, a payment most could ill afford, yet only a minority stood to benefit, since most female factory workers were young and unmarried. Many industrialists, too, evaded paying their share.

'Practical feminism' has been controversial among historians. Franca Pieroni Bortolotti saw this trend (which she dismissed as 'reformist feminism, typically bourgeois') as evidence of a watering down of feminism away from Mozzoni's ideological clarity and emphasis on equality.[27] American historian Donald Meyer too, in a comparative study, was dismissive of the UFN's approach.[28] Buttafuoco, in contrast, challenged this interpretation, arguing that, to understand practical feminists, we need to look at what they did, not just what they said.[29] Buttafuoco saw the UFN as having many values in common with 1970s feminism (of which she herself was, politically, a product), in other words, a belief in gender equivalence rather than sameness, in 'equal but different'. 'Practical feminists', she argued, were social maternalists who believed that welfare would not just alleviate social distress but also lead to civil and political rights for women. At the heart of this lay a belief in the value and importance of women's maternal role.[30]

Even Buttafuoco admits that some of their activities looked banal, just like philanthropy, and that the emphasis on maternity was, in part, a defensive strategy against feminism's detractors who said that it made women unnatural.[31] But, in her view, their aims were anything but traditional. Through their public role in welfare, practical feminists believed, women would gain confidence and self-awareness, and would raise the consciousness of other women. Thus, such activities would help forge a new kind of woman, shaping and elevating both activists and their clients. Moreover, in their welfare work, practical feminists felt they could demonstrate women's potential for citizenship, their fitness for positions of public and political responsibility. Citizenship, in this analysis, was not simply neutral, for such welfare work would show new ways to run the country to the benefit of both sexes: the whole of society, they believed, would be improved by the increased influence of women and the extension of female and domestic virtues. For them, feminism was a way of remaking the world, not just winning rights.

Feminism as duty: Catholic feminism

Catholic women were another, very different, group who exalted women's maternal role and focused on welfare work.[32] In this period, worried by encroaching secularism and the rise of socialism, the Church took an active interest in attempting to offset the social ills caused by economic growth. The Papal Encyclical *Rerum Novarum* (1891) had led to the launching of 'social Catholicism'. Many young Catholic women threw themselves into this new work, seeing it as a route to a religious revival. By Italy's 'Belle Époque' at the turn of the century, women were active in various 'social Catholic' initiatives, including trade unions, mutual societies and welfare organisations.

Although not all in the Church accepted an active role for women, others, particularly Christian democrats, encouraged it. They believed that women, who were proving the more enduringly devout of the sexes, should be mobilised to stem the tide of secularisation and, in particular, the advance of atheist socialism. In short, women were to be the vanguard in the Church's stand against modernity. The term 'Catholic feminism' began to be used, although this implied no desire to reduce gender inequality: women were deemed equal only on a spiritual, not a terrestrial, level. The idea was not to change women's condition but for them to help the Church in its mission to re-Christianise the family and stem the increasing atheism of men. In short, 'Catholic feminism' meant not new rights but new duties for women, new ways to serve God. Women were to carry out these duties without being taken away from their true mission as wives and mothers. There was, for example, a new emphasis on the role of mothers in instilling religious and moral values in their children. The adoption of the term 'feminism' in the context of welfare work was understandable given the importance of welfare for many secular feminists, although, of course, for them it was a route to women's emancipation. The official position of the Church hierarchy could not have been more different. 'Catholic feminism' was not, therefore, just a mild version of lay feminism, but its diametric opposite, for lay feminism itself was a sign of modernity, against which the Church was doing battle.

Catholic feminists generally agreed on things like improved education (particularly religious education) and legal reforms like the introduction of paternity searches, but otherwise their views varied. Some remained true to the position of the Church hierarchy, emphasising duty and the gulf between them and other 'feminisms'. Elena Da Persico and her magazine *L'azione muliebre*, for example, whilst attempting to give middle-class Catholic women a better understanding of the world and campaigning for issues like child protection, never wavered from full support of the official line that supernatural gender equality made earthly equality irrelevant. Although such women called themselves feminists, feminism, for them, meant restoring female dignity and enhancing women's moral and religious role, not rights. In 1906, for example, *L'azione muliebre* opposed individual female suffrage, instead advocating the compromise position of the family vote.

But 'Christian feminism', with its emphasis on the value of the feminine, ended up having an effect on some activists, who found that their faith became a route to emancipatory ideas. Partly through contact with the feminist movement and through welfare and union work, they drew closer to the positions of secular feminists, on certain issues at least. Prominent among these were a group of young Milanese activists associated with the Fascio Femminile Democratico Cristiano (founded 1901), the magazine *Pensiero ed azione* (founded 1904) edited by Adelaide Coari (a young, fervently religious, primary teacher with a social conscience) and the Federazione Femminile Milanese (founded 1905 and eventually with a membership of 20,000). Many of these activists were involved in things like organising workers and founding vocational schools. Coari and others from the Fascio, encouraged in their activism by 'modern' clerics such as Monsignor Radini Tedeschi, initially toed the official line of 'feminism as duty'. However, whilst essentially never abandoning this position, they increasingly embraced some of the demands of secular feminism, including suffrage. Voting, of course, could itself be construed as a duty, another way for pious women to combat socialism. Even they, nonetheless, never advocated divorce, nor did they question the importance of the family (but then, neither did other feminists).

Coari and the Milanese Catholic feminists forged links with secular feminism. In 1907 they organised a conference open to all, even socialists, to discuss those parts of the feminist programme that Catholics could support without compromising their faith, like equal pay, workers' education, paternity searches and even the vote (in local elections). The conference was well attended and much common ground identified, although there were disagreements too, such as a dispute between Majno and Da Persico over whether unmarried mothers should be able to benefit from maternity funds. In 1908 some Catholic women attended the first national women's conference.

Unity and fragmentation: the CNDI and the 1908 Conference

Behind the 1908 conference was the Consiglio Nazionale delle Donne Italiane (CNDI – National Council of Italian Women), the Italian section of the International Council of Women, founded in 1903 in Rome.[33] From the start the CNDI aspired to dominate the women's movement and to represent it internationally. Although ostensibly secular, interclass and apolitical (women's issues, it argued, were above such divisions), it was in fact a conservative organisation which aimed to stem social upheaval not foment it. Its membership was dominated by aristocratic and upper middle-class women, mostly anti-socialist supporters of the ruling Liberals. The Queen was its patron and its founders included the Duchess of Aosta, Princess Letizia di Savoia and Countess Gabriella Spalletti Rasponi (CNDI president from 1903 to 1931). Many of its leaders had close associations with the political elite, indeed some were married to Liberal parliamentary deputies. Many of the feminists who subsequently became Fascists came from this organisation, such as Teresa Labriola (head of the CNDI legal section) and Daisy di Robilant.

The CNDI had branches all over Italy and affiliated to it were numerous women's associations, not all of them feminist. They included Catholic groups and welfare organisations with no ambition to challenge the patriarchal order. From 1907 to 1911 its newspaper (unofficially, given that it presented itself as unaligned) was *Vita femminile italiana*. One source estimated its membership in 1912 at 16,000.[34]

The CNDI was active in various fields and created sections to focus on different branches of its activities, including Education, Legal Affairs, Work, Hygiene and Emigration. It campaigned for legal reform and actively promoted the 'cultural elevation' of women, running libraries and so on. Before the First World War, however, it did not openly call for suffrage (although some CNDI members, like Maria Montessori, did so individually). This was because the CNDI considered that women were not yet ready to vote. Often it spoke as much of duties as rights and it was increasingly patriotic. Like the UFN, however, the CNDI did believe that through welfare and other initiatives women could prove their worth and demonstrate their capacity to take a place in the public sphere. Although many CNDI members were influenced

LA **DOMENICA** DEL **CORRIERE**

Anno . . . . L. 8 – L. 10,–
Semestre . . . . . . » 2,75 » 5,25

Si pubblica a Milano ogni Domenica
Dono agli Abbonati del "Corriere della Sera „

UFFICI DEL GIORNALE:
Via Solferino, 28
MILANO

Anno X. — N. 18   3 10 Maggio 1908   Centesimi 10 il numero

Il primo Congresso delle donne italiane a Roma : la seduta inaugurale nella sala degli Orazi e Curiazi in Campidoglio.
(Disegno di A. Beltrame)

Illustration 2 The inaugural session of the first Italian National Women's Conference, organised by the CNDI in Rome in 1908.
(Reproduced courtesy of Fototeca Storica Nazionale Ando Gilardi.)

by Catholic values, it always presented itself as secular and lacked formal links with the Church. Membership was open to non-Catholics.

Many activities of the CNDI and its affiliated groups were welfare initiatives of various kinds. Some of their initiatives were similar to those of the

UFN (they too, for example, ran an information bureau in Rome) and they similarly emphasised maternal welfare. Many CNDI activists, however, saw welfare differently from the UFN, as a means of social control that could prevent unrest, and they emphasised morality and discipline. Although CNDI activists did hope to improve conditions for the poor, the defence of class interests was often apparent in their approach. Funding for the CNDI Maternity Fund (founded in Rome in 1907), for example, came solely from charitable donations and subscriptions from worker members: neither the state nor employers were asked to contribute.

One of their more original ideas was the Industrie Femminili Italiane (founded 1903),[35] which promoted traditional female handicraft activities like lacemaking. This aimed to help free women from the brutal exploitation of the sweated trades. It offered support to numerous small initiatives (workshops and training schools) all over Italy. It was run in a commercial manner (albeit assisted by donations and the volunteer labour of the organisers) but with a welfare aim: to offer paid employment to poor women. The main role of the central organisation was to promote sales of the handicrafts on international markets.

In April 1908 the CNDI organised the first national conference for the women's movement. It was attended by delegates from a rainbow of different political views (about 1,400 delegates from approximately 70 organisations), including socialists, radicals, moderates, Catholics, representatives of foreign organisations and even royalty. It had six sections (Education and Instruction, Welfare and Social Insurance, Women's Moral and Legal Condition, Hygiene, Art and Literature, Emigration). The most publicly visible feminist event in this period, it saw wide-ranging debate on a spectrum of issues. This moment of unprecedented unity, however, quickly gave rise to an irreparable rift.

Minor disputes arose over questions like whether the state should contribute to maternity funds. On this issue the different sides did not necessarily align according to organisation: the advocates of state contributions included Schiff, Labriola and Coari. Much more serious was the dispute over religious education. Some Catholic feminists were present (as individuals rather than as official representatives), reassured by promises that certain topics would not be aired, including divorce. They were appalled when the socialist Linda Malnati broke the pre-conference agreement by tabling a last-minute motion to ban religious education in primary schools, replacing it with the study of comparative religion. After a heated debate, a vote overwhelmingly passed Malnati's motion. This abruptly ended co-operation between Catholic and secular feminists. When, in 1912, the CNDI organised a conference on education, various other groups, including the UFN, were represented but not Catholic women.

Despite Coari's strong defence of religious education at the conference, this proved the beginning of the end for Catholic feminism. Young and politically naive, Coari dug her own grave when she subsequently included reports of the debates at the UFN's conference held in Milan in May 1908 in her paper *Pensiero ed azione*. She even recommended Bebel's *Women and Socialism* as holiday reading (albeit to help Catholic women understand the opposition). Soon her opponents in the Church hierarchy, and some of her erstwhile supporters, moved against her. As a fervent believer, who had always professed utmost devotion to Papal authority, she chose her faith over her feminism and closed her newspaper. The Federazione Femminile similarly folded. This ended 'Catholic feminism' (although many practising Catholics, without close links to the Catholic hierarchy, did continue to play a role in feminist organisations).

The idea of a national Catholic women's organisation had been around since 1900 but it was only in April 1909 that this was finally inaugurated as the Unione fra le Donne Cattoliche d'Italia (UDCI – Union of Catholic Women). To avoid a repeat of what had just occurred, the new organisation, headed, from 1909 to 1917, by the tireless, authoritarian and uncompromising Princess Cristina Giustiniani Bandini, was placed firmly under Vatican control and instructed to stick to a spiritual mission. Pius X explicitly stipulated that its role excluded, 'politics or calls for rights which are in direct opposition to the providential mission of women'.[36] Its aim was not to improve women's lot but to defend Christianity. As Cecilia Dau Novelli has noted, the Vatican decided this organisation was needed to counter the threat posed by the rise of secular feminism.[37] In theory the UDCI was strictly subordinated to the Church hierarchy, but, with such a loyal organiser at its helm, the Vatican allowed it a degree of autonomy.[38] This enabled it, despite its apolitical remit, to do far more than just run prayer meetings. It carried out welfare activities, campaigned for religious education in schools and against divorce, advocated the minimum wage and even helped create all-female trade unions (for telephonists, seamstresses, nurses and tramworkers). It had numerous committees, even in small towns, and educated its members via readings, conferences and training courses. In theory, although it drew a number of other organisations into its sphere, it was centralised and hierarchical (since the Pope thought this easier to control). In practice, some local committees went their own way. Whilst never espousing feminism, it did help modernise the role of Catholic women, offering them an active extra-domestic role. It grew quickly: by 1912 there were 180 committees and 30,000 members.

The Pope, in reality, had never supported female suffrage. He had made this clear in May 1906 in audiences with Camilla Teimer and Elena da Persico. To Teimer he said that he was in favour of female education and women's welfare role, 'but not female voters, not members of parliament. . . . Yes, there is nothing wrong, on the contrary there is much to admire, in a feminism which aims to elevate women socially and intellectually, but God preserve us from political feminism!'[39] Essentially, the Pope had tolerated Catholic feminism rather than supporting it. Nonetheless, both Coari and Giustiniani Bandini were interesting role models, assertive women who took a prominent role in the public sphere. Both, in their own way, helped pave the way for the political role of Catholic women later in the century.

'A leap in the dark': the vote and the suffrage committees

In 1861, only a tiny minority of male Italians had suffrage rights but a series of reforms modified this. In 1882 the wealth and education qualifications were lowered. This enfranchised all middle-class and some working-class men and increased the electorate from half a million to two million. In 1912 the vote was extended to all literate men over 21, illiterate males over 30, and all others who had completed military service. No women obtained the vote in this period, although the question was much discussed. In the decades after 1861 the issue of suffrage, for at least some categories of women, was debated a number of times in parliament and in 1888 a parliamentary committee declared itself in favour of (certain) women voting in local elections. This, however, was overruled by Prime Minister Crispi.

All sorts of arguments were mobilised against female suffrage,[40] including the oft-repeated fear of the sexes 'promiscuously' mingling at polling stations (even some supporters of suffrage advocated women voting by proxy) and worries that women were too weak and impressionable to cope with being intensely lobbied as electors. Some argued that women would just obey their husbands, thereby giving married men an extra vote, or, conversely, that if they voted differently it would foment domestic strife. Some baldly stated that women's place was in the home, not in the turbulent world of the electoral rally, or that they lacked the capacity to understand the issues. Others said that women were still ill-prepared to vote or considered female suffrage, as Giolitti put it, 'a leap in the dark'. Even many socialists opposed it, fearing that women would vote for the Right. Some reformist Catholics supported it, believing that women would vote for them.

Overall, there was more support to enfranchise women in local than in national elections. Local matters were seen as closer to women's 'natural', domestic concerns. There was, however, no explicit ban on female suffrage in national elections in the 1848 Statuto and in the 1859 and 1882 legislation (although the assumption was that they would not do so), whereas for local elections this was explicitly stated. In pre-unification Lombardy, Veneto and Tuscany a tiny number of propertied women had been able to vote (via proxies) and some early suffrage campaigners tried to build on this precedent. This failed, although some concessions were made. From 1877 women were allowed to be legal witnesses, from 1890 administrators in charities, and from 1893 members of *collegi dei probiviri* (arbitration boards for minor labour disputes). From 1910, female business owners could vote to elect Chamber of Commerce officials, and from 1911, women could both vote and be candidates for elected roles in schools.

As such an overarching issue, the vote became a rallying point that brought feminists together. In 1897 the magazine *Vita femminile* had first proposed a national suffrage committee but this came to nothing since, as yet, feminists were not very focused on this question. Some, particularly those connected with the PSI, believed that women were still unready for it. More education was needed first. Things really took off, however, in 1904, when the Republican parliamentary deputy Roberto Mirabelli presented a women's suffrage bill. This stimulated a flurry of activity and debate.

From 1905 onwards suffrage became a core issue for feminists. Other activities, like welfare, continued, but increasingly feminists believed that only with the vote could their other demands be met; 1905 saw the foundation of local *comitati pro-suffragio* (suffrage committees) composed of representatives of different feminist organisations, which rapidly spread across Italy. Some of the committees (in Turin, for example) admitted members of both sexes. In 1906, the Roman committee proclaimed itself to be national (the Comitato Nazionale Pro-Suffragio Femminile – CNPSF) and joined the International Women's Suffrage Alliance. Its president was Giacinta Martini Marescotti, wife of a Giolittian deputy. *L'alleanza*, edited by Carmela Baricelli, was, albeit unofficially, its newspaper.

The suffrage committees organised talks and other activities and urged women to attempt to enrol on provincial electoral registers, on the grounds that the legislation governing general elections did not specifically exclude them. In some areas, women were successful in registering. Subsequently, however, courts ruled against them in all cases.

The Rome committee launched a suffrage petition, drafted by Mozzoni. Signatures were collected all over Italy and it was presented to parliament in early 1907. Mirabelli's bill, however, was defeated in February 1907 (Republicans and Radicals had supported it whilst Socialists had proved ambivalent) but the parliamentary debate on it did lead to Giolitti setting up a commission to investigate the feasibility of enfranchising women in local elections. This focused on trying to identify categories of women who could be trusted to vote, by compiling statistics on things like female education and numbers of women active in the public sphere, in trade unions, charities and so on. The commission came to nothing as it concluded that the impact of giving women the vote was too uncertain.

In 1909, a new tactic was proposed by some younger suffrage campaigners like Teresa Labriola, imitating a technique tried in Britain, to offer active support to the campaigns of 50 deputies they had identified as favourable to their cause (what Labriola described as founding a 'feminist-suffragist party'). This strategy caused a rift in the suffrage committees that led to the demotion of the president and a takeover by Labriola. It angered the socialists, who had no interest in supporting non-socialist deputies.

A further, more serious fracture (Buttafuoco called it the 'first real rupture' of the women's movement[41]) came over the question of the Libyan War in 1911–12. Some increasingly patriotic feminists, particularly from the CNDI (despite the fact that it claimed to be essentially pacifist), rallied to the imperialist enterprise. Labriola was among those who backed the war, deluding herself that the government would grant women suffrage in return for this display of loyalty.

This created a split with the socialists. At the PSI conference in Modena in October 1911, Anna Kuliscioff asked socialist women to leave the pro-suffrage committees. This became official PSI policy and 'dual militancy' was condemned. Membership of feminist associations was declared incompatible with PSI membership. This hugely weakened the suffrage committees. Their already small membership dwindled, making it increasingly implausible that they could speak on behalf of all Italian women. By 1913 the Lombard suffrage committee, for example, had only 190 members.[42]

Even before this radical split, the suffrage issue had created friction between the PSI and feminists. Although many campaigners had looked to the PSI for support, its attitude had been luke-warm and sometimes overtly hostile, particularly as some feminists were willing to fight to enfranchise certain women only. It was, in fact, only after this latter idea had been raised in the 1908 conference that Kuliscioff threw herself into a campaign for universal suffrage. Before this, even she had lacked interest in the question, judging women too politically immature to vote, and her attitude had done nothing to help socialists like Malnati who did want to co-operate with the suffrage committees. By 1910, however, Kuliscioff was willing to openly challenge her own partner, the leading socialist parliamentarian Filippo Turati, in what she famously called a 'family disagreement', when he argued that universal male suffrage had to be won first. He also maintained that female voters would be a conservative influence, damaging to socialist interests. Only in 1911, at the Modena conference, did the PSI finally commit itself to supporting female suffrage and instruct its deputies to vote for it, whether for local or for national elections.

In the parliamentary debate on the extension of the franchise in 1912, female suffrage was again aired (the amendment was presented by Turati and fellow socialist deputy Claudio Treves) but shelved for the time being (48 deputies voted for it and 209 against). Adding female voters would have further radically increased the size of the electorate, and the parliament had neither the confidence nor the will to take this step.

The 1912 electoral reform made the question of women's suffrage seem even more anomalous now that even illiterate men could vote. Some suffragists were spurred on by this. Kuliscioff and other socialist women, for example, waged a campaign for the vote in the *Difesa delle lavoratrici*. Some more conservative feminists, however, became uncertain, fearful of adding yet more poor people of either sex to the electoral rolls. After 1912 the debate continued but, by the outbreak of the First World War, Italian women seemed no nearer than ever to obtaining political representation.

'Exemplary lives': sexuality and the women's movement

Most feminists were sexual puritans. A few advocated birth control, to ensure that maternity was never enforced but chosen, but the majority shunned this issue (or at most described contraception as a necessary evil), calling instead for male restraint. Most believed that women's primary role was motherhood, and sexuality itself inherently bad. This attitude is perhaps not surprising given that most men did nothing to encourage their wives to enjoy sex.

Through their campaign for paternity searches feminists did assert women's right to dignity in motherhood even if unmarried. However, although not all were themselves wives and mothers, feminists of all types generally supported marriage as an institution. A good example of this was the wave of hostile criticism that greeted Sibilla Aleramo's pathbreaking novel *A Woman* (1906), in which the protagonist leaves her marriage and is therefore forced to abandon her child with her husband. This was seen as abhorrent by many feminists. Ersilia Majno, for example, strongly criticised the book as self-indulgent and the behaviour of the protagonist as selfish, a selfishness that feminists needed to rise above. Majno believed that feminists needed to have 'exemplary lives' and that this was the wrong sort of role model.[43]

This puritanical approach also created problems at the Asilo Mariuccia, a residential home run by the UFN in Milan, which aimed to assist girls and adolescents to escape or avoid prostitution. Here, the organisers' moralising approach created a gulf between them and the young women they were attempting to 'redeem'. The feminists saw morality and modesty as essential (trying, for example, to stop the residents even speaking about sex) whereas, for many prostitutes, economics was more important. They found the feminists condescending: many of them just wanted board and lodging and had no desire to be converted into prim young ladies by middle-class feminists.[44]

Assisting or 'redeeming' prostitutes had long been seen as a feminist issue.[45] As early as the 1870s some, including Mozzoni, had been involved in abolitionist campaigns against the prostitution laws. They argued that the regulations were ineffective in improving public health and were humiliating for the women themselves. They criticised the fact that health checks were imposed on prostitutes but not on clients and the fact that the state profited from evil by taxing brothels. Prostitution, many of them felt, was neither necessary nor inevitable: instead, men should control their sexual urges.

At the beginning of the twentieth century, feminist involvement in this question took a new direction. Spurred on by lurid tales about the trafficking of women, feminists joined international campaigns against the 'white slave trade'. Italy's Committee against the White Slave Trade, founded in 1901 by a group of Milanese women, soon became a national organisation, with Ersilia Majno at its helm. It took a broad approach, looking not just at the economic causes of prostitution but also at factors like rape, incest and legal issues such as the need for paternity searches to make single mothers less vulnerable.

Catholics too became involved in this issue, founding the Comitato Italiano per la Protezione della Giovane (Italian Committee for the Protection of Young Women) in Milan in 1902. This association, which aimed to protect young women from falling into prostitution, grew quickly, particularly in the North, and became, effectively, Italy's first national Catholic female organisation. The Catholics, however, had no interest in the civil rights of prostitutes or the iniquities of the sexual double standard and shunned feminist proposals for sex education to warn girls about prostitution.

An uphill struggle

First-wave feminism in Italy was a diverse and fascinating movement. Its activities and demands were varied. Some feminists wanted timid reform. Others, as Teresa Moglia put it in 1907, aspired to 'transform society from top to bottom'.[46] Like many other European feminist movements of the time, however, the Italian movement's achievements were limited. By the outbreak of the First World War, although there had been some minor successes (such as women being allowed to be administrators of charities) there had been no significant legislative reform, nor had the movement attracted a mass membership (although its sympathisers were certainly more numerous than its activists). Moreover, many women's associations had a great continuity of leadership and the same names cropped up again and again in different organisations and publications. This suggests that there were problems with inspiring the younger generation, a problem that made it easy for Fascism to later dismiss feminism as old-fashioned, belonging to a bygone age.

The explanation for this weakness lies in a number of factors. These include Italy's deeply divided and malformed political system, the smallness of its middle class, the fact that there was little tradition of women working together in an organised manner, and the level of female education. The pressure of 'respectability', moreover, made it difficult for women, particularly the unmarried, to take an active role in the public sphere. Many were even afraid to have it known that they had subscribed to a feminist periodical, sheltering behind initials or pseudonyms in subscription lists. Italian ideas about appropriate gender behaviour certainly made suffragette-style antics unthinkable and it was not by chance that many of its leaders came from atypical 'outsider' groups. The opposition to feminism, moreover, was strong: the unholy alliance between science and religion, both preaching female inferiority, was highly problematic and the divisive impact of both the Vatican and the PSI in instructing their followers to cease co-operating with other feminists undermined attempts at unity. Far from all women, moreover, supported feminism. Much press coverage did little to help: feminists were regularly lampooned by male journalists. The legal weakness of women also hampered efforts to win more rights. Married woman, for example, could not even subscribe to periodicals without their husband's 'marital authorisation'. Inevitably many feminist publications were short-lived. Large numbers of women, particularly in isolated rural areas, doubtless never even heard of feminism in this period. In short, the task of feminists was an uphill struggle.

However, although feminists did fail to remake Italian society in a new mould, they fought with courage and commitment for what they believed in. They may never have engaged in dramatic direct action like the British suffragettes but neither did other European feminist movements. They did succeed in bringing the 'woman question' to the fore and, had parliamentary democracy not collapsed in 1922, it is probable that many of their demands would have been met fairly quickly, as was demonstrated by the reforms of 1919. But this was not to be, for soon the rise of Fascism changed everything.

Apart from the question of religious education, which caused rifts with Catholics, the most divisive factor for the movement was war: first the Libyan War and then the First World War. Only a tiny number of feminists actively campaigned for Italy's intervention in the Great War but many middle- and upper-class feminists were to rally to the war effort once Italy became involved.

3

On the 'Home Front': World War One and its Aftermath, 1915–20

Many historians have concluded that wars are limited in their ability to emancipate women. They may open up new roles but these are usually temporary. Wars may appear to subvert the gender order, but, with peace, it is restored, often with a vengeance. Periods of warfare often bring an exaltation of traditional gender roles with men portrayed as warriors and women as mothers, symbolic guardians of peace, normality and the home, which soldiers protect by their fighting and can return to when hostilities end. Indeed, the Higonnets have argued, invoking the image of the 'double helix' to explain the enduring constancy of gender differentiation in wartime, that, in both world wars, women only stepped temporarily into the 'male sphere'. Meanwhile male activities were still construed as socially more important.[1] This idea, which suggests no real change at all, is perhaps too rigid, although it does have resonances for the Italian experience. As for other countries, the issues are complex. In Italy, some, albeit fairly limited, change brought by World War One did outlive the ending of hostilities and there were opportunities for women to prove their worth in both paid employment and voluntary work. But lasting change was limited.

For Italy, the Great War was a traumatic event that both forged and revealed the inadequacies of national identity.[2] Italy joined the war in 1915 after prolonged, heated debate about whether to intervene, a debate that tore the nation apart and created a rift along which post-war politics would later align. Although Italy did eventually decide to fight (alongside France and Britain), after a sustained campaign by a minority of extremely vocal 'interventionists', many Italians remained opposed to going to war. Italy's war experience was terrible for soldiers but generally better for civilians compared with the Second World War. In the Great War, the battlefront and 'home front' were quite distinct: few non-combatants actually witnessed the fighting. The only exceptions were those living near the front lines or in parts of the Veneto invaded by the Austrians after the defeat of Caporetto in 1917. Here women experienced some of the horrors of war. In the occupied territory, as the research for a post-war

Royal Commission revealed, rapes, including terrible incidents of drunken gang-raping, or of very young girls or elderly women, were common.[3]

Elsewhere in Italy, life went on more or less as normal, to the extent that some middle- and upper-class people continued to take seaside holidays throughout the conflict. This does not mean that civilians experienced no changes in their lives. Many suffered a good deal. The war dragged on far longer than expected, real wages fell and many ate more poorly than before, something with potentially dramatic consequences for the millions for whom hunger was a feature of everyday life even in peacetime. Due to the inefficiency of the government, bread, the mainstay of the diet of many of the poor, was only rationed from September 1917, making shortages common. Loaves were frequently bulked with other ingredients rendering them virtually inedible. Resistance to disease fell and the death rate from illnesses like TB rose. It has been estimated that about 600,000 additional civilian deaths occurred during the course of the war, a similar death toll to that of the battlefield.[4] Moreover, vast numbers of Italians (estimates range from 375,000 to 650,000) of both sexes died from 'Spanish flu' in 1918–19. Italy was poorly equipped for this terrifying epidemic, lacking sufficient medical supplies or even gravediggers.

The concept of the *fronte interno* (home front) was, of course, born in this conflict. In Italy, it was used as a mobilising notion by interventionists from 1915 with the aim of rallying the whole nation to the war. In the new 'modern' warfare of this conflict, where logistics were as important as the valour of combatants, a nation's military might was now directly linked to its economic prowess and its ability to mobilise the support of civilians. This was highly significant for women, who were asked to contribute to the war in a parallel effort to that of soldiers, making it a catalytic moment for ideas about women and the nation. Welfare work was presented as patriotic activity and widows and 'mothers of the fallen' as suffering for the nation. All this helped legitimise the idea of a political role for women and, as some feminists argued, their right to suffrage.

Men and masculinity[5]

Although many did fight, far from all Italian men were called up. Some were too old or too young. Others were exempted as workers in essential war industries. Some volunteered enthusiastically, dreaming of heroism and glory. Their illusions were soon shattered. Much of Italy's war, as on other fronts (albeit here mainly in mountainous areas), involved men awaiting death or injury in filthy trenches, and there were few real battles in the traditional sense. About 600,000 Italian soldiers were taken prisoner, 100,000 of whom died in captivity of diseases like TB or simple starvation. Italian men's war memoirs reveal experiences similar to those of soldiers of other combatant nations. They remember passivity and daily tedium interspersed with terrifying episodes of horror. Diaries and letters show that most soldiers' main aim was simply to survive. For many, particularly peasants, who had mainly been reluctant conscripts, it was an incomprehensible experience. Most, moreover, felt misunderstood when they got home because censorship meant that few civilians fully grasped what was taking place at the front. Many returned physically disabled or with deep psychological problems.

The very virility of Italian men was, moreover, cast into question both by the passivity of trench warfare and by the terrible, humiliating rout of Caporetto with its mass, disorderly retreat. Only the *arditi*, the shock-troops who carried out daring missions, could return home with a glamorised memory of war. All of this made the conflict unsettling for traditional notions of masculinity and one way to view Fascism's emphasis on militarism is as an attempt to remedy this.

It is, therefore, impossible to see this war as positive for Italian men. Approximately 650,000 soldiers (precise figures will never be known) died, about 500,000 were permanently physically or psychologically injured, and a million more were wounded. For some women, however, the period brought new opportunities in employment and voluntary roles. But even for many women this was a difficult period, marked by anxiety, hunger and privation. For some, particularly those who lost loved ones, it was a dark, traumatic time.

Widows

For many women, the war was a time of waiting anxiously without reliable news of their menfolk, often for months or even years. Many had to care for husbands or sons who returned home maimed or sick. About 200,000 were widowed.[6] As women who had left their father's home but were no longer under the control of a husband, war widows were seen as problematic. Many were young, potentially sexual women. One solution to this was to cast them, alongside the 'mothers of the fallen', in the role of heroic victims who represented the nation's ritual mourning in post-war commemorative ceremonies, a conservative role that echoed Catholic images of suffering womanhood.

Widowhood could have 'emancipating' aspects for women who became heads of families thereby acquiring various legal rights. However, for many, the grief of bereavement was accompanied by economic distress. Widowhood could be economically disastrous for the poor as female wages were so low. Even for middle-class women it could have a dramatic impact as many of them lacked employment experience and had not expected to have to earn a living. Some of these problems were attenuated by the gradual emergence of a welfare system, one that helped pioneer the idea of state responsibilities in welfare.

After initially assisting widows by supporting voluntary organisations in the field, the state then intervened more directly with financial subsidies. From 1918 even 'widowed' fiancées became eligible for payments, reflecting the social importance of the *promessa* on the road to wedlock. The subsidies were, however, small and quickly eroded by inflation. Many widows had to seek help from charities. Eventually, they began to organise, founding the Associazione Madri e Vedove dei Caduti in Guerra (Association of War Widows and Mothers of the Fallen) in 1917, which lobbied for financial help as well as promoting widows' importance in the rites of public mourning.

Welfare work

Widows were far from the only recipients of welfare. During the war, a large number of middle- and upper-class women threw themselves into providing assistance for soldiers and their families. Many of them embraced this opportunity with enthusiasm. Adele Reverdy, for example, wrote to her sister in 1916 that: 'I can't wait to get started, because by making some little sacrifice in this way, I'll feel less useless and passive amid all this feverish activity going on around me.'[7] From early 1915, civil preparation committees mushroomed all over Italy with, as their motto, Prime Minister Salandra's words: 'Those who do not lend their arms to the nation, must give their minds, their possessions, their hearts, their renunciations, their sacrifices.'[8] The committees were founded and run by local elites, all acting in an unpaid capacity, but many lower middle-class people, such as primary teachers, got involved too, as did some priests.[9] Where local elites failed to spontaneously establish one, local authorities stepped in. Even municipal committees relied on volunteer labour and donations, although they could also levy extraordinary taxes.

The government entrusted these committees with all forms of war-related civil welfare, rendering them semi-official bodies. They co-ordinated the activities of pre-existing, more specialised welfare organisations in their area, many of which, of course, were women's associations. From July 1915 the committees gained responsibility for handing out state subsidies for soldiers' families without other means of subsistence. Some also offered their own, local subsidies. Ostensibly apolitical, many were in practice run by the pro-war elites and quickly became active propagandists for the war. Indeed, as Andrea Fava has argued, their aim was often less to help the needy (although they certainly did this) than to rally the population to the war effort and, at the same time, to watch out for signs of defeatism.[10] In their work, the borders between welfare and social control were fragile: often material assistance was leavened with propaganda. As the war went on, government supervision of the committees and other welfare organisations increasingly tightened.

Because of their pre-war welfare experience, the committees actively encouraged women to work with them. Where the women's movement was strong, such as in large northern cities, women preserved their autonomy by creating their own sections. Elsewhere this proved more difficult. The welfare activities women did in this context included rolling bandages, collecting wool, making warm clothes for the troops, assisting soldiers' families and running nurseries for their children. Women ran information offices to help families keep in touch with male relatives at war, organised refreshment stalls for troops in transit at railway stations, sent relief parcels to the front, ran soup kitchens, assisted orphans and refugees and did plenty of fundraising. They organised 'weddings in absentia' so that fiancées could qualify for subsidies while awaiting the return of soldier grooms. Some became *madrine di guerra*, corresponding with prisoners of war, although this aroused the comments of moralists (particularly in the Catholic press) who feared that impressionable girls would forge relationships with soldiers.

Women were also active in campaigns to limit waste, such as finding new uses for old cloth and newspapers. They promoted the cultivation of 'war vegetable plots'. Foreshadowing what would happen in the 1930s, peasant women were particularly targeted as both producers and consumers of food and, indeed, as potential saboteurs of food production. Women involved with these campaigns mainly did home visits and fundraising, whereas most of the actual talks were given by men.[11]

Even Catholic women were active in war welfare. The UDCI, increasingly a mass organisation with about 50,000 members grouped into 300 committees by January 1917, became involved in a whole range of initiatives in addition to spiritual assistance. These included helping war orphans, training nurses and creating and running nurseries and afterschool activities for the children of soldiers.[12]

Feminism and the war

The question of intervention or neutrality, which deeply divided Italy during 1914, cut transversally across women's associations. No single organisation adopted a clear anti-war stance. Many feminists opposed the war but, as the previous chapter showed, some had already begun to abandon pacifism in rallying to the Libyan War. Even before the First World War broke out there was some, albeit limited, feminist discussion of the idea of wartime civilian service for women, as an equivalent to the call-up for men.[13]

In 1914, a few feminists could be found among those actively calling for intervention in the new conflict.[14] Their reasons varied. The most high-profile and vocal figure was Teresa Labriola, who wrote copiously in the press and published numerous patriotic pamphlets. In October 1914 she resigned from the CNDI because it rejected her proposal to spread propaganda to use only Italian goods. Labriola, who had embraced the rising doctrine of nationalism, was increasingly anti-democratic.[15] Others, including a handful of socialist women, spoke instead of a democratic war against the reactionary central European powers or of the sufferings of the people of Belgium. In early 1915, these interventionist socialists (who included Anna Kuliscioff) aired their views in *La difese della lavoratrici* until party leaders purged the paper's editors to return it to a neutralist line.[16] The (by now elderly) Anna Maria Mozzoni also supported intervention. Together with many other democratic patriots, she saw the idea of Italy fighting alongside the democratic powers as a completion of the Risorgimento.

Most feminists, however, were neutralists. When war broke out in Europe in 1914, many were depressed or appalled at the news. However, although some did remain pacifist throughout the conflict, many increasingly fell back on talk of sexual difference and how women's humanitarian mission could symbolically oppose male barbarism. Women, they felt, could safeguard values of peace and humanity amidst the horror of warfare. This was, however, interpreted as a call to welfare not pacifist civil disobedience. Not unusual was the attitude of Alice Schiavoni Bosio of the CNDI who, despite describing the war as 'a barbarous anachronism of the times' and women as 'naturally pacifist', argued that Italian women had a duty to the 'great mother' of the nation.[17]

Once hostilities commenced, even many feminists who had been, or still essentially were, neutralist, became involved. This meant that the war served to exacerbate the class divide between women. Whilst many of the poor protested against war, many middle- and upper-class women mobilised for it. Even Ersilia Majno and Linda Malnati, socialists who had both opposed intervention, did welfare work assisting soldiers' families.

The nature of pre-war feminism, with its emphasis on welfare and on women proving their worthiness for citizenship, rendered this more or less inevitable. The war offered an unprecedented opportunity for women to demonstrate their capabilities and some were proud to be asked to help, their experience, honed by years of pre-war welfare activities, needed at last by the authorities.[18] Some threw themselves into such work with enthusiasm, others with ambivalent feelings about the overall purpose and meaning of the conflict. Even though the aims of many feminists differed from state plans, they generally proved faithful followers of orders and tended not to voice criticisms.

The war brought much of the feminist movement together in home front activities, albeit not without rivalries and tensions between different groups and tendencies.[19] Some feminists became involved even before Italy actually entered the war, although initially the UFN held back. The CNDI and its affiliates took a leading role. As early as August 1914, it was calling on its members to compile lists of women who could offer their services to keep things running while men were at war.

The war spawned many new women's associations, large and small, local and national, too numerous to analyse or even list here, for war work. In some cases, women worked alongside men but this does not necessarily mean that they took a back seat. One of the most important war welfare organisations, the Federazione Nazionale dei Comitati di Assistenza (National Federation of Welfare Committees – FNCA), was formed from a merger between a male-run committee and a committee uniting all the Milanese feminist organisations (except the UFN). The FNCA, which eventually expanded to other Italian cities, had an organising committee with equal numbers of men and women and even dual presidents and treasurers, one of each sex.[20]

As time went on, war work changed the feminists themselves. Many of them gradually moved from their initial ambivalence to embrace the aims of the conflict, particularly after 1917 when fear of invasion gave a new sense of urgency to civil mobilisation. Activity, which had somewhat flagged during 1916 as volunteer fatigue set in, intensified in the charged post-Caporetto atmosphere. Patriotism also helped some make sense of an apparently pointless conflict, a war that was like none that had gone before. Working with the committees brought feminists into contact with the anti-socialist, nationalist Right and this helped erode their commitment to democracy.

Particularly in the latter part of the war, women's activities went far beyond simple humanitarian assistance to include a good deal of propaganda. They produced vast numbers of pamphlets and got involved in activities like encouraging people to donate gold for the war effort and sign up for national loans. They visited munitions factories to urge reluctant industrialists to employ more women. Some were directly involved in committees to sign up female labour.

The extent to which the feminist movement changed can be seen in the fact that, in May 1918, various prominent feminist organisations gave their support to the National Anti-German Conference. This, among other things, called for the internment of Germans and Austrians resident in Italy (even those with Italian nationality) and the seizure of their property.[21] By the last year of the war even some UFN members had embraced the idea of repressing 'internal enemies'.[22]

Buttafuoco has portrayed this dramatic capitulation of feminism to war-time patriotism as that of a weak movement swept along by the strong currents of the time.[23] There is much merit in this argument, although it is true that other, much stronger movements (in Britain, for example) did likewise. The rallying of some Italian feminists to the war, moreover, was not devoid of calculation: some believed that wartime responsibilities could lead to civil and political rights. Service in war was, of course, a good terrain on which to base claims because, since the French Revolution, citizenship had often been seen as linked to bearing arms for the nation. Women all over Europe had seen suffrage rights denied them precisely on these grounds.

Some interventionist feminists began to argue that women needed to be integrated into the nation for them to contribute properly to the war effort. Some even called for recognition of their work as a kind of auxiliary military service, with badges, uniforms and decorations. In 1917, at the FNCA second conference, there was a proposal that unmarried women and childless widows aged 14 to 48 should be compulsorily mobilised for the home front.[24] This would have given official recognition to what women were doing but the government failed to adopt the idea, despite the fact that some men, too, wanted a female call-up, albeit as part of the 'anti-shirker' campaign, which aimed to mobilise all non-militarised Italians.[25] The feminists never, however, called for women to actually fight.

In October 1917, a National Women's Conference held in Rome, to which all feminist organisations were invited, called for suffrage as well as reforms like paternity searches. Not all feminists agreed with this approach. Some were wary of making demands at a time of national emergency or just stated that there was no correlation between patriotic mobilisation and suffrage. Others remained troubled and confused by the war. Some, notably many female supporters of the Republican Party, considered it selfish to make demands. Women, they argued, should 'give without asking' in such times.[26]

Red Cross nurses

One prominent way that women could 'give' in this war, was by volunteer nursing. Red Cross nurses became iconic figures of the time, symbolic mothers who carried out a 'mass *maternage*' of the wounded and dying. Nursing before this had been a rough and ready profession with little or no training. Hospitals cared only for the poor and chronically ill. Their overworked and badly paid nurses had a reputation for dirt and ignorance, apart from those who were nuns (about 40 per cent in 1902), who were seen as more moral and disciplined. Many lay nurses were male, although nursing was being gradually feminised in this period.[27]

Red Cross nursing emerged at the beginning of the twentieth century in Italy.[28] Prior to this, women had been involved in the Italian Red Cross

Illustration 3   Group of volunteer Red Cross nurses in 1915.
(CRI Archive, Rome. Reproduced by kind permission of the II. VV Ispettorato Nazionale.)

(CRI – founded 1864) only as fundraisers. At the turn of the century, however, women's nursing courses were set up and by 1908, when the terrible earthquake hit Messina, about 500 women were ready to try their hand in the field. In the Libyan War, some CRI women served on a hospital ship.

During the Great War, CRI nurses became deeply involved in caring for the sick and wounded. By May 1915, about 4,000 women had received some CRI training. Most were unmarried, childless women from the very highest echelons of society. Many were patriotic monarchists and some had links to the CNDI.

In April 1915, a member of the royal family, Duchess Elena D'Aosta, was appointed as CRI National Inspectress. No mere figurehead, she intervened energetically to raise standards, and, although 'Haughty, harsh, unpopular at court', she was 'loved and respected by the nurses'.[29] Notwithstanding her efforts, hostility to CRI nurses persisted. Many worried about 'moral risks': any form of intimacy with soldiers or doctors was intensely frowned upon (an incident when nurses danced with officers, for example, was much criticised) and in this respect Italian nurses were far more restricted than their counterparts from places like Canada and Britain.

Despite opposition to their involvement, many Italian women wrote of their fervent desire to do their bit, inspired by a mixture of patriotism and a desire to infuse their lives with new meaning. Some, however, admitted in their memoirs that they went partly to assuage feelings of abandonment as their men went to the front. Maria Navoni, for example, wrote that, 'I needed the intense work to console myself, by consoling others.'[30] A few simply wanted the glamour and prestige of a CRI uniform. Whatever their initial motives, however, memoirs suggest that many of these women enjoyed themselves and took pride in their achievements.

Their actual role was usually restricted mainly to the cleaner parts of nursing like bringing meals, reading letters to patients and offering moral support. They did, however, have physical contact with the sick: they cleaned and dressed wounds and assisted at operations, all difficult tasks given the kind of warfare involved. Apart from often gruesome wounds, some patients had frostbite or gangrene or were victims of gassing. Some were literally crazed with terror. Volunteer nurses were not normally expected to clean wards, although at the front some ended up doing even this. Nurses' duties included the painful task of writing to the families of the deceased. CRI nurses proved themselves particularly useful in the 'caring' aspects of nursing (as emphasised by the 'Nightingale model' they followed), preserving a reassuring hierarchy which left the 'technical' aspects to male personnel. Although relations with their patients were usually good (some patients fell in love with CRI nurses), some volunteers were moralistic in their approach – lecturing their captive audience of the wounded on the dangers of drink and brothels and attempting to quash 'subversive' talk.

Initially CRI nurses worked mainly in local hospitals, in hospital trains or in first aid posts in railway stations. By 1916, however, some were at the front. Here the pace of work was frenetic, living conditions often primitive and the risks potentially great – from both infectious diseases and explosions. Nonetheless, some women were keen to get to the front. The reality was often tougher than they had anticipated. Many were not properly ready, in terms of either training or psychological preparation, for what they were to face. A few went home within days. Some, moreover, proved a difficult workforce. Although many were adaptable, others were resistant to accepting orders from 'social inferiors' and some were reluctant to take on less glamorous tasks like night shift work.

It was a mixture of such problems and a good dose of general prejudice against women that made many doctors and hospital orderlies hostile to them. This did not prevent CRI nurses being used, for they were needed: Italy quite simply lacked sufficient medical personnel to manage without them. Moreover, many CRI nurses worked hard and eventually won the respect of doctors.

Voluntary work, whether as nurses or in the more mundane activities of the committees, meant that women were involved in welfare activities on an unprecedented scale. For other women, actual employment opportunities opened up. But the distinction between welfare and paid work was sometimes blurred, as the example of garment-making shows.

Employment

Although the Italian economy did grow and modernise during the war, the largest single group of female 'war workers' was engaged in a traditional female occupation – making clothes. About 600,000 women made uniforms for the armed forces in workshops or as outworkers. Approximately 200,000 knitted woollen garments and 400,000 stitched uniforms.[31] Such work was vital because unprecedented quantities of military clothing were required: much of the fighting took place at high altitudes where warm clothing was necessary all year round. The military authorities, however, underestimated the importance of uniforms, seen as a lesser priority than arms and munitions. Moreover, the sector was poorly organised: attempts to get proper national control of the work fell foul of rivalries between ministries and departments.

Uniform manufacture was run in a strange manner. The labour force was not employed directly by the state. Instead, the chance to earn by making military clothing was offered primarily to the needy and presented as a form of welfare. Production was mostly managed by welfare organisations, mainly women's committees, and farmed out to female outworkers. Women, it was argued, could do the work in spare moments between housework and childcare. This system inevitably caused problems since the needs of production (urgent given that soldiers were dying from cold) and the welfare approach contradicted one another. Recruiting by need rather than skill meant that much work was shoddily done. As volunteers, the organisers were under no obligation to turn up and rarely had business skills.[32]

Although the supply of women willing to make uniforms varied according to local labour markets, in some areas huge numbers queued up for the work, testimony to the desperate plight of many civilians. Even lower middle-class women sought this work. Economically vulnerable in the war, sewing discreetly at home, even for a pittance, was a good option for them, since extra-domestic employment could compromise their respectability and class status.

Recruiting women to make clothes seemed an excellent idea as many organisers simply assumed that any woman could sew and knit. They were often surprised, however, by how few of those who sought work actually knew what to do. In practice the only women already skilled in this work were middle-class ladies (for whom sewing was an accomplishment they learned as a normal part of their upbringing) and professional seamstresses.

The notion of a market wage was ignored when fixing rates of pay. In parts of Tuscany, at the end of 1915, wages averaged about six lire per month, the price of twelve kilos of rough bread.[33] Wages were presented as merely a supplement to other income like state subsidies or the produce of a smallholding. The ample labour supply also kept wages down. It was difficult for the workforce to demand higher pay or even complain if work was lacking due to insufficient raw materials (a frequent problem) because ostensibly they were just receiving charity.

This system was fairly dysfunctional: a more professional approach focusing on training and mechanisation would have produced more uniforms. Many soldiers received insufficient clothing, often wearing the same filthy flea-infested garments for weeks on end. Some became sick, hypothermic or frostbitten as a result. However, although the whole enterprise was compromised by the government's strategy of mingling welfare with military needs, it did have advantages for the authorities. It kept costs down and enabled the armed forces to use the unpaid labour of the organisers. Given that undistributed stockpiles built up, the shortage of military clothing was probably due as much to disorganised distribution and shortages of fuel and raw materials as to this system.

Ultimately, as Beatrice Pisa argues, the middle-class female organisers performed badly. They neither established any sort of minimum wage nor grasped the need to rationalise production. Instead, many just viewed the work as a way of returning poor women to the 'naturally feminine skill' of needlework, their lack of knowledge of it being a sign of the degradations of modernity.[34] Overall, uniform manufacture provoked no public debate for it fitted neatly with expectations of female roles.

This was also true of the work of the many women who continued in the same occupations as before the war. Female employment only became controversial where women appeared to move into hitherto male work roles in factories, public transport or offices. As Barbara Curli has argued in her excellent study of women's wartime work, it was precisely such new and visibly modern types of employment that structured post-war debates about female employment.[35] Statistically, however, they were only a small percentage of economically active women in this period. Numbers of women in 'auxiliary factories' producing arms and munitions, for example, rose from 23,000 at the end of 1915 to 198,000 by August 1918 (only 21.9 per cent of the total workforce). This was far less than those making uniforms but their importance as symbolic harbingers of change greatly outweighed their actual numbers.

Although Italy faced the challenge of modern warfare with a level of economic development far behind that of certain other combatant nations, the impact on women's employment was, in some respects, similar. In Italy, as elsewhere, women rarely directly substituted for men, instead tending to move into new work roles produced by wartime expansion and new patterns of work organisation. A good example of this was munitions. Initially, many employers feared that unskilled female workers might damage machinery. But government pressure gradually led to the recruitment of women. Once they had started work in this sector it continued, their presence outliving the war. They rarely actually took over what had previously been seen as 'male jobs', instead moving into new (mainly lighter, unskilled) roles, spawned by the changing patterns of work organisation, with more subdivision of tasks, precipitated by the expansion of production.

Male workers, of course, opposed 'substitution'. It was feared (wrongly) that women would not fight for workers' rights. More importantly, men replaced by women faced call-up papers. In factories with 'auxiliary' status, male workers were subject to military discipline. If they left their jobs they were considered deserters.

On public transport, women did directly substitute for men. Often photographed, tram-conductors became a staple feature of the iconography of the home front. Since their employment was considered temporary, they were given only a few days' training. The work was hard, the hours long and the pay low. Turnover was high. This was due partly to women themselves seeking more palatable alternatives but also because many of the poorly trained women ended up being sacked. The reasons for dismissal ranged from what was termed 'maternal' behaviour (such as allowing barefoot children on board), to a range of crimes and misdemeanours like lateness, absenteeism, theft, sitting down on the job, drinking (including conductors who 'leave the tram to drink in taverns') or even 'keeping the tram stationary while she did her shopping'. Some behaved even more badly. One 'possibly drunk' conductor, for example, while 'screaming threats and insults', slapped a passenger.[36] Those who stuck it out until the end of the war were summarily dismissed to make way for returning veterans.

Very different from the unruly ticket collectors was the new army of 'white-blouse' workers. Recent improvements in female education ensured a supply of qualified candidates for this work. These women did not directly replace men but moved in at a time of expansion which was accompanied by a major reorganisation of the workplace. Nineteenth-century office practices, where each clerk did a range of tasks, were replaced with a 'modern' organisational structure with clear roles and hierarchies. Women were assigned the more boring, repetitive tasks like typing and telephony, whilst men retained the more responsible, interesting jobs, a division of labour that survived the war. Drawn more by the respectable, clean nature of the work than by the pay, many female clerks remained long after the ending of hostilities. Unlike tram-workers, white-blouse workers proved competent and loyal.[37]

For many women, wartime employment just meant staying on the land. Although some women did desert farming (agriculture did worst where new industrial opportunities became available, like Lombardy – particularly on the fringes of urban areas), millions remained there. In reality this was the sector where women were most likely to do 'men's work'. About 2,600,000, mostly young and strong, peasant men were called up over the course of the war and farming also lost labour to industry. In this situation, many peasant women simply experienced heavier workloads as they struggled to do their own, already onerous, tasks plus those normally done by men, like ploughing. As one woman recalled: 'All the jobs that men did, I did them too. I even stacked sheaves, unloaded grain, and helped with the threshing when the machine came.'[38] Such work was tough and far from 'emancipating', although some did use agricultural machinery for the first time, or learned to manage accounts and market their produce. Some female sharecroppers or small proprietors found themselves in charge. In many households, however, the traditional hierarchy remained intact. As one peasant woman remembered: 'At home, the old folk were still in charge.'[39]

Women did well on the land in this period, their output exceeding expectations (mainly because, driven by the need to survive, they were willing to tackle almost any task), although production held up best in types of farming where women had expertise, like poultry and olive-growing.[40] Paul Corner has even argued that, in Lombardy, the financial situation of some peasant families improved. Here, rising agricultural prices, which yielded good profits on the black market, together with enhanced opportunities for women in factories, particularly in silk production, enabled some families to reduce their debts.[41] Southern agriculture did less well, as it was harder for women to substitute for men there.

Another pre-existing group whose workload increased were prostitutes. In the early part of the war, brothels proliferated in areas near the front and clandestine prostitutes also gathered. This led to fears about disease. To remedy this, compulsory health checks and forcible internment for treatment for infected prostitutes were brought back. Soldiers were also checked and given treatment where necessary. Official military brothels were created near the front lines. The conditions for the women who worked in these places were often appalling. One doctor reported finding women who were forced to have sex with about 80 clients a day.[42]

Social Protest

Overall, although the war did provide new opportunities for some women, for many this was a time of hunger, distress and anger. As a result, the home front was in ferment for much of the war. Despite special legislation to repress it, there was widespread unrest in both rural and urban Italy, in which women were often the main, in many cases the only, protagonists.[43] This was not due to some sort of 'innate female pacifism' but because women risked less. Male strikers could be sent to the front whereas women were usually only fined, since prison would disrupt their families too much. The level of unrest grew as the war dragged on, particularly after the end of 1916. Many protests were violent and some had quasi-insurrectionary dimensions, such as the enormous protest in Turin in August 1917. Begun by women angered by flour and bread shortages, the upheaval lasted five days, spreading to engulf entire working-class communities. About 50 demonstrators were killed, 200 injured and 900 arrested.

Women played leading roles in many industrial strikes. In 1917, for example, despite being only a minority of the workforce, 64.2 per cent of strikers in auxiliary factories were female.[44] The strikes, often spontaneous events not controlled by the labour movement (indeed union leaders were often hostile to them), were mostly at least nominally about pay or work conditions but also sometimes about broader questions such as food shortages. Anger was exacerbated by the fact that the rich were perceived to be doing better, able to afford luxuries on the black market. Working conditions and pay, moreover, worsened in many factories as military discipline gave employers a free hand. Many strikes were quite openly anti-war. The Socialist Party, however, offered no real leadership. Their wartime slogan, 'neither support, nor sabotage', was far from helpful to protesters.

Peasant women were similarly involved (indeed, if anything, had even more of an important role) in numerous protests, evidence of a new confidence (as well as poverty) while men were at the front. The Italian countryside had been far from an idyllic, tranquil place before the war and this situation continued but now the leading protagonists were female. Rural unrest, as Giovanna Procacci has argued, was essentially women's unrest in this period.[45] Thus occupations of uncultivated land in the South, often in defence of 'moral economy' questions (like the loss of grazing rights on common land), did not begin, by any means, in the war, and women had been involved before, but this was the first time women played such leading roles.

The war added numerous new grievances. Many were angered at the loss of husbands and sons, snatched away to die for a nation few identified with. Apart from the emotional distress caused, the absence of adult males could mean grave economic hardship. The government subsidies were totally inadequate and quickly eroded by inflation (the lira lost about 80 per cent of its value during the war). Anyone who owned even a minute plot of land received no subsidy, nor did families of deserters (which included soldiers who had actually been killed or captured but were believed to have deserted). Moreover, as socialist deputy Cabrini stated in parliament in March 1917, 'civil assistance isn't reaching smaller towns, where the wealthy classes don't want the welfare tax legislation applied'.[46]

Such problems gave rise to numerous spontaneous protests about food shortages, the smallness or uneven distribution of subsidies, the lack of leave for soldiers and the inefficiency of the authorities. Many rural protests were around 'war questions' such as attempts to prevent the departure of men for the front. They often followed the traditional model of pre-industrial agitations, with processions, demonstrations and riots. Typical actions involved crowds of women invading town halls to destroy call-up papers, the looting of shops, and the besieging of police stations or the homes of the rich.[47] In 1917, for example, groups of women from nearby rural areas gathered in Vaiano in the province of Prato, where they urged women employed in war industries to strike and not support the war by substituting for men. This sparked off a week-long protest by peasant women, female factory workers and even children, which spread rapidly to surrounding areas. The protestors built barricades, cut telegraph wires and hurled stones at the police.[48]

Some unrest was about imagined rather than real problems, but even these protests show how deep-rooted suspicions were of the state. In one protest by thousands of Tuscan women, for example, the grievances included compulsory vaccinations, believed to be a means of killing off extra mouths to feed, and requests to sign forms to obtain subsidies. Many believed that if they signed for the following year it meant they had approved the continuation of the fighting for a further year.[49] Even the subsidies, although essential to the survival of many families, caused anger, as they seemed a poor exchange for absent men. Some felt that accepting subsidies made them complicit in the war.

Some protests were quite successful. Land occupations, for example, often led to compromise solutions in which peasants did well. Eventually the escalating level of protest forced the government to recognise the need to do more than just heavy-handedly suppress the opposition. This was particularly true after Caporetto when Salandra's policy of expecting the nation to simply obey (or face fierce repression if they did not) began to be replaced by an understanding of the need to raise civilian morale.[50] Greater attention began to be paid to the welfare of the population, wage levels in factories and the supply of food. This, coupled with continuing repression of 'agitators', did lead to a slight decline in the level of protest, although it far from ended.

The aftermath of war

As in other countries, women's role changed a great deal during the First World War. Although here, as elsewhere, many changes were subsequently wholly or partly reversed, women's increased visibility in the public sphere and new talk about their importance to the nation did create the impetus for legal reform. In the ferment of 1919, women gained new legal rights and almost won the vote.

By this time there was much support for female suffrage. A number of politicians during the war had voiced support for it, particularly for local elections. By 1919, things had advanced further. The founding document of the new mass Catholic party, the PPI, for example, included female suffrage. Women, they hoped, would vote for the Church and keep socialism out. On 9 September 1919, the Chamber of Deputies passed a female suffrage bill (with 174 votes in favour and only 55 against). This law was only to be applied to the next elections, not the ones looming that year. It also denied suffrage to prostitutes. These restrictions, however, proved irrelevant as parliament was dissolved before the legislation could be approved by the Senate. The following year, the Chamber again voted for female suffrage (this time in local elections only) but this bill similarly ran out of time.[51]

More successful was Ettore Sacchi's bill to reform women's legal position, presented to the Chamber in February 1917, which became law in July 1919. This abolished the 'marital authorisation' and allowed women to practise all professions and to take up public employment. As stipulated in the regulations for the law (published the following year), however, there were exceptions for roles deemed particularly important. Women still could not, for example, be magistrates, diplomats or police officers, nor could they aspire to a long list of civil service jobs (mainly, but not exclusively, in the higher grades). Despite its importance (these considerable limitations notwithstanding) the law roused little public interest at the time, appearing to many a kind of automatic reward for women's war work.[52] Indeed, in Sacchi's presentation of the bill, he described it as such, although it clearly was also the result of a longer, more gradual change of attitudes and the example of similar reforms being enacted in other countries at the time.

The marital authorisation had, in fact, already been eroded during the war. In January 1917 it was declared unnecessary for financial transactions related to war loans. Other changes, too, had slightly altered the legal subordination of women. In a break with the terms of the Civil Code, subsidies for soldiers' families were paid directly to women, not their husbands.[53] The 1919 legislation went much further: married women henceforth had full juridical powers (although men kept *patria potestas*). The 1919 legislation also meant that women could now practise law (although in parliamentary discussions some advised them against doing so). Lidia Poët, now aged 64, finally managed to register as a lawyer.

The campaign about lawyers was highly symbolic but provided only a handful of jobs. By 1921 there were 85 women lawyers. Numerically more significant was a decree of 23 October 1919 that offered permanent contracts to all those who had been taken on temporarily during the war in the central state administration, albeit with various loopholes, introduced the following year, which excluded women from more prestigious work roles.

Some other women kept their jobs but many did not and there was a great ideological and actual backlash against female employment. The backdrop was inflation and a collapse of employment in war-related industries, a difficult context in which to defend women's jobs. In this atmosphere, heated polemics arose in the press about certain types of working women, particularly criticising the new, highly visible white-blouse *signorine*.

Those in the uniform workshops were all sacked. Seen as only receiving charity anyway, they were deemed without rights. Many of the munitions workers ceased work quickly: 27 per cent were expelled from war industries in December 1918 and January 1919, compared with only 4.5 per cent of the male workforce.[54] Even unemployment payments were used to underscore the temporary nature of women's war work. In Bologna, for example, only women who had been employed since before the war obtained unemployment benefits if they were made redundant.[55] For some, particularly lower middle-class women whose husbands earned a family wage, the end of the wartime 'world turned upside down' may have been a relief as now they no longer needed to work. For many, however, the ending of hostilities just meant a return to old economic problems. Unlike the classic picture of women as a 'reserve army of labour', many did not become economically inactive after the war but continued to seek employment in changed circumstances, hit, for example, by the crisis in textiles. Thus for some, it meant not stopping work, but changing jobs and often earning less.

The situation for widows was particularly difficult. Legislation emphasised the importance of jobs for war veterans but not for widows and the renewed emphasis on the family and women's role as wives and mothers was unhelpful for those without a husband. Marrying again was rarely an option: men were in short supply. Many were, therefore, forced to rely on state pensions that frequently only arrived after long bureaucratic delays.

Some European historians have challenged the idea that the First World War actually increased female employment.[56] Although it is difficult to get a clear picture, this may also be true to a degree in Italy. That women did new types of employment in this period is undeniable. And that some women who did not normally work began to work, such as lower middle-class women who stitched uniforms, is also clear. However, the vast majority of female war workers were peasant and working-class women who, otherwise, would have been working anyway.

That said, in terms of the legacy of the war for women, it is important to distinguish between what actually happened and what was believed to be happening, for what was new was not women's work itself but perceptions of it. Despite talk of 'substitution', the old rule of ensuring that women's work, whatever it was, had lower status, was generally adhered to. To many, however, change seemed great, and this aroused much hostility. There was a chorus of disapproval in the press about the selfishness of female factory workers, said to be frittering away their new-found wealth on indulgences like silk stockings. One commentator, for example, wrote: 'There is a whole class of not very nice women who, in Milan at least, dress extravagantly and spend madly.'[57] Male workers sometimes accused the new female workers of being 'prostitutes' and even the socialist press teemed with articles about women stealing men's jobs and preening themselves while men died at the front.[58] During the war, the PSI abandoned its pre-war support for female employment, instead repeatedly asserting the idea that a woman's place was in the home. It is perhaps not surprising that so few women joined the party in this period (only about 1,000–1,500 in 1917).

Many other voices joined the socialists in their condemnation of women's employment, for working women had become increasingly visible. Previously the only women who tended to get their pictures in the press were exceptional figures like royalty, actresses or criminals.[59] During the war, photographs of women frequently appeared, often portraying them in novelty work roles like tram-conductors, barbers (described by the press as 'Figaros in skirts'[60]) or munitions workers. These images created a misleading impression of the actual numbers involved in such activities: the far greater numbers in traditional employment were more rarely shown. Another much photographed group were the CRI nurses, generally seen in sanitised, posed photographs without blood or corpses, visual depictions whose main aim was to reassure the public that the wounded were being well cared for in a clean, orderly environment.[61] This did not prevent, however, the circulation of many unofficial postcards depicting nurses as flirtatious and sexual.

One of the most pervasive and evocative images of women in the war, in both official and non-official representations of the period, was, however, the mother. In one respect, maternity featured less in women's lives than before: the birth rate dropped from 31.7 per thousand just before the war, to 24 in 1916 and 18.1 by 1918. But the mother with babe-in-arms was not, of course, the one celebrated here but the mother of adult soldier sons. The image of the war mother was tinged with historical significance, evoking the *madre risorgimentale*, devoting her support behind the lines to the 'nation in arms' and willing to sacrifice her sons to the cause. At the same time, in many public and private representations, and, indeed, as their letters reveal, in the minds of many of those in the trenches, the figure of the mother also signified consolation, a reassuring refuge in a time of horror and distress, something elemental, protective and nurturing.[62]

After the war, social protest continued apace, for 1919–20 was the *biennio rosso*. Although the gender dimensions of this period of enormous tension and ferment have, to date, been little studied, it seems clear that women did play a role in both the rural and urban unrest of the time.[63] Some took part directly in land occupations and strikes. More were involved in food protests. But their role was generally much reduced compared with the wartime situation. In particular, when organised labour once again took charge, women tended to be marginalised. There were other factors too. In the widespread agitations among sharecroppers of the immediate post-war, for example, once the hierarchical family structure was reinstated, men represented the household in negotiations. During the dramatic episode of the 'Occupation of the Factories', many of the firms affected were engineering factories with predominantly male workforces and women were relegated mainly to supplying the strikers with food.

The impact of war

In some respects the First World War did mark a real change in Italian women's lives. Women got the opportunity to try out new work roles, some of which outlasted the war. Women went out to work in factories and offices and dealt with money and the economy in unprecedented ways. Red Cross nurses ventured far from their families into new and challenging situations and even many peasant women broke down the barriers of their narrow existences to go to market or to reinvent themselves as munitions workers. Clothes became much less restrictive. Gone were the pre-war whalebone corsets and cumbersome skirts. By 1919, hemlines had risen and female dress was altogether more practical, opening up the potential for women to engage in new activities, such as sports. The new emphasis on the role of women in the nation created a new language in which to demand the vote.

However, because some of these changes were temporary, the lasting effects were less than they promised to be. For many women, the ending of hostilities just meant a return to old gender roles. For millions, moreover, the Great War had not been an exciting time of new opportunities but one of hunger, fear, disease and loss. Although legal reforms of considerable importance were passed in the ferment of 1919, they excluded the most important one – the vote. The perception of change was, however, great. Some women had stepped into men's shoes and proved that they could manage. For many men this was disturbing. The war, moreover, changed the direction of Italian feminism. Many feminists moved to the right, a trend that was to prove significant in the near future. Increasingly, moreover, the role of women in the war was remembered and celebrated not as the tough munitions worker making shells, nor the angry peasant boldly trying to halt the departure of troops to the pointless slaughter of the trenches but, instead, as the elemental, archaic figure of the stoic mother sacrificing her sons for the *patria*. This 'mother of the nation' was soon to become a pervasive image during the Fascist dictatorship.

4

'Exemplary Wives and Mothers': Under Fascist Dictatorship

In 1922, amidst tumultuous upheaval and near civil war in parts of the country, Benito Mussolini seized power. By 1925 Italy was in the iron grip of dictatorship. A considerable historiography now exists on the role and experience of Italian women in this period, much of it in English. Italian historians of women have been more reluctant to tackle this topic, seeing it as unpalatable compared with themes like the heroic deeds of women in the Resistance. Early writings (notably Piero Meldini's pioneering work published in 1975[1]) tended to portray women under Fascism as the hapless victims of an aggressive, violent and patriarchal regime. Other studies focused mainly on anti-fascist women or on evidence of female dissent, such as striking rice-weeders or textile workers.[2] More recently, the work of Victoria De Grazia[3] has convincingly demonstrated that this was a period of complex and contradictory changes for women and that, despite the regime's patriarchal ideology, for some it was a time when new, more modern roles and opportunities emerged.

Ideology

The Fascists paid far more attention to gender roles than the Liberals had done and intervened much more in the private sphere. Fascist speeches and propaganda, redolent with echoes of the recent war, tried to recover male pride, which had been delivered a vital blow by the defeat of Caporetto and the failed imperialist ventures of the Liberal period. As the magistrate Giuseppe Maggiore summed up in the late 1920s: 'Fascism is male. It loves danger . . . it is made of hard rock, unlike the sweet paste of crystallised fruits which – like a woman's soul – hides stones that can break your teeth. . . . Fascism is, in a word, a forger of virility against any effeminacy and softening of the spirit.'[4]

Fascism exalted an exaggerated virility, defined as military, soldierly values, which it contrasted with a vision of women as 'angels of the hearth', devoted to producing large broods of children as future troops for the regime's military adventures. Of course, as the preceding chapters have shown, an emphasis on the importance of maternity was nothing new in Italy. Motherhood had been stressed in political discourse ranging from Risorgimental celebrations to feminist ideas. The Fascist approach to motherhood distinguished itself by its persistent emphasis on the sheer quantity of babies produced, and by the way in which motherhood was explicitly linked with militarism, although the latter idea does at least in part date back to World War One. Under Fascism, this idea was summed up in the often-repeated slogan: 'Maternity is to a woman what war is to a man.'

Mussolini himself was paraded as the ideal man: sporty, soldierly, virile and tirelessly energetic. His own attitude to women was dismissive. In the late 1920s, for example, he candidly said in an interview with a female journalist: 'Women are a charming pastime, when a man has time to pass . . . but they should never be taken seriously.'[5]

Much Fascist gender ideology hinged around the pro-natalist 'demographic campaign'. Mussolini even referred to the falling birth rate as the 'problem of problems'. This led to unprecedented official attention to women, who were now supposed to devote themselves to being 'exemplary wives and mothers'. Propaganda hammered out the idea that motherhood was a service to the nation. The ideal woman was portrayed as rounded and rural with many children, the so-called *madre prolifica* (profilic mother). She was contrasted with the *donna crisi* (crisis woman), the modern, lipsticked woman, selfishly neglectful of her national, maternal duties. Mussolini even launched an 'anti-slimming' campaign, for women should have 'maternal' curves. This backward-looking ideology, however, was in itself contradictory, for whilst seemingly consigning women to a purely domestic role, it also asserted their value to the nation. This eventually gave rise to new opportunities for women in the public sphere, particularly in the PNF (Partito Nazionale Fascista – Fascist Party) and its mass organisations.

Fascists increasingly argued that feminism was an outdated relic of a bygone era when individual rights were considered important, something the new generation of Fascist women should reject. Such individualism was dismissed as irrelevant: Italians now all had only duties to the nation, not rights. In this, men and women enjoyed a bizarre equality: both had duties, neither had rights. Their duties, however, were separate and gender-specific, for Fascism firmly upheld male privilege.

Because motherhood was supposed to be women's core mission, there was considerable criticism of female employment, in speeches and writings – criticism that escalated in the period of the economic depression. Condemnations of female employment were, of course, quite consistent with Church teachings and, overall, Catholic gender ideas, with their emphasis on female submission and the overarching importance of marriage and the family, were quite acceptable to the Fascists. The main difference lay in the regime's insistence on the imperialistic and warfaring purpose of women's maternal duty. Otherwise, Church and regime were in broad agreement (if not always on the details) on many issues relating to gender. The essential conservatism of the Fascist approach to gender was therefore only reinforced by the signing of the Lateran

Illustration 4   'Prolific mother' and her seven children.
(Reproduced courtesy of Fototeca Storica Nazionale Ando Gilardi.)

Pacts in 1929, when Church and state found themselves, after seventy years of hostility, talking to each other once again.

Fascist ideas on gender can be seen in a battery of propaganda, in speeches at rallies, in the press and in radio broadcasts. The impact of all this is, however, not simple to assess. Some women were more exposed to propaganda than others. Those who were middle class and literate had far more exposure than working-class or peasant girls and women. Women in remote sharecropping households, or in villages lacking roads and electricity, remained relatively distant from the world of speeches and rallies, although the regime eventually did try to reach out even to them. The regime, moreover, despite its totalitarian pretensions, did not have a monopoly on ideas about women. Throughout the *ventennio* there were, instead, a series of competing discourses about gender, some reinforcing, others contradicting or more subtly challenging, the regime's official ideology.

Even Fascists themselves put forward a range of views. Different Fascists embraced the regime's official gender ideology to varying degrees. Discordant views were often aired by women who were active supporters of the regime, although this became progressively more difficult as the regime entrenched itself in power. Even in the 1930s, however, it is still possible to find the Fascist women's press defending female employment and denouncing the idea that female employment and education had anything to do with demographic decline.

The demographic campaign

The birth rate was indeed, as the Fascists believed, falling. It had begun to decline towards the end of the nineteenth century but initially only among the northern urban middle classes. By the early twentieth century, this trend had spread to the northern working class. In the southern, agricultural region of Apulia, for example, the mean number of children per marriage in 1900–9 was 4.99 whereas in Piedmont it was only 3.82. By the interwar period, even some of the northern peasantry were beginning to have slightly smaller families. The decline was not yet dramatic and the falling death rate meant that the population was not actually shrinking. Despite this, the situation was portrayed as a national emergency by the Fascists, who vigorously attempted to stem the tide of population change. Mussolini exhorted Italian women to have many babies so that the Italian population would grow from its level of about 40 million to 60 million by the middle of the century.

A number of factors contributed to the launching of the populationist panic. Important, as elsewhere in Europe, were the ideas of social scientists who, enthused by new ideas about eugenics and Darwinian notions of the survival of the fittest, believed that attention needed to be paid to the size and quality of population. The work of Corrado Gini, published before the Great War, was particularly influential in fostering the idea that population decline was a problem. The war itself, with its huge death toll, and the subsequent influenza epidemic, further fuelled such anxieties.

Fascists argued that Italy's prowess in warfare was dependent on the size of its population and that, without an increase, it would be unable to stand up to the other European powers. As Mussolini intoned in his Ascension Day speech in May 1927, which effectively launched the demographic campaign, 'what are 40 million Italians compared with 90 million Germans and 200 million Slavs . . . or 46 million Englishmen and 450 million in the Colonies?' The 'battle for births' was closely linked to imperialism, for it was supposed both to create cannon-fodder for the army as well as explain why Italy needed an empire – to create living space for the expanding population. Mussolini put this starkly: 'If we decrease . . . there will be no empire. We will become a colony.'[6]

The demographic campaign interwove with and reinforced other elements of Fascist policy like the ruralisation campaign, since peasants were the most 'prolific' Italians. Moreover, the type of peasants most praised in official rhetoric, those who, like sharecroppers, lived on the land in large households and who, for the regime, were a symbol of social stability, were generally the peasants with the largest families. In the Ascension Day speech, rural Italy was praised for its demographic vitality, whilst cities like Milan were lambasted for their sterility.

The 'battle for births' underpinned Fascist gender policy. It created a convenient ideological rationale for curbing women's presence on the labour market. It also fitted well with the backward-looking aspects of Fascism, harking back to a bygone (and largely fictitious) past when women's role was primarily maternal and domestic, unsullied by modernity. The campaign tied in with Fascist notions of masculinity. Nations with growing populations were seen as young, thrusting and virile. At the same time, it created a new role for male Fascist activists in the late 1920s when Mussolini was trying to get control of his own supporters. The demographic campaign gave the *squadristi* (the violent thugs who brought Fascism to power) a new role, as fathers.

To encourage Italians to breed more, the regime indulged in its usual love of display and propagandistic excess. Public ceremonies and rallies full of stage-managed pageantry, speeches and writings were all used. From 1933, a 'Mother and Child Day' was staged annually on 24 December, when 'prolific mothers' were publicly honoured for the numbers of their offspring. These events featured prize-giving ceremonies and sentimental touches like gently rocking cradles laden with fruit.

There was also a battery of pro-natalist and pro-marital measures. These included the 'bachelors' tax', which aimed to promote early marriage by levying a higher rate of tax (graduated according to age and income) on unmarried men aged between 25 and 65. Marriage was also encouraged by lowering the age at which each sex could marry, and the age of consent, and by measures like preference in state employment for fathers of large families. There were prizes and benefits for 'prolific mothers', such as tax reductions and various local benefits like free medical care, tram tickets and school meals. To qualify, a family had to have at least seven or even ten living children, a very high level, particularly given the prevailing high rates of infant mortality. In practice, only a minority of families benefited from these provisions.

In the 1930s, essentially in response to the fact that the other measures had failed, marriage loans and family allowances were tried, at a time when the regime's attention was particularly concentrated on warfare with the invasion of Ethiopia. State employees had already begun to receive family allowances in 1928 and these were extended to industrial workers in the mid-1930s, initially only to those who had been forced, by the economic recession, to cut their working week to 40 hours. Soon, however, this benefit was available to all industrial workers and, in 1937, to waged farm-workers. The marriage loans, modelled on those introduced in Nazi Germany in 1933, were for low-income couples aged under 26. Until 1938, even Jews were eligible in Italy. These interest-free loans (of 1,000–3,000 lire) had to be repaid at a rate of 1 per cent per month, starting six months after marriage. The debt was progressively cancelled with the birth of each child. Couples who remained childless paid higher repayments after four years.[7] These measures were less successful in Italy than in Germany partly because the sums involved, and the percentage of the debt cancelled per child, were lower. Only a small number of Italian couples took out loans.

The Fascists also adopted repressive measures against fertility control. This effectively meant condoms (for those who could afford them), abortion, *coitus interruptus*, restraint or just marrying late.[8] Women's knowledge of birth control when they married was often non-existent: sex education for girls was extremely unusual and many brides were ignorant and inexperienced. The attitude of one peasant woman from Piedmont (born in 1918 and married in 1938) was doubtless not unusual: 'Sex was sin. . . . We grew up knowing nothing about sex, or with the wrong information. . . . Yes, we saw the animals, but we didn't understand. . . . I was so unprepared for marriage . . . I didn't dare get undressed . . . I felt no attraction, nothing . . . I couldn't, I couldn't. . . . He went after other women. I couldn't blame him.'[9]

Doctors did nothing to illuminate women, often sharing the view that only men were supposed to enjoy sex. Only a few voices spoke openly in favour of birth control. In 1911, two socialists, Luigi Berta and Secondo Giorni, had published *L'arte di non far figli* (The Art of Not Having Children). An unsuccessful attempt by Catholic morality campaigners to prosecute it as obscene had boosted sales to 27,000 copies. Under Fascism, texts like this were outlawed as it became illegal to publicise birth control methods. The new legislation was enforced by the police, who investigated chemists and newspaper advertisements. They also clamped down on abortion.

Even in Liberal Italy, abortion was illegal and punishable by a prison sentence. Prosecutions, however, were rare and, although reliable statistics do not, of course, exist, it is clear that abortion was widespread. Far from being the last resort of the unmarried pregnant girl of fiction, both married and unmarried women had abortions. This was partly because many, even including some priests, believed that it was not wrong to abort in early pregnancy. Fascism, however, tried to stamp abortion out, tightening up the legal situation in the Public Security Laws of 6 November 1926. This legislation was further reinforced by the Rocco Code of 1930, which defined abortion as a crime against 'the integrity and health of the stock'. Medically motivated abortions to save a woman's life were, however (contrary to Church teaching), permitted. Although the legislation was not much more rigorous than that already on the statute books, it was considerably more rigorously applied. Judges, however, proved reluctant to impose it and consistently handed down lenient sentences, which, Denise Detriagache has argued, suggests a widespread acceptance of abortion in society.[10] The question of abortion was also tackled by the regulation of medical professionals. A law of 1927 obliged them to report miscarriages to local medical authorities. This campaign targeted in particular the activities of midwives.

In interwar Italy, about 95 per cent of women gave birth at home. Many births were attended by midwives. Peasant women, in particular, were rarely attended by a doctor. One rurally-based midwife recalled: 'They would call the vet for a cow, because a cow was important. Not for a wife, because they could get another one and she'd bring a dowry too. No, no, for the vet they found the money, not for the doctor.'[11] Although midwifery training had begun to be available, many midwives were still untrained 'handywomen'. Under Fascism there was a sustained campaign to train and professionalise them (enrolling them, for example, in a Fascist trade union) and to carefully watch over their activities. One reason for this was the fact that many seem to have been willing to perform abortions. When, for example, the house of midwife Caterina B. was searched by the police, they discovered 'a complete kit of drugs and catheters suitable for abortive practices'.[12] Midwives' help could be very important as many of the methods used by those attempting to perform their own abortions, which included the insertion of metal rods and even poisons, were dangerous. Their illegal activities were, therefore, often welcomed in local communities. The police in the village of Susegana (Treviso) needed, 'months of careful probing and investigation as public opinion has closed ranks behind a dense veil of silence', to uncover information about an abortionist midwife.[13] In another northern village, local women openly rioted against the arrest of an abortionist doctor.[14] The attitude of the Fascist state to abortionists can be seen in the type of punishment meted out to those who were caught: some were sent to *confino politico* (internal exile for political dissidents), rather than ordinary prisons. This demonstrates just how seriously the state took the idea that 'anti-demographic' acts amounted to political, anti-Fascist behaviours. *Confino politico* was, moreover, also sometimes used for another 'anti-demographic' group, homosexual men.[15]

In terms of its stated objectives, the demographic campaign was a dismal failure. The birth rate continued to decline. Abortions too continued to be common. One reason for the continuing decline in family size was doubtless the fact that the financial and material incentives offered were far too limited to offset the real cost of raising extra children. Marriage loans and family allowances were potentially more effective but, because of the outbreak of war soon after, it is impossible to know how successful they might have been. It is, in fact, notoriously difficult to change demographic behaviours through state intervention, particularly crude and ill-thought-out measures like these, due to cultural reasons. This aspect emerged, for example, in Luisa Passerini's oral history research among working-class people in Turin. Some saw having many children as irresponsible and the pro-natalist propaganda as offensive. One man recounted: 'Once, at a meeting . . . they wanted us to make babies . . . to go home and jump on our wives. What? There's already enough poverty, good grief. Well, that's something I just can't accept.'[16] Some Fascist interventions, moreover, may have backfired. As Chiara Saraceno has argued, the maternal welfare policy 'may have had an unintended effect: insofar as it promoted children's needs, the program may have encouraged parents to have fewer of them'.[17]

Maternal welfare

Although some improvements had been made to the National Maternity Fund in 1917, when Fascism seized power, maternity services were still extremely limited. In 1925, the Fascist state launched the Opera Nazionale per la Maternità ed Infanzia (National Mother and Child Agency – ONMI),[18] which aimed to reduce infant mortality and to ensure that the next generation of Italians was raised 'rationally and scientifically'. Often presented as part of the demographic campaign, ONMI was, in fact, founded before the real onset of the populationist panic.

ONMI, a 'para-state' organisation, inspected, co-ordinated and supervised the work of local organisations concerned with maternal and child welfare, such as charities and orphanages. It also provided direct assistance for poor and vulnerable pregnant women and new mothers, assistance that aimed to fill in the gaps left by such institutions. This included medical care, free meals, handouts of milk powder and layettes and an educational campaign in childcare methods. Much of its work was organised by 'Committees of Patrons', groups of local worthies, including many women. At first, the work of these committees consisted largely in home visits by female volunteers, who distributed advice together with subsidies, in cash or kind. In the early 1930s this system was abandoned. Cash subsidies were slashed and funds concentrated on more professional provisions, with the aim of creating a national network of obstetric and paediatric clinics.

ONMI policymakers saw themselves as committed to a 'modern' conception of welfare, 'technocrats' who were 'engineering the social' in the service of the state. ONMI, they argued, was quite different from charities which just provided benevolent help to needy individuals, stemming from the moral obligations of the rich towards the poor. Instead, they believed, ONMI's assistance would further the collective purposes of society and the state.

The ability of ONMI to reshape welfare provisions along these lines was seriously undermined by financial constraints. Although it received some state funding, as well as a percentage of residence taxes and the bachelors' tax, this was never sufficient and it also had to rely on donations. Consequently, there were huge regional imbalances in provisions. Volunteers continued to be widely used: ONMI could afford few properly paid staff. This made it, despite the 'modern' language of its ideologues, a hybrid, half way between a state welfare programme and a politicised charity. Many of the women assisted may have seen little difference between 'Fascist welfare' and old-fashioned charity, apart from the intrusiveness of the Fascists' innumerable snooping home visits. ONMI was also far from an embryonic 'welfare state' in that it stressed duties, not rights. Mothers and children were not given guarantees of assistance. The only exceptions were unmarried mothers.

Due to the influence of social scientists, who increasingly emphasised the rights of the child and the importance of the maternal role, the centuries-old system of anonymous abandonment of unwanted babies in the *ruota* (wheel) was in decline.[19] Under this system, unmarried mothers had been able to abandon their babies in order to salvage their 'honour' and a future chance of wedlock. This was considered preferable to abortion, despite being effectively a 'massacre of the innocents' (most foundlings died), because the babies could be baptised and their immortal souls safeguarded. Already by the turn of the century, anonymous abandonment was becoming increasingly difficult, although in the South many wheels stayed open due to the intensity of the 'honour code'. In northern Italy, some homes became maternity hospitals, where women gave birth then nursed their babies.

The Fascists introduced national reforms for the first time. In 1923 the 'wheel' was outlawed and attempts were made to improve foundling homes by means of inspections and so on. Because reformers argued that the existing system encouraged abandonment by assisting only foundlings, in 1927 subsidies were introduced for unmarried mothers who agreed to nurse their babies. The mothers were actively encouraged (although not coerced) to recognise their child. Their right to secrecy was respected. Although, in many respects, an enlightened policy, it worked badly due to funding shortages. The subsidies, never particularly generous ('Amelia', interviewed by Luisa Passerini, called them 'a paltry help'),[20] were reduced in 1933, forcing many women to turn to charities. Moreover, the policy was implemented unevenly. In practice, some *ruote* were still functioning a decade later. Another big problem was that no real long-term help was offered to mothers after babies were weaned. By the fall of Fascism, in many regions, mortality rates among illegitimates remained barbarically high. For ONMI, too, the subsidies were problematic as they virtually bankrupted the organisation. Even after 1933, when ONMI's contribution was reduced to a third, they continued to drain funds.

Although short on finance and material assistance, in the sphere of propaganda ONMI was energetic. With its army of home visitors and its supervisory powers over other organisations it was in an excellent position to spread the Fascist message on motherhood and the importance of 'improving the race'. Activities were all to an extent infused with propaganda and this aspect was reinforced by the widespread role of the Fasci Femminili (see Chapter 5) as volunteer labour. By the late 1930s, women who wanted to use ONMI facilities needed party membership.

Political considerations aside, ONMI was a fairly ineffective organisation. The regional disparities, the reliance on poorly qualified staff, the funding problems and local resistance to central policy all go a long way to explaining why, with a few regional exceptions, it had little discernible effect on Italy's high rates of infant mortality. Infant mortality did fall during the *ventennio* but no more quickly than in the previous two decades.

Education

In 1923, compulsory education for both sexes was extended to five years. According to official figures, numbers of girls at primary school rose at roughly the same rate as boys, stabilising at about 47 per cent of overall enrolments (3,879,479 in 1928–9 and 4,850,058 in 1937–8).[21] Female illiteracy rates improved from 30 per cent in 1921 to 24 per cent in 1931 (compared with 24 per cent and 17 per cent for males) although regional variations persisted. In Calabria in 1931, for example, 56 per cent of women were recorded as illiterate compared with a mere 5 per cent in Lombardy.[22] Overall, getting girls into primary education was seen as positive by the regime since, along with reading and arithmetic, they received a good dose of Fascist propaganda, including about their domestic and demographic mission.[23] Post-primary female education was considered more problematic. Here, girls were advancing steadily. Although many middle-class girls still attended private schools, by 1920–1, 30 per cent of the 57,289 *ginnasi* pupils and 18 per cent of the 16,644 *licei* pupils were female.[24]

The 'Gentile reform' (the collective name of a cluster of decrees passed in 1923) tried to stem this tide by reducing the number of teacher training colleges and by introducing a three-year *liceo femminile*, a dead-end girls-only grammar school, offering no route to university. Gentile himself was no friend of feminism, dismissing it as an 'egalitarian illusion, a false and ridiculous ideal of the woman-man',[25] and his new schools offered, in addition to some humanities tuition, mainly 'feminine' subjects like domestic science and singing. The *liceo femminile* failed because, by this time, middle-class parents wanted a good education for their daughters and preferred to send them to a proper *liceo* offering university entrance. Only 374 girls ever enrolled at a *liceo femminile*. In 1928 they were abolished.

Other tactics were also deployed to discourage girls from moving up the educational ladder, such as the imposition of discriminatory fees in secondary schools and teacher training colleges. From 1929, for example, boys could get total exemption from teacher training school fees.[26] The small numbers of male primary teachers (only 22 per cent in 1927) worried some Fascists. Boys, they felt, needed virile role models in the classroom.

Bottai's School Charter in 1939 again tried to tackle female educational progress through new three-year secondary 'institutes' aimed at 'spiritually' preparing girls for a future as housewives or nursery school teachers. Girls, however, were not to be excluded from other schools so what impact this would have had in the long run, had the war and the fall of the regime not intervened, is uncertain. Higher middle school fees for girls were also included in the Charter.[27]

Despite these various attempts to restrain them, the rise in numbers of girls and women in secondary and higher education continued apace. By 1931, 53 per cent of girls (compared with 65 per cent of boys) attended middle schools (the comparable figures in 1901 had been 23 per cent and 28 per cent respectively). In the elite *ginnasi* and *licei*, where overall numbers were increasing, the proportion of girls also rose. By 1937–8, 32 per cent of the 92,653 *ginnasi* students and 26 per cent of the 33,899 *licei* students were female.[28]

Attending a mixed *liceo* was still slightly uncomfortable for girls. One *liceo* pupil in the 1920s later recalled: 'We girls had few, quite formal, interactions with the boys, we addressed each other with the formal *Lei*, even in class.

It wasn't proper to speak to them in the corridor or walk with them on the street.'[29] In some areas, however, rising female enrolments enabled the creation of girls-only classes with separate entrances and timetables and this, in turn, encouraged more girls to attend.

In teacher training colleges, numbers of female pupils rose almost three-fold (although the gender ratio altered as boys flooded in to these institutions). In 1922–3, there were 2,225 male and 26,769 female students. Already in 1929–30, the numbers of male students had increased to 5,192 whilst female enrolments had dropped to only 19,180. By 1938–9, however, numbers had risen dramatically to 42,753 males and 71,439 females.[30]

In higher education women's presence rose both in absolute numbers and as a percentage of the student body, which itself was expanding. In 1922–3, 12 per cent of students were female.[31] This rose to 17.4 per cent in 1935–6 and 29.9 per cent by 1942–3. Female enrolments at university tripled in the 1930s from 5,987 in 1929–30 to 18,174 in 1939–40,[32] although drop-out rates were quite high. The most popular subjects remained those that could lead to teaching. In 1934–5, according to Maria Castellani, head of ANFAL (National Fascist Association of Female Artists and Graduates), 602 women graduated in humanities and philosophy, 174 in mathematics and physics, and 341 in education. Another popular subject was pharmacy with 288 women graduating in the same year whereas only 83 graduated in medicine and 113 in law and political science.[33]

At all levels, therefore, female enrolments in education were rising. This suggests that, government policy notwithstanding, the education of daughters was increasingly seen as important by many parents, often as a kind of 'insurance policy' in case they did not marry. This was a real possibility: stark demographic statistics demonstrated that there were far from enough potential husbands to go around. The scarcity of employment in the period of the world depression, moreover, made acquiring qualifications seem particularly important. In turn, better education opened the door to new employment opportunities for some.

Employment

It was middle-class women who were the main targets of legislation against female employment during the *ventennio*. The perennial oversupply of suitably qualified candidates for posts in state employment and the professions was exacerbated in this period by rising numbers of graduates and the prevailing economic climate. For many middle-class men, the increasing numbers of well-educated young women were far from welcome on the labour market. The Fascist backlash was also shaped by perceptions of what had happened during the Great War. As was argued in Chapter 3, many were influenced by press reports that women (selfishly seeking wages to squander on trifles) had stolen men's jobs while they fought at the front. The Fascists presented work as essential to both male pride and demographic success. In 1934, for example, Mussolini argued that work was potentially dangerous for women and might make them sterile, whereas for men it was a source of 'great physical and moral virility'.[34]

Demographic reasons were repeatedly invoked in discussions of female employment. Some women, even Fascists admitted, did need to work for financial reasons, but their maternal mission meant that they were not to aspire to careers. Instead, they should be content with jobs that men did not want. Under Fascism, it was no longer acceptable to talk of links between employment and female emancipation. Where women did attempt to defend their right to work, it had to be phrased in language that stressed their need to help their family or children.

The Fascist government began introducing discriminatory laws soon after coming to power. A particular target was education. The legislation aimed not to stop women teaching but to exclude them from certain positions. In 1923, women were banned from headships of state middle schools, and in 1925 this was extended to private middle schools. In 1926, the recruitment of women to teaching posts in *licei* and teacher training colleges in certain subjects (those deemed particularly prestigious), such as Italian literature, history, philosophy and Latin, were blocked (although those already in post were not sacked). Further legislation in 1934 excluded women from various roles in technical schools.

Such legislative measures did nothing to prevent the increase in numbers of female teachers, but it did help confine them to the lower ranks. By the mid-1930s, according to Castellani, only 25 per cent of primary heads were women and 10 per cent of secondary heads. A handful worked in higher education. Further down the career ladder, however, schools teemed with women: 100 per cent (14,899) of nursery teachers were female, 81 per cent (88,470) of primary teachers and 44 per cent (5,186) of secondary teachers.[35] Where women were permitted to compete for jobs, they did well. In 1937, for example, women successfully won state competitions for 112 out of 162 new posts available in *ginnasi superiori* (upper middle schools).[36] The majority of women teachers, however, were still to be found earning low pay in the challenging conditions of primary education, although those who did find work here were lucky. By 1938, the expansion in numbers in teacher training colleges meant that there were 100,000 unemployed primary teachers.[37]

Life was comparatively easier for those in the graduate professions although here too competition was intense and far from all the new cohort of young women graduating from *licei* and universities actually got the jobs they trained for. There were, nonetheless, growing numbers of female professionals. According to Castellani, by 1931 these included 795 doctors, 30 dentists, 180 lawyers, 436 pharmacists (and 260 pharmacists' assistants), 15,514 midwives, 500 qualified nurses, 51 actuaries, 195 engineers, 182 journalists, 391 writers, 517 accountants as well as smaller numbers of women in various other professions.[38] Census figures record far higher numbers of nurses (39,646 in 1936 in addition to nuns) but most of these presumably were untrained, since the state only introduced nurse-training in 1925, and some, of course, were men. Fascist legislation did not directly discriminate against female professionals, unless they wanted to work in public administrations, although they were often criticised in the press and male prejudice made it difficult to operate in systems that required social connections and patronage networks.

One response to the growing threat of female professionals was to attempt to channel women into exclusively female occupations. The Fascist Party championed this idea by founding three women's residential colleges in Rome, to train domestic science teachers, rural primary school teachers and factory social workers.[39]

Much larger (and growing) numbers of women worked in the tertiary sector, particularly in shops and offices. By 1927, 70 per cent of shop assistants were female. Predominantly from working-class backgrounds, they earned exploitatively low pay and often lacked job security.[40] Lower middle-class women were more likely to go into clerical work. The growing army of female officeworkers generally did the least prestigious, poorest-paid jobs and they, too, were often on temporary contracts. A survey of 8,000 female clerical workers in 1932 revealed that 80 per cent of them were employed in menial work roles like typing. Only 3.5 per cent were university graduates.[41] Although they were often criticised in the press as spoilt, modern women working to buy luxuries, many, in reality, struggled in genteel poverty. Their wages (too low to permit them to live independently) were often essential to maintain dependants such as aged parents or (in the case of war widows – given priority in the public sector) children. Most white-blouse workers were single: only 22 per cent were married in 1936.[42] Some firms did have a marriage bar, but it met with official disapproval. For example, an attempt to impose it in a Milanese telephone company in 1926 was overturned after the sacked women successfully appealed to Mussolini. Astutely cloaking their protest in demographic rhetoric, they wrote: 'Losing our jobs we shall also lose those necessities of life which enable us to raise our children. Did we err in legalizing a sacred tie and showing ourselves obedient to your directives *Duce*, by procreating and preparing for the nation new young reserves?'[43]

Various measures specifically targeted women's tertiary-sector employment, to limit either numbers or career progress. Women's presence was particularly controversial in the public sector and the early post-war years saw a backlash against what was perceived as an advancing tide of *signorine*. In 1923, all employees in state administrations who had started work during the war (mainly women) were sacked, with the exception of certain war-related categories, including war widows (providing they had not remarried). In 1926, women were excluded from permanent positions in the Postal Ministry.[44] From 1933, invoking 'women's maternal duties', all branches of the state administration were permitted to exclude women from competitive examinations for new posts or to place a ceiling on their numbers. The Ministry of Education, for example, in 1934 complied by excluding women totally from competitive examinations for 'A Grade' jobs and limiting them to a third of 'C Grade' positions.[45] Despite such measures, numbers of white-blouse workers continued to grow. In public administrations, swelled by the burgeoning Fascist bureaucracy, the proportion of women declined only slightly, whilst actual numbers rose. Public administrations employed 129,142 women (and 343,195 men) in 1921 and 160,804 women (528,054 men) in 1936.[46] Numbers of female sales assistants rose even more, from 138,743 in 1921 to 294,218 in 1936.

The most notorious attack on female tertiary-sector employment was the decree law of 1938 which placed a ceiling of 10 per cent on the recruitment of women in non-manual jobs in both the private and public sectors. Public administrations were allowed to ban women totally from work roles as they saw fit. In small businesses, no women at all were to be recruited. There were, however, loopholes. Family members working in small businesses were exempt and the legislation as a whole did not affect jobs classified as 'particularly suitable for women'. When the list of these was issued the following year, it turned out to include practically all the jobs that women actually did, like typing, filing and telephony or, in shops, sales of household wares, women's clothes and so on. Once again, this measure aimed to safeguard workplace hierarchies rather than to expel women wholesale. Moreover, because the Sacchi law of 1919 had established the principle that almost all professions and public employment were open to women, both the 1933 and 1938 legislation, which contradicted it, were presented as temporary 'exceptions to the rule' necessitated by the economic crisis.[47]

For millions of poorer women, including many married women, work remained a necessity. For them, the Fascist government tried to offset the negative impact that work supposedly had on their reproductive capacities by new protective legislation. Some of this meant changes, like improvements to maternity leave and the provision of nurseries and breast-feeding rooms, which, somewhat ironically, potentially encouraged women's extra-domestic labour. But other legislation was more likely to have the opposite effect. A law in 1934 created a new category of 'female minors' (aged 15–20) who, together with children of either sex under 15, were banned from jobs deemed heavy, dangerous, or dirty. The regulations accompanying this law, published in 1936, listed numerous jobs which neither 'female minors' nor boys under 15 could do, or which they could only do if special health and safety precautions were taken. It also limited the length of women's working day, banned them from underground mining, reinforced the ban on night work and established differential scales for the maximum weights that male and female workers were allowed to lift.

The impact of this law was limited by the fact that many employers ignored it. Moreover, women employed in categories exempt from the legislation vastly outnumbered those covered by it. Excluded categories included servants, members of the employer's family, outworkers and most peasants (although the maximum-weights clause did apply to agricultural work). These categories were also excluded from most of the improvements in maternity protection. This suggests that legislators were just as worried about female competition in factories as about the dangers to future mothers' health. Significantly, 'female minors' were precisely the age group most likely to do extra-domestic work. The legislation reinforced the idea that, even though it was accepted that many women needed to work, their real value lay in their reproductive potential. It also made employing women slightly more expensive, gave men a monopoly in certain types of work and reinforced the gendering of work roles.

Admittedly census figures do show a slight decline in the percentage of women in employment from 33.3 in 1921 to 30.1 in 1936. The biggest drop was between 1921 and 1931, a period when male employment rose and the percentage of 'economically active' women plummeted from 33.3 per cent to 23.5 per cent. After that, the trend was reversed. The census of 1936 shows women's employment rising and men's falling,[48] probably due, at least in part, to the effects of the Ethiopian War. To what extent this overall downward trend had anything to do with Fascist campaigns and legislation is, however, uncertain, for the decline in female employment in official statistics began long before the rise of the blackshirts and continued until the 1970s. Apart from the protective legislation described above, there was no real attempt to banish working-class women from the labour force and even the attack on middle-class women mainly aimed to prevent women from rising up the career ladder, rather than actually preventing them from working. Quotas in particularly desirable occupations often did no more than freeze the existing situation since few women had actually risen to such heights. It is difficult, moreover, to disentangle the effects of Fascist policies from broader changes in the economy, such as the crisis in the textile industry, particularly in this period of world economic depression.

Once again, at least part of the explanation for the apparent changes may be the unreliability of the statistics. Even the census compilers themselves admitted this: a note in the report on the 1931 census warned that they could claim no great accuracy with regard to female employment in agriculture, commerce and crafts.[49] It is certain that many recorded as 'housewives' in the 1930s were actually doing at least some sort of paid employment and the decline in the official figures may partly just reflect an increase in numbers doing marginal, temporary, or seasonal work.

As Ornello Vitali has demonstrated, figures for peasant women should be treated with particular caution.[50] Although, according to the census, only about 1.5 million women were 'economically active' in agriculture in 1931 and almost 2.5 million in 1936, farming undoubtedly remained the largest employer of women. Vitali argues that many 'housewives', in reality played an important role in the productive activities of farming households, particularly in households that were resident on the land they tilled. Silvia Salvatici's excellent study of peasant women under Fascism, based on qualitative sources, demonstrates this amply.[51] Under Fascism, peasant women's lives had effectively changed little from the situation described in Chapter 1, and their contribution to the household was still great. It seems safe to assume that even Vitali's recalculations, which put numbers of 'economically active' farmwomen at about four million, are (as he himself admits) a conservative estimate.

A further 2.4 million women were recorded by the 1931 census (and 2.8 million in 1936) as 'economically active' in non-agricultural sectors. Many of them worked in industry. According to the 1936 census, about 25 per cent (1,377,373) of the industrial labour force was female. Major employers of women were the paper industry (50.7 per cent of the workforce), leather (40.8 per cent), chemicals, food processing, mechanical industries and printing. The most important sector, however, was still textiles (where 75 per cent of the workforce was female), a sector in serious crisis in these years. In some textile firms, such as those making the new 'artificial silk', economic pressures, together with the disappearance of real trade unions, led employers to impose terrible, dangerous working conditions.[52] But this period also saw the increased employment of women in new light industries, mainly born in the war, where they worked in much cleaner surroundings, doing repetitive, tedious tasks like assembling products.[53] Large numbers, only partially visible in the census, continued to do outwork manufacturing of various kinds.

Hotels and inns employed a good number of women (127,217 in 1936), as did a whole range of not particularly modern jobs like dressmaking and domestic service. Numbers of servants, previously declining, rose. In 1936, 10.5 per cent of all women classified as 'economically active' were servants. Numbers grew from 380,614 in 1921, to 469,510 in 1931, and 554,076 in 1936. There were probably many more part-timers who went uncounted. In 1936, 95 per cent of servants were female.[54] Numbers were swelled by rural women migrating to urban areas during the agricultural crisis. Despite Fascism's legal restrictions on internal migration, it continued apace as many, spurred on by economic distress, found ways round the measures. Maids, moreover, were exempt. Life for servants was harsh, characterised by endless toil, lack of personal freedom and poor pay. Nonetheless, the wages of these female migrants often constituted a vital resource for many peasant families and, on their return home, they could act as a force for modernisation, as people who had 'seen the world'. One specialised category of servants was wetnurses, still employed, even as late as the 1930s, by some wealthy mothers. Some of these peasant women actually moved into the homes of the rich, leaving their own babies at home.[55]

Under Fascism, unlike most other occupational groups, servants were not unionised. This was because domestic service was not considered real employment but woman's natural mission, and, as such, a category with 'few rights and numerous duties'.[56] Servants, together with farmwomen, were excluded from much of the protective legislation and social insurance introduced in the *ventennio*. It was not until 1942 that servants at last got the right to a weekly day off, paid holidays and redundancy payments.

Prostitution remained the 'career' (or at least something to resort to in hard times) of some women. In 1923 the regulation of prostitution was tightened, reaffirming the compulsory registration of prostitutes and brothels. Any woman who refused to undergo a medical check for venereal disease was presumed infected. From 1926 the police were empowered to round up any women lingering in a public place on suspicion of soliciting. Those picked up ran the risk of a night in the cells, a humiliating medical inspection and a police record. This legislation, theoretically aimed at rounding up 'clandestine', unregulated prostitutes, was often used to harass even women whose papers were in order.[57]

Exemplary wives and mothers?

The stubborn persistence of widespread female employment, the forward march of girls in education and the steadily shrinking size of the family all add up to a picture which poorly matches the Fascist ideal of the 'exemplary wife and mother'. There were other trends too, in this period, that undermined the Fascist ideal, trends that could be broadly summarised under the heading 'modernisation'.

In the family, some change was perceptible. Admittedly, the extended, hierarchical, peasant family far from disappeared. Indeed, numbers of share-cropping families actually grew with the Fascist policy of *sbracciantizzazione* (decasualisation) in the countryside. However, Fascist anti-migration laws notwithstanding, this was a period of progressive urbanisation that enabled some women to escape the restrictions of the peasant world. In urban areas, marriages were increasingly 'companionate'. The expanding numbers of middle-class girls at co-educational schools and university, and their greater partici-pation in the labour market, moreover, somewhat increased the chances of the sexes meeting and getting to know each other before marriage. Marriage was, however, still more or less every girl's ambition: spinsters were still regarded with derision and enjoyed little personal freedom, condemned, in many cases, to never leaving home. Family law was not substantially altered. Although a new version of the Civil Code was issued in 1942 it contained no particularly significant innovations as regards the position of women.

In northern working-class couples, where wives worked full-time, there is some evidence of men taking a share of household tasks. One Milanese fac-tory worker remembered: 'If I got home late he used to prepare the food and if I got home first then I used to do it. . . . He also used to get the child up in the morning and dress her and take her to my mother's, because I had to go out first. He always made the bed . . . he kept the house clean and tidy. I used to start in the evening and he finished off in the morning.'[58] Even these men, however, never did the most onerous tasks like laundry and, in the vast major-ity of Italian families, housework remained entirely woman's work. House-work was still very laborious: many homes lacked even basic amenities (only 20 per cent had flush toilets in the 1930s) and only the very rich had domestic appliances.

Women's dress, in urban areas at least, changed roughly in line with inter-national trends, becoming increasingly sporty, practical and less class-specific, although most clothing was still made at home or by seamstresses. Fascism did make its own interventions in dress: it promoted uniforms, tried to ban foreign words for clothing and even set up the Ente Nazionale della Moda (National Fashion Board) to promote Italian fashions. Despite this, fashionable women continued to view Paris (with some inspiration from Hollywood) as the most important guide to what to wear.[59]

Women's leisure activities were still constrained by the burden of domestic duties, the cost of going out and notions of respectability. Girls still needed a chaperone to go dancing or to the cinema and women were effectively excluded from many centres of social life, like bars and cafés. The regime offered its own mass leisure activities in the shape of the Opera Nazionale Dopolavoro (National After Work Organisation) but this, too, was mostly fre-quented by men. For women, however, leisure opportunities were expanding. Forms of commercial leisure were becoming increasingly important. Radio broadcasting, born in the 1920s, brought entertainment into the home for middle-class women (others listened in communal facilities) and Hollywood films fed the dreams of many (particularly young, urban) women. Despite Fascist campaigns to encourage Italians to watch Italian, not foreign, films, imports from across the Atlantic were popular. Such films brought new, glamorous, 'modern' images of womanhood that jarred with the Fascist ideal of the rounded, maternal homemaker. Magazines for women of various types also proliferated ranging from the party's official publications to the new glossies, filled with fashion and advice columns. This was when some glossies which were to prove very long-lasting, such as *Gioia* and *Grazia*, were born.[60] Many magazines contained messages that, if not explicitly anti-fascist, were far from harmonious with Fascist gender ideology.

Perhaps unsurprisingly, attitudes were changing, particularly among the young. One survey of 1,003 mainly lower middle-class girls (aged 14–18), in 1937, found that most of these Roman teenagers planned to work after leaving school. They showed only modest interest in future motherhood (considering one or two babies quite enough) and even less in traditional female pursuits like knitting.[61] They listed their favourite pastime as the cinema. They were also very interested in sports, a new female activity, offered primarily by the Fascist Party youth groups. Somewhat perversely, in spite of deluges of rhetoric stressing women's domestic and maternal mission, a contribution to the modernisation of female lives in this period was made directly by the policies of the regime itself, through its mass mobilisation of millions of girls and women.

5

Doing their Duty for Nation (or Church): Mass Mobilisation during the Fascist *Ventennio*

The Fascist *ventennio* sounded the death knell for Italian feminism. Some women initially continued to belong to autonomous organisations but these gradually disappeared. Considerably greater numbers frequented Catholic groups and a few were active in clandestine anti-fascist groupings. By far the largest female organisations in this period, however, were Fascist. Fascism politically mobilised women and girls on an unprecedented scale, in vastly greater numbers than previous political parties had done. In November 1920, for example, the PSI had only a few thousand female members (about 2 per cent of their membership) and, by December 1921, only a few hundred (about 1 per cent of the membership) had joined the new Communist Party. About 15 per cent of the membership of trade unions (whether Catholic or socialist) was female by 1920. At most, tens of thousands belonged to feminist organisations. Such figures pale into insignificance when compared with the Fascist mobilisation.

Rival allegiances: non-fascist organisations and anti-fascist women

The Fascists did not immediately close down autonomous women's organisations. This happened only gradually. For example, the Federazione Italiana Laureate e Diplomate di Istituti Superiori (FILDIS – Italian Federation of Female Graduates) lasted until 1935, when it was swept aside to make way for the analogous but Fascist ANFAL (founded 1926). The UFN managed to survive, despite its left-wing politics, by focusing exclusively on welfare. It was shut down in 1938, ostensibly because Fascist welfare programmes had made it redundant; in reality, because it had many Jewish members. A rather different case was the CNDI, which, with its anti-socialist and patriotic membership, openly embraced the new regime. In 1922, just after the March on Rome, Countess Spalletti Rasponi sent Mussolini a telegram saying: 'In this sacred hour italic renewal consiglio nazionale donne italiane confidently applauds Italy's great future.'[1] After this, the CNDI adapted well to the new political circum-stances although eventually its international links made even it unacceptable.[2]

Opposition political parties, of course, were simply suppressed. Some women continued to think of themselves as communists, socialists or liberals. Only a handful, however, were actively anti-fascist, engaged, for example, in the illegal distribution of leaflets or newspapers which attempted to present a counter-view to Fascist propaganda. Women constituted only a small minority of anti-fascist activists but, given the poor record of the parties of the Left in recruiting women in the past, this is hardly surprising. The price could be very high for the brave few who chose this difficult life: 748 women were tried for political crimes by the Special Tribunal (founded in 1926) and others by ordi-nary courts. In total, about 500 women received sentences for political crimes under Fascism. Some spent much of the *ventennio* in prison or in 'internal exile'. Others went abroad. The communist former textile worker and future parliamentary deputy Teresa Noce (code name 'Estella'), for example, took ref-uge in Paris, from where she travelled repeatedly to Italy on dangerous under-cover missions.[3] Other women, although not necessarily linked to organised political groupings, staged open protests or went on strike, both illegal under Fascism. There were quite a large number of strikes among, for example, sea-sonal rice-workers and women employed in the beleaguered textile industry.

Such open or clandestine anti-fascist activities were later to be symbolically extremely important as they showed that not all had supported Mussolini. They also helped sow the seeds of the wartime Resistance. Only very small numbers of women, however, were involved. Numerically much more impor-tant were the organisations for Catholic women which flourished under the protection of the Vatican.[4]

In contrast to Pius X's disapproving attitude to female activism, Benedict XV encouraged it as part of the Church's attempts to adapt to the changes that had taken place in the war and the advent of mass politics. In 1919, in a speech to Catholic women, he stated that, given the 'changed conditions of the times', there was a need for an extra-domestic role for women in the service of the Church (albeit never forgetting their familial role). Unlike her predecessor, Maddelena Patrizi Gondi, who succeeded Giustiniani Bandini as UDCI Presi-dent in 1917, never had to justify its existence. This papal support was enough to override the opposition of some of the Church leaders. Pius XI, enthroned in 1922, continued to support the organisation of Catholic women and they in turn rallied to his aim to re-Christianise society and shore up the family.

An important innovation in this period was the fact that the Catholic organ-isations began to mobilise girls as well as adult women. In October 1918, a middle-class Milanese woman, Armida Barelli (1882–1952), became UDCI vice-president with the task of running a new youth section. The *sorella mag-giore* (big sister) of the Catholic organisations was not a nun but had, in 1913, taken a vow of lifelong chastity to dedicate herself to a lay apostolate. When asked by the Pope to become vice-president, she protested that: 'I've never travelled alone, I've never left my mother.'[5] In fact, she was far less inexpe-rienced than this suggests, having already proved her considerable abilities in helping organise the simultaneous ceremonies to consecrate the Italian armed forces to the Sacred Heart in 1917 and in fundraising for the foundation of the Catholic University of Milan. In her new role, Barelli was soon tirelessly travelling the length and breadth of Italy.

In 1919, the UDCI became the Unione Femminile Cattolica Italiana (UFCI), with two wings, the Unione Donne di Azione Cattolica (UDACI – Union of Catholic Action Women) and the Gioventù Femminile (GF – Female Youth – led by Barelli). A few years later a third section, the Universitarie, was added. As a branch of Catholic Action (AC), the UFCI was subordinate to the Church hierarchy.

With its new, innovative youth section the UFCI grew rapidly. Already, by the time of its first congress in 1919, the GF had 700 groups with 50,000 members and UDACI about 70,000. By 1922, GF had 220,000 members in 4,360 groups all over Italy, and by 1925, there were 15,800 GF groups with 330,000 members, in 281 different dioceses. By 1939, GF membership had reached an impressive 863,000. The section for older women grew too, although more slowly. By 1925, it boasted 3,162 groups with about 160,000 members, mainly housewives, and by 1931, about 6,000 groups with over 250,000 members. Although numerically somewhat smaller than the Fascist mobilisation of girls and women, the Catholic organisations do testify to the enduring importance of Catholicism in the lives of many Italian women in this period.

UDACI welcomed women over 35. Initially GF was open only to those aged 16 to 35 but soon this age group was renamed the Effettive and joined by new girls' sections: the Aspiranti (aged 12 to 16) from 1920, the Beniamine (6 to 12) from 1923, the Piccolissime (4 to 6) from 1933 and even, in 1937, the Angioletti (birth to 4).

Although Catholic women's groups, like the Fascist groups, promoted women's maternal role, they took a firmer stand against modernity. Their mission was to fight secularisation and to provide social and religious training for the future mothers of Italy. They promoted a very traditional view of gender roles, opposing women's emancipation and aiming to curb manifestations of immodesty or modern behaviour among women. Women were urged, for example, to reject fashions with shorter skirts. Outwork was actively promoted as a way of combating the rural–urban shift. Extra-domestic work and too much female education was also criticised, for women's role, they argued, was essentially maternal and domestic. It was repeatedly stressed, as one writer in the *Bollettino dell'UFCI* put it in 1920, that: 'only *the Christian apostolate* can call us out of our homes'.[6]

The Catholic organisations offered their members a range of activities, usually organised by class, with separate activities for workers, for middle-class housewives, and so on. The main activities of its local, parish-based groups were religious, including meditations, spiritual exercises, talks on religious matters and so on. The members were, however, supposed to also carry the organisation's message beyond the meeting room. Particularly in the 1930s, they did a good deal of welfare work, such as assisting needy children. Some women were very active. Lucia Banti, a middle-class GF member involved in such welfare initiatives in Florence, remembered that, in the 1930s, 'I worked as a volunteer, but I worked as much as someone who was paid.'[7] Catholic activists also assisted servants, particularly in order to protect young women from the dangers of seduction or prostitution on their arrival in cities. In ministering to servants, they emphasised the idea of service and dutifully carrying out orders as well as the importance of religious observance.[8]

The UFCI was dominated by aristocrats and upper middle-class women at the higher levels. Lower middle-class women held the intermediate ranks and working-class and peasant women, including many servants and housewives, formed much of the mass membership. Many of the GF leaders were young, middle-class, fervently religious, unmarried women like Barelli herself, often with a good level of education.

The GF had a hierarchical structure, with a president in most dioceses and a president and treasurer in each local branch. Innumerable courses (usually lasting a week) were run for these leaders, teaching them in their thousands how to, for example, speak in public. Some women were specifically trained as 'propagandists' whose role it was to travel around giving lectures. The training courses were wide-ranging, covering topics like women's work or how to inculcate religious values in the membership (one important theme being the cult of the Sacred Heart). There were also spiritual retreats. During training, women were urged to learn self-control and to eschew traditional feminine traits such as vanity and sentimentality, instead concentrating on religious ideals, their supernatural destination and, of course, obedience to the Church hierarchy.

Many of these leaders were extremely active. Apart from daily devotional activities, they busied themselves organising meetings, attending courses and conferences, helping organise 'religious culture competitions' and going on pilgrimages all over Italy. Sometimes they went to stay temporarily in other areas in order to help set up new sections. In short, although these organisations preached female submission, domesticity and a rejection of a political role for women to their members, for many of the leaders they brought a not inconsiderable degree of personal emancipation. Particularly in the case of unmarried women, whose lives otherwise would have been hemmed in by endless restrictions, the transformative effects of such activism were potentially great.

With their capillary network of groups all over Italy, their parish-based structures and their welfare activities, the Catholic organisations were an imposing and highly successful force. They reached out to large numbers of women, offering them female social networks and a chance to reinforce their faith. They strengthened the hold of the Church over women and represented the only real alternative, during Mussolini's dictatorship, to the Fascist organisation of women.

Fascist women: the Fasci Femminili

Initially it was by no means clear whether women would have a role in the new Fascist movement. The vast majority of early Fascists were male. Many, fresh from the male camaraderie of the trenches, were ill-disposed to accepting a disrupting female presence. Right from the start, however, a few women rallied to the new movement.[9] Initially numbers were small. There were only nine women at the movement's founding meeting in Piazza San Sepolcro in Milan in March 1919. Tiny numbers of largely young, petty bourgeois women, like the '*squadrista* heroine' Ines Donati, who took part in various types of direct action like strike-breaking, were directly involved in the violence of the time.[10]

Women like Donati joined mixed (almost all-male) groups (the Fasci di Combattimento) but soon some Fascist women began to organise separately. Women-only groups (initially called the Gruppi Femminili Fascisti and later taking the name Fasci Femminili – FF) quickly appeared.[11] The first was founded in March 1920 in Monza (Milan) and was followed by others, mainly in northern and central urban areas. Like the male 'Fascists of the First Hour', the members of these groups included both those who saw the new movement as one which would radically transform Italy, as well as more conservative elements, largely from the traditional elites, who valued Fascism mainly as a means of defeating the 'red threat'. These early groups had many urban lower middle-class members but, even at this stage, the leaders were often from a higher social milieu, being upper middle-class or even aristocrats.[12] Many of the early leaders had previous experience of public life in political or philanthropic organisations. For some of them the events in Fiume had proved formative in drawing them to right-wing politics, and indeed some of them saw themselves primarily as irredentists rather than Fascists. Many were unmarried or widowed or with children already grown up. In keeping with their generally higher social status, their average level of education tended to be somewhat higher than that of the male hierarchs of this early period.[13]

A substantial number of the early leaders were feminists of various kinds, particularly from the CNDI. Many of them had been drawn along the path to Fascism by the shift that had taken place in the feminist movement during the First World War and it was only a small ideological step from their patriotic wartime stance to the new blackshirt movement. Their role in war work, moreover, had given many a taste for an active public life.

In general, however, women who became Fascists in the early period, whether feminists or not, chose to do so more as members of their class than of their sex. Undoubtedly many middle-class women were, quite simply, convinced by Fascist politics and, together with others of their class, believed that Mussolini could save them from the Bolshevik menace and restore the honour of the nation. Angela Maria Guerra, a Fascist sympathiser from the start and later a party activist, remembered: 'That's when I became a Fascist . . . being a Fascist in 1920–21–22 meant loving order, justice, respect. It meant respect for crucifixes in schools, respect for the symbols of the Nation, respect for property and the family.'[14] Similarly, Elisa Lombardi, who later became director of the Fascist women's sports academy, recalled: 'There was nothing to criticise about Fascism when it started, when there was the revolution . . . in Italy, after the war, they spat at soldiers, my brothers couldn't walk around in uniform.'[15] Moreover, none of the other political parties had so far delivered substantial improvements to female rights. For many nationalist and irredentist women who also thought of themselves as feminists this new movement seemed as good as the rest on gender questions. Indeed, at first the new movement did not seem particularly misogynous and its early programme even promised female suffrage.

Many male 'Fascists of the first hour', however, were far from encouraging towards the women's groups. They regarded Fascism as fundamentally masculine. Such men wanted women to confine themselves entirely to support roles. In 1921, when the Fascist movement officially became a political party, draft regulations were drawn up for the women's groups that defined them as internal sections of the Fasci di Combattimento. They were placed under the control of the male heads of each Fascio and confined to propaganda and welfare work.

Despite this, somewhat paradoxically, the general disinterest of the hierarchs in them gave early female Fascists a degree of autonomy. They were left to organise their own conferences and even to lobby for feminist demands. Their press in this period, when open debate was still possible, was an odd mix of patriotism and feminism and, as Stefania Bartoloni has noted, often expressed 'positions that were later persecuted by the regime'.[16] At the end of 1924, in the aftermath of the Matteotti affair, Mussolini appointed the former Red Cross nurse and 'Fascist of the first hour' Elisa Majer Rizzioli to a new position of Inspectress of the Fascist Women's Groups with a seat on the Party Directorate. She was a patriot and moderate feminist who aspired to real power for PNF women.

Mussolini's choice of a feminist (even a moderate one) annoyed many male hierarchs. Their hostility to her was reflected in the new FF Regulations drawn up by the Party Directorate. Although a congress of Fascist Women held in Milan in June 1924 had drafted their own Regulations, which would have given women far more equality in the party, their proposal was ignored and a different document imposed which removed the last vestiges of female autonomy.

Suffrage was granted, in a cruel gesture, to certain, limited categories of women in November 1925, just as democracy itself was disappearing. This gave the vote in local elections to women over 25 who had been decorated for war service or for civil merit, to soldiers' widows of 'good moral conduct' (excluding separated widows), to mothers of war dead, to literate heads of families, to those who had satisfactorily completed elementary education, and to literate women who paid 100 lire in taxes per annum. Those eligible had to specifically request enrolment on the electoral lists. This law, passed in 1924 before the Fascist coup d'état, was supported by Mussolini (albeit stating, during his speech in favour of it, that, 'I don't believe that women have the power of synthesis, and so they lack the capacity for great spiritual creations'[17]). It potentially enfranchised about 1,700,000 women (compared with 9 million male voters) but it was irrelevant. Local councils were replaced by the unelected Fascist *podestà* in 1926.[18]

Majer Rizzioli herself did not last long. At the end of 1925, Party Secretary Roberto Farinacci closed down her newspaper the *Rassegna femminile italiana*[19] and, in January 1926, abolished the Women's Inspectorate, forcing Majer Rizzioli herself to resign. After this, the Women's Fasci were directly controlled by the (male) Party Secretariat. The attack on Party feminists was not confined to Majer Rizzioli. During the mid- to late 1920s various troublesome local leaders who had attempted to resist the sidelining of women in the party, like Pia Bartolini of Bologna who spoke explicitly of 'Fascist feminism', were ousted.

Augusto Turati, Farinacci's successor from March 1926, was hardly more encouraging to Party women. His attitude can be seen in a circular he sent to all the FF Secretaries in May 1926, rebuffing a demand from women to be allowed to wear black shirts. It stated bluntly that: 'The black shirt is the virile symbol of our revolution and has nothing to do with the welfare tasks that Fascism has given women.'[20] Turati appointed Angiola Moretti, previously Majer Rizzioli's clerical assistant, as Secretary to the Women's Groups. Only twenty-seven years old, Moretti was too young to have dabbled much with feminism and ambitious enough not to cause trouble.

This clampdown on 'feminist Fascists' coincided with the launching of the demographic campaign in 1927 and the deluges of propaganda about women's maternal role. Here feminists found themselves caught in a slippery trap because of their own preoccupation with the social value of maternity. Thus, for example, when ONMI was founded, some felt that at last things for which they had long campaigned were being granted.

Not all feminists became Fascists (it was largely the more moderate and conservative among them who did so) and, of those who did, some ceased to support it after the last vestiges of democracy vanished in 1925. Others, however, continued to be involved although often at the cost of a degree of torment and confusion. Many felt betrayed by the new laws limiting female employment and by the fact that Mussolini had promised them the vote and then snatched it away. Some, such as Teresa Labriola,[21] rationalised their conversion to Fascism by speaking of 'Latin feminism', supposedly an Italian reformulation of feminism. This stressed, unlike 'sterile foreign doctrines' which emphasised individualism and equal rights, the importance of women's maternal duty to family and nation. As De Grazia has argued, however, male and female Fascists saw these things differently, for 'Latin feminists saw [sexual] difference as meaning complementarity and collaboration between men and women, whereas Fascist men understood it to mean sexual hierarchy and female subordination.'[22] Feminism itself was increasingly portrayed as old-fashioned or a foreign doctrine unsuited to Italy.

The class composition of the FF membership has never been systematically researched but the existing evidence suggests that it was predominantly middle or upper class. In the 1930s, as membership increased, the class base widened slightly but even in this period there were still many aristocrats in higher-ranking leadership positions. There were also many professionals (mainly teachers) and middle-class housewives who took organisational roles at all levels. Particularly in rural areas the majority of local leaders were primary teachers.

In 1930, even Moretti's post was abolished, and central party control was further tightened in May 1931, after which, nominations for local fiduciaries had to be approved by Party Headquarters. This done, women's activities were allowed to expand. The background to this was the transformation of the party itself in the early 1930s, when it became increasingly bureaucratic and depoliticised. Under the unintelligent and unimaginative Achille Starace (PNF leader for most of the decade) a massive membership drive was launched for the party and its ancillary organisations. In the new policy of 'going to the people' the women's groups proliferated rapidly. From 1932, it became compulsory for every local party branch to have an FF. One was to be automatically created wherever the local party had at least ten female members aged over twenty-two. Each local FF section was run by a Secretary and she was supervised by a Provincial Fiduciary. This all-female chain of command was, however, always subordinate to the male Party hierarchy and the tasks and duties of Fascist Women were simply assigned to them from above.

With this structure, the PNF became the first Italian political party with a truly mass female membership. The novelty of this mobilisation should not be underestimated. For all its rhetoric about 'exemplary wives and mothers', with this attempt to recruit millions of women, the regime did something quite new. Women now were asked to actively demonstrate their support for Fascism and play a role in forging the 'consensus' the regime desired. This meant, essentially, welfare work.

In dedicating themselves to welfare, Fascist Women were similar to many (non-fascist) female activists elsewhere in interwar Europe. Indeed, Fascist Women themselves displayed considerable interest in the activities of foreign women and, despite the regime's nationalistic ideology, continued to send delegations to international women's conferences throughout the *ventennio*. The way in which Italian women followed this broader European trend was, however, conditioned by the context in which they found themselves: dictatorship, the suppression of free speech and civil liberties, and extreme nationalism leading to imperialism and war.

Fascist welfare frequently differed from the sort of welfare activities in which many middle- and upper-class women had been previously involved, whether feminists or not, more in its propagandistic messages and the scale of its operations than in its precise activities. It is clear that many Fascist Women who were engaged in running Party welfare programmes genuinely believed that they were doing 'good works', offering a helping hand to those in need. Many of the causes Fascism asked them to support, like running holiday camps for poor and sickly children, seemed a perfectly worthwhile outlet for their energies. Fascist welfare was, however, stripped of any emancipationist ideology. It was to be selfless service by an army of dutiful women carrying out orders for the greater good of the nation.

Fascist Women did welfare work during the entire *ventennio*. In the 1920s this was deemed largely a peripheral activity, something relatively unimportant which could be safely left to them. In the context of the world economic depression, however, it took on new importance as a central plank in the regime's attempts to forge a consensus or at least to prevent the eruption of open unrest. From the early 1930s, Party women provided the volunteer labour required to enable the Fascist propaganda machine to sing the praises of how caring the regime was. This made them essential agents of Fascist domestic policy. Without their voluntary work, Party welfare schemes would have collapsed. Welfare activities, furthermore, provided a useful channel into poorer homes. While distributing powdered baby milk or packets of vegetable seeds, Fascist Home Visitors brought propaganda into the heart of millions of families.

In the field of welfare, Fascist Women were very active. Even in the late 1920s their activities included running sewing workshops, teaching domestic science courses, distributing milk and layettes to impoverished mothers and staffing holiday camps. In the 1930s their responsibilities increased vertiginously. A Fascist Woman might find herself engaged in, amongst other things, running information centres for peasant women or servants, staffing stalls for migrant rice-workers at railway stations, visiting welfare recipients at home, assisting medical staff in paediatric or obstetric clinics, or even inspecting chicken coops for poultry competitions.

Particularly in northern and central areas, many sections were a hive of activity. The level of activity is particularly impressive given that most of it was run on a shoestring, for the party offered the FF very little funding. Most of their budget, apart from income from membership fees, had to be raised by running lotteries or lucky dips, begging for donations from local wealthy persons, requesting special levies from the membership and so on.

Italy's invasion of Ethiopia in 1935 brought new challenges. It led to a shift both in FF activities and in the language used to address women. The best known example of the mobilisation of women for this imperial war was the public sacrifice of wedding rings in the ceremonies of the 'Giornata della Fede', which seemed only to confirm women in traditional roles. But the war effort also led to women being called to the service of the nation on the 'home front' in other ways. In response to the League of Nations sanctions, party activists attempted to mobilise all Italian women, as both consumers and producers, for the autarky campaign and propaganda stressed their central role to the national cause. The FF were also assigned the role of bringing assistance, solace and propaganda to soldiers' wives.

In this period the Party women's press was swept along in a flood of warfaring, patriotic rhetoric. Women were exhorted to make sacrifices, including the sacrifice of their own sons. Even after the actual sanctions ended, the autarky campaign, which proved a useful mobilisation tool, was not abandoned and women continued to be urged to do their bit for the nation. This period also saw the creation of courses to prepare young women for 'colonial life' as wives in the new Empire, instructing them in things like specialised types of first aid and camping skills.[23]

Despite the expansion of their duties, Fascist Women never obtained any actual political power. In the late 1930s, however, the increased level of activity, created in particular by the autarky campaign and the growth in membership numbers, led to the announcement of a new salaried rank of National Inspectress. The main task of these new officials was to ensure that central policy was carried out locally and they remained excluded from the real corridors of power. Those appointed to these new positions were, at least initially, Party stalwarts with years of unpaid service as Provincial Fiduciaries behind them.

After the outbreak of the Second World War, Fascist Women made other, albeit small, political gains. In 1940, for the first time, Provincial Fiduciaries got a seat on PNF Provincial Directories and on provincial 'corporative' committees which helped oversee local economic affairs. In symbolic terms at least, this was significant, for the Corporate State was in theory the Fascist substitute for democracy. It was also in this period, just after the outbreak of World War Two, that the FF at last got their own Central Committee.

Such slight widening of their political influence did not, however, fundamentally change their subordinate position in the party pecking order and the only sphere where Fascist Women ever had real power was over other, poorer, women, the recipients of Party welfare. Eventually it was decided to recruit such women into the party. The class composition of the FF was safeguarded by creating two separate, dependent sections: one for peasants and one for working-class women.

The Massaie Rurali and SOLD

The foundation of the section for peasant women marked a turning point as previously the PNF (like most other political parties before them) had shown little interest in rural women, apart from waged farm-labourers like rice-weeders. But such waged workers, many of whom had previously been members of socialist trade unions, represented only a small percentage of the millions on the land. In 1933 a special section of the Fascist farming unions was founded for women peasants, headed by a retired schoolteacher, the former socialist, *sansepolcrista* and political maverick Regina Terruzzi. The following year this was absorbed into the Party itself as the 'Massaie Rurali' (Rural Housewives) Section of the FF.[24]

This Section developed an extensive training programme that aimed to improve the lives of rural women without altering rural class relations, land tenure arrangements or the gender hierarchy of the rural household. As its founding Statute declared, it also aimed to 'make (rural women) appreciate all the advantages of life on the land, as a means of opposing the harmful trend towards urbanisation'.[25] Members were trained to carry out 'women's agricultural and household activities' in a 'modern and rational' manner, supposedly following the tenets of the 'rational farming' movement (the application of Taylorism to agriculture). To encourage the take-up of training, numerous competitions were held. Most of the courses and competitions focused on domestic science, hygiene and childcare and on what were seen as female roles in agriculture like poultry farming and vegetable gardening. The peasant members were also subjected to numerous lectures on political themes.

From 1935 onwards, the section was heavily mobilised for autarky. Peasant women were urged to play a key role in the anti-sanctions campaign, increasing production for the national cause by, for example, raising greater numbers of rabbits and chickens to replace imported meat, and gathering wild herbs to be used as medicines. They were also trained in new 'autarkic' craft and cultivation techniques.

An analogous section for female workers, the Sezione Operaie e Lavoranti a Domicilio (SOLD – Section for Women Workers and Outworkers), was belatedly created in 1937, quite clearly modelled on what was seen as the successful example of the Rural Housewives. As its name suggests, the membership included factory workers and outworkers but it also actively recruited working-class housewives and domestic servants, the latter a category virtually untouched by the regime's other mass organisations. SOLD members were offered outings, sports activities and short holidays. They could enter competitions, receive handouts and cut-price goods and follow training courses. Like the courses for rural women, these combined propaganda with practical instruction, mostly in domestic science, childcare and hygiene but in some cases offering professional training or basic literacy education.[26]

Although training and welfare heavily dominated the day-to-day activities of both sections, in practice party hierarchs saw such aspects as simply enticements to encourage women to join. The real aims of both sections were political, part of Starace's broad plan to gradually find a niche in the PNF for every single category of Italian according to class, gender and economic sector. He, quite literally, aimed to put the entire nation into Fascist uniform. In many respects, of course, such blanket mobilisation could only be achieved at the expense of any real sense of political commitment. Starace, however, was optimistic, arguing that the sections could enable the party to bring Fascist politics into the heart of every poor urban and rural family. This was an interesting proposition in its own right since it portrayed women as a key to the political mobilisation of whole families and households. This was quite new: pre-fascist politicians had made little or no attempt to court female support.

Joining the Party

The extent to which Starace's plan really succeeded is debatable. In numerical terms, it was extremely successful. In 1929, FF membership was already about 100,000 and by 1940 this had soared to around 750,000, and to over a million in 1942. Even larger numbers joined the Rural Housewives section: its membership grew from 225,094 in 1935, to 895,514 in 1937, nearly 1.5 million in 1939 and over 2.5 million by late 1942, making it one of the largest of all the Fascist mass organisations overall. Even the latecomer SOLD had signed up an impressive 1,514,860 by July 1942.

The reasons why such large numbers joined were varied and differed according to the period and to women's class and position in the organisation. In the case of poorer women, the meaning of membership is far from clear as those who joined the two subordinate sections were offered only a passive role in the party. Many of them, particularly peasant women and domestic servants, were politically totally inexperienced. This, of course, was less true of urban industrial workers, who were more likely to come from left-wing families. Although some members of both sections may have joined out of a sense of loyalty to the regime, many others may have not had much understanding of the issues at stake or may even have joined in spite of the political message. In many cases, opportunism or material needs were clearly significant motives. One Emilian peasant woman, for example, horrified the FF leader who tried to recruit her when she admitted that: 'I'll get myself a Rural Housewife card, just as I'd have the communist one if they gave me something to eat.'[27] Some women joined to obtain employment: servants seeking work in labour exchanges, for example, were vetted by SOLD organisers who, under the guise of offering professional and 'spiritual' guidance, scrutinised their political and moral suitability. More broadly, by the late 1930s the Party card had become a prerequisite for access to welfare benefits and services previously open to all, earning it the nickname of the 'bread card'. Although considered equivalent to full PNF membership, joining the sections was cheap and entailed the purchase of only a neckerchief and badge, rather than an expensive tailored FF uniform.

Without denying that there were at least some committed Fascists among the members of the sections for poorer women, it is, undoubtedly, among the FF members that the greatest number of 'true believers' were to be found. In the 1930s and 1940s propaganda increasingly depicted Fascist Women as almost mesmerised by the glories of Fascism and the godlike person of the Duce. They were frequently praised for their disciplined devotion, their blind and unswerving loyalty and their desire to serve the regime with any sacrifice that might be required.

It is indeed possible to find women who fit this picture, women who believed fanatically in the regime and its politics. This was true of Laura Marani Argnani, Provincial Fiduciary in Reggio Emilia and eventually National Inspectress, whose writings were drenched with the Cult of the Duce and declarations of total unquestioning loyalty to him. According to one former student from the teacher training college she ran, 'she had an obsession that filled her whole head: her head was full of the Duce, she adored him. She was in love with the Duce.'[28] Similarly, even defeat in war could not shake the beliefs of Angela Maria Guerra, a Fascist since 1920. At her trial in 1945 she boldly stated that: 'I was, I am and will continue to be a Fascist.'[29]

It does need to be stressed, however, that not all FF members were so loyal. Even for middle-class women, opportunism and material factors could be significant. For public-sector employees, party membership was a prerequisite for employment, and teachers were expected to take an active role in local party activities. In the early years of Fascism it is still possible to talk of women consciously choosing to support the regime, for alternative political paths were still open to them. This is less true of the 1930s when many FF members came from a whole new generation. They had grown up under the regime and been indoctrinated with propaganda at school and by the Party youth groups from an early age. By the time they moved up into the adult Party the regime seemed normal, just a fact of life, immovable and unchanging. In this context anti-fascism of any sort was hard to imagine and, for many rank-and-file members, simple conformism, the hallmark of the 1930s, certainly played a role.

Conformism, however, is not enough to explain why women sought leadership positions. As Helga Dittrich-Johansen has argued, even among female leaders levels of commitment were far from uniform and the motives for taking up organisational positions varied over time as well as according to generation, class, region and rank in the party hierarchy. Some who took leadership roles did so out of genuine political commitment. For others, the incentive may have been the potential for social advancement the Party could offer.[30] For many, the real spur was doubtless simply the desire to find some extra-domestic activity to absorb their energies. As the regime took over and refashioned charities and other welfare organisations to its own ends, many of the volunteer activities women had previously done in other contexts now became party work.

For a small minority, the motives included economic ones. Some opportunities for paid employment emerged although mostly only towards the end of the *ventennio*. Before this there were a few women employed in the central FF Office in Rome and Party responsibilities could open the door to forms of paid employment, particularly directorships for children's summer camps. From 1938 the Party began to employ salaried 'Rural Housewives Technical Leaders', and the National Inspectresses, appointed from 1937, also received a monthly wage for their work. It was not until 1940, however, that FF provincial leaders were, at last, conceded salaries.

The majority of FF leaders were unpaid. At lower levels, the party seems to have considered a sense of importance and the satisfaction of doing their 'duty' to the Nation sufficient reward for women's time. Even Regina Terruzzi, who took on the not inconsiderable task of setting up the Rural Housewives section, was paid nothing whatsoever for her labours. All over Italy thousands of local section secretaries or 'nucleus leaders' (the lowest rank in the pecking order) soldiered on unpaid, often in difficult circumstances. Some of them may have accepted these positions because they found the challenge genuinely interesting. Others, particularly primary teachers, found it hard to refuse. It needs to be noted, furthermore, that even those who took on paid positions were not necessarily economically driven. In the case of the Inspectresses, for example, some, like Clara Franceschini, former Provincial Fiduciary in Pavia, needed the money, but for others non-economic motives were clearly foremost. Countess Laura Calvi Roncalli, from Bergamo, was so rich she donated her entire salary as National Inspectress to charity in 1942.[31]

For paid and unpaid alike, various forms of training were gradually introduced, such as short courses for 'Fascist Home Visitors' or for 'assistants and directors of children's holiday camps' and *turni di servizio* (service rotas) whereby Provincial Fiduciaries were briefly transferred to another province to observe their organisational methods. Once the Provincial Fiduciaries became paid officials, a two-month-long national training course for new recruits was introduced. More in-depth education for a select few was available in the elite female sports academy (see below) and at the Sant'Alessio PNF women's college which, from 1937, stopped training rural primary teachers and instead began to turn out Technical Leaders for the Rural Housewives.[32]

The Girls' Organisations

It was on girls and young women that the Fascist mobilisation had the most modernising impact. Fascism mobilised huge numbers of them in gender-segregated youth organisations, graded, like the boys' analogous groups, into age-structured ranks.[33] Girls aged 8–12 joined the Piccole Italiane (Little Female Italians) and those aged 13–18 the Giovani Italiane (Young Female Italians). Initially these groups were run by the FF, but in 1929 they were placed, along with the boys' groups, under the wing of the Ministry of Education. In 1937, the youth groups for both sexes became part of the Gioventù Italiana del Littorio (GIL – Italian Youth of the Lictors), with four different ranks for girls. The Giovani Fasciste (Young Female Fascists), for the 18–21 age group, was

Illustration 5   Athletics competition, Parco Cervi, Reggio Emilia, 1940.
(Photographer Renzo Vaiani. Reproduced courtesy of Fototeca Panizzi, Reggio Emilia.)

effectively a youth section of the FF. Girls aged 15–17 now joined the Giovani Italiane, those 8–14 the Piccole Italiane and 6–7-year-olds could sign up in the Figlie della Lupa (Daughters of the She-Wolf).

Unlike their male equivalents, whose activities were mainly pre-military, the girls' groups did plenty of 'demographic activities' like domestic science classes and 'doll-drill', where they learned childcare techniques to prepare themselves for their future maternal role. They also played group games, listened to lectures, watched films and followed training courses on topics like gardening and first aid. Older girls did welfare activities like the FF. They were also, of course, subjected to a good deal of propaganda. In the GIL, Fascist culture courses were added and the chance to participate in the Ludi Juvenili, in which sports and cultural competitions were staged.

Many of the activities for Fascist girls were potentially very appealing, offering opportunities for sociability outside the family including excursions and the chance to do sports, particularly gymnastics. As an official press release put this, in 1932, they did sports because, 'Fascist women need to be physically healthy, to become mothers of healthy children.'[34] Sports for boys and girls were kept rigidly separate. Although the regime undoubtedly put more resources into male sports activities, much was provided for girls, particularly graceful, artistic forms of gymnastics, which were considered suitable as they avoided making them too 'masculine'.

Teachers for these new sporting activities were trained at the elite sports academy in Orvieto, founded in January 1932 as a female version of the male academy in Rome. The Orvieto Academy trained PE teachers for both schools and the girls' organisations. By 1943, 800 young women had completed the prestigious training there. Their respectability was guaranteed by numerous restrictions, including usually only being allowed to go out in a group to Mass or to a sports event. Nonetheless, the Academy, in many respects, represented the most modern face of women during the regime. The students featured frequently in official propaganda, gracefully throwing javelins or engaged in synchronised gymnastics routines (often dressed in short shorts). They put on displays at many big political events and marched confidently in formation, smartly turned out in their neat distinctive uniforms, at party rallies around Italy (and, in 1937, in Berlin). During their three-year course, in addition to sports-related subjects, their curriculum included a good dose of political education as well as subjects like anatomy, hygiene, choral singing, domestic science and religious education. The Academy was quite expensive but a few grants, available to categories like war orphans, widened its social base. A sprinkling of girls from poor backgrounds were, as a result, included in the student body, which mainly comprised girls from educated, lower middle-class families, daughters of clerks or school teachers and a few wealthier students.[35] Afterwards, employment was guaranteed, a most unusual thing at the time.

The Academy offered a few young women extraordinary opportunities. Even when interviewed recently, former students had fond memories of their time there, a period they remembered as one of freedom and enjoyment. They also felt important, a female elite of the era. One former student, for example, remembered, 'the joy of going to do the exercises, endless people praising you . . . and, well, I liked it, I was a show-off, eh! When I came back to Verona, I used to walk around in my uniform and so on, and everyone looked at me.'[36]

Even for the ordinary girls and adolescents they went on to teach, sports activities represented a new opportunity, something that took them out of their families in unprecedented ways. Many girls from the youth organisations, too, performed in public at mass, choreographed events. This could create tensions in families. Agnese Pitrelli, for example, born in Brindisi in 1929, recalled:

> My parents were furious when I put my uniform on and went to the Fascist youth meetings, because women weren't supposed to go out. My mother was outraged at the idea of women putting themselves on display. Marching together, taking part in parades and gymnastic displays was scandalous for people with a traditional mentality. But I loved it.[37]

There were also young women in the Gruppi Universitarie Fascisti (GUF – Fascist University Groups). Although the GUF had both male and female members, activities were usually separated by gender and indeed the female members (the *gufine*) had to put up with a good deal of hostility from the men in this organisation. The *gufine* did sports activities, followed courses on topics like childcare and did welfare work like the FF. They also eventually participated in national cultural competitions, the Littoriali di Cultura (founded in 1934 but admitting female contestants only from 1939), which involved oral and written presentations on set, mainly political, topics.

Membership of the girls' organisations was high at 2,385,060 (for 8–18-year-olds) by October 1936, and 2,698,082 (8–21 age group) by 1942.[38] This membership, however, was predominantly middle-class, particularly among older girls, as generally only school pupils joined and, of course, few girls from poor families stayed on for post-elementary education. From 1939, membership was compulsory for schoolchildren.

Membership levels were higher for girls in urban than rural areas and in northern than southern provinces (something that was also true for the FF and its two dependent sections), probably due to cultural factors in the South. Because of the link between membership and school attendance, numbers were lowest in the higher age brackets. Overall girls' membership was lower than boys' but this was accentuated in the higher age groups due to the larger numbers of older boys at state schools.

As with the organisations for adult women, levels of active participation and motivations for joining varied greatly. Some girls joined out of conformism or because teachers expected them to. Many others, however, were happy to get involved, either because infused with enthusiasm for the regime (children being, after all, notoriously impressionable) or because of the opportunities for sports and social activities. These were particularly attractive for middle-class girls, who otherwise led fairly restricted lives as parents tried to protect their 'respectability' until they were safely married.

Towards the future: the legacy of the *ventennio*

The sheer scale and scope of the Fascist mobilisation of women and girls was something quite new in Italian history. By dint of a combination of propaganda and material and social incentives, millions of them were persuaded, cajoled or, in some cases, forced to join the Fascist Party. The expansion of Catholic organisations, the only other mass organisations for women in this period once feminism and free trade unions had gone, was also striking in these years. The Catholic and Fascist mobilisations mirrored each other in some respects. Their ideologies were far from identical although they did agree on some issues, particularly the importance of maternity. Both were anti-feminist, whilst at the same time both created substantial new spaces for female activism in the public sphere.

The pattern of female mobilisation in this period had repercussions for the future. In some ways, it is possible to argue that it acted as a kind of brake on future progress, a hindrance to the development of women's politics once democracy returned. It created a precedent that was hard to shake off, namely the mobilisation of women in single-sex groups, operating within, and subordinate to, large male-dominated organisations and with a marked emphasis on welfare activities. This pattern was followed by the major post-war political parties. In other respects, however, the interwar mobilisation was modernising, for both the Catholic and Fascist organisations helped render the idea that women should be mobilised en masse seem quite normal and doubtless helped pave the way for women to start voting and standing for political office after the war. The Church, of course, was one beneficiary of this as, once mass democracy returned, it was in an excellent position to gather the votes of many of the new female electorate for the new Christian Democratic Party. Another important factor in convincing post-war politicians that women were ready for an expanded role in the political arena was the new roles for women, particularly in the Resistance movement, which emerged during the Second World War.

6

War Comes to Women, 1940–45

The Second World War was a complex and difficult time for Italian women. During the five years that Italy was at war, Italians fought both for and against Nazi Germany and were invaded by both sides. Italians also fought each other. In the 1943–5 period, after the Allied armed forces had invaded from the south, the front line inched slowly up the length of the Italian peninsula.[1] The northern half of the country suffered both Nazi repression and the lacerating effects of a bloody civil war. Thus, for women, the situation could not have been more different from the Great War since, in the latter part of this new war, the distinction between the home front and the battlefront became blurred. Although no reliable figures exist of war-related civilian deaths, it is certain that they were extremely high, possibly as high as deaths among the military. Many civilians were injured or died in air-raids. Others starved to death, perished from diseases related to malnutrition or were killed by the occupying forces.

During this often terrifying period many women became unprecedentedly active in the public sphere. Some did so in a political cause, as partisans or as die-hard followers of Mussolini. Others were forced out of the safety of their homes by the situation around them, driven by the need to survive in very difficult circumstances. Many fled their homes to escape bombing or racial or political persecution. Many worked, some of them in new forms of employment.

Until recently the historiography on the role of women in this period has been very uneven with most research on one topic alone – the Resistance. Since the 1990s, however, historians have begun to look at the experience of other women too. This new research has demonstrated women's very active role in this period. It also brings out the terrible levels of suffering endured by civilians. This shift in the historiography puts women in a more central place in the history of the war. Unlike much Resistance historiography, much of this new writing has a profoundly anti-war message. Some historians have also recently turned to the hitherto unpopular topic of female 'collaboration' with the RSI (Italian Social Republic – Mussolini's puppet government in 1943–5) and the Nazi occupiers.[2]

The 'mobilisation' of civilians and women's employment

Italy joined the Second World War on 10 June 1940, at a time when a Nazi victory appeared both imminent and inevitable. At this point nothing, it seemed, could stem the inexorable advance of the German armed forces. Hitler, many believed, would soon be in London and peace was just around the corner. The vast majority of Italians, therefore, were not greatly alarmed by the outbreak of war, confident that it would be over in months. Lulled into a false sense of security by propaganda about the prowess of the Italian armed forces, many felt no sense of urgency about the need to mobilise civilians. Even many Fascist officials seem to have been taken in by the regime's own propaganda. Thus, as many historians have emphasised, the Italian 'home front' was only half-heartedly organised. Civil defence measures, such as the building of air-raid shelters, were neglected and employment mobilisation plans scarcely put into action. There was no call-up of women. Italy was not, in any case, able to gear up fully into a 'war economy' as it lacked coal and steel, both of which it had to import from Germany. Consequently, the need to mobilise new workers was reduced.

Even at this stage, however, the attitudes of women and men seem to have differed. Some reports on public opinion gathered by Fascist police spies suggested that many women were far from enthusiastic about the war. On 23 May, for example, a police report from Genoa stated that, 'most people are quite calm, apart from women of all classes who are always opposed to intervention'.[3] Maria Luisa Faita recalled her mother's reaction, as they listened to the news of the outbreak of war on the radio: 'Into the silence of the square (Mussolini) shouted: "Do you want it?" Thousands of voices roared "Yes." At that moment my mother drew her hands to her mouth, said "No" and burst into tears.'[4]

Initially, for many civilians the war seemed distant. The battlefronts were far away and, although some bombing started quickly, the first air attacks were fairly small and ineffective and affected only certain areas. In many regions life went on much as normal. Although the experience of the First World War had demonstrated the need to mobilise civilians in modern warfare and plans for this had been devised soon after the Fascists took power, when war broke out the plans were not implemented.[5] Given that victory appeared to be at hand, forced mobilisation of civilians seemed a pointless, costly and potentially unpopular exercise. Moreover, in the early phase of the war at least, where production did expand, most employers could easily fulfil new labour requirements from the (male and female) unemployed. Firms were also usually able to retain much of their existing labour force by registering them as key workers exempt from military service. Many men were not initially called up either, since mobilisation into the armed forces began slowly. Indeed, insufficient military equipment was available to make a faster call-up possible at this stage.

At first, therefore, civilian mobilisation amounted to declaring some work-ers 'mobilised' (and thereby subject to increased discipline) and compiling lists of civilians available for war work. The task of registering women aged 18–70 (along with adolescents of both sexes aged 14–18) was given to the Fascist Party, with the Ministry of Corporations listing men. On 5 June 1940 a bill was approved by the Council of Ministers to enable men employed in state administrations to be replaced by women or pensioners. On 29 June, the quotas on female recruitment in public sector white-collar employment, intro-duced in 1938, were suspended indefinitely. In April 1943, a list of jobs was issued for which it was forbidden to employ men, such as waiters, cashiers, tram-conductors and so on. As in World War One, women were once again encouraged to work on public transport, in offices and to deliver the post, as before with temporary contracts 'for the duration'. They were not, how-ever, compelled to do war work of any kind, either in the public services or in war industries. By 1941, once it was clear that the war would be longer than expected, more attempts were made to mobilise civilians, but to little effect.

Many women, however, did work a great deal, and, for some, their work-loads and responsibilities increased. In particular, many peasant women found themselves with much to do. 'Giulia', for example, a Tuscan sharecropper's daughter, found her dreams of becoming a dressmaker dashed as her farm-ing workload massively increased when her brother was called up. Both she and her mother had to take over agricultural tasks normally reserved for men.[6] Particularly after the first year of the war, when larger numbers of men began to be called up, some new opportunities emerged for women in industry and services as the labour market tightened. Although, to date, this phenomenon has not been properly studied, it is clear that it was happening. One study of 22 war-related firms in Bologna, for example, found that, between December 1940 and March 1942, the female workforce increased by 96 per cent com-pared with only 31 per cent for male workers.[7] In these firms, nevertheless, women remained a minority with about three times as many men as women on the shop floor by the end of this period.

Such changes were largely not officially co-ordinated by the authorities. In September 1941, for example, a mere 73,000 of the six and half million women and children the PNF had registered as available for war work were recorded as in employment.[8] Many employers clearly preferred to have their existing workforce exempted rather than take on new, inexperienced staff.

'Civilian mobilisation', therefore, generally just meant greater control over existing workforces. Admittedly, from early 1942, there were attempts to force some to work with the institution of the 'servizio del lavoro' (work service) but this tended to be only applied to Jews (excluded from the armed forces by the 'race laws' of 1938) and 'shirking' middle-class men. In practice, work was only found for a few of them and by late 1942, those doing compulsory work service numbered 169,938 men and 10,674 women.[9]

By 1942 there was a labour shortage in some industries and more attempts were made to encourage women to work, but even at this stage they were not compelled to do so.[10] By late 1942, a period of much bombing, the biggest problem was to prevent existing workers from fleeing urban areas, and more and more civilians were declared 'mobilised' simply to keep them at work. By December this included all industrial workers. By this time about two million men and half a million women had 'mobilised' status.

The FF increased their activities in this period but this was mainly limited to war-related welfare and training of various kinds. Typical courses included vegetable gardening, to help women till the 'gardens of war' in urban green spaces, and poultry farming, for the many women who tried to raise chickens and rabbits on city balconies. Once again, some girls and women became *madrine di guerra*, writing to soldiers and sending them parcels at the front. Some FF members played a role in UNPA (Unione Nazionale Protezione Antiaerea – National Union of Anti-aircraft Protection), founded in 1934, volunteering and training to help with what little air defence did exist for civilians. In contrast to certain other nations in this conflict, however, women were not recruited into the armed forces. The only Italian women who went to the battlefront were, as in World War One, Red Cross nurses who nursed the wounded in various theatres of war, including on the Russian front.

Everyday life, 1940–43

Initially everyday life went on much as normal for many civilians. Even as late as 1941, in some areas the summer social life of the wealthy continued on beaches and in country houses. Gradually, however, the situation deteriorated. For many women, this increasingly became a difficult and disorientating period. Many lost loved ones or suffered distress or injury in bombing raids. Women's lives became filled with new responsibilities.

Many Italian cities were heavily bombed in 1942 and early 1943 once the Allies were able to attack from the Mediterranean. At this point the inadequacy of the regime's preparations became glaringly evident, with a huge shortage of air-raid shelters and ineffective cover of anti-aircraft guns. Air-raid defence was supposed to be organised by UNPA. As a poorly funded para-state organisation, it provided only patchy cover. In May 1939, according to Aurelio Lepre, Italy's public and private shelters between them had room for only about 300,000 people. Many of those that did exist proved totally inadequate.[11] Some were just cellars. Others were purpose built but proved little protection against the larger bombs used later in the war. Sometimes the overcrowding led to deaths from suffocation in the shelters themselves. A blackout of lights was quickly imposed and civilians were urged to buy gas masks but the extension of other civil defence provisions such as shelters and sirens happened only slowly.

The myth of the invincibility of the Italian airforce was soon shattered. The first civilians died during the second night after Italy joined the war, when Turin was bombed. This was only the beginning. Various places, including Genoa and a good number of cities in the South, such as Naples and Cagliari, all experienced considerable bombing in 1940 and 1941, although many other cities, including Rome and Milan, remained unaffected in this period. Raids escalated greatly in late 1942, when large northern industrial centres like Milan, Turin and Genoa as well as other targets like Naples were attacked.

Rome, however, was not bombed until July 1943. In many parts of Italy the death toll and the numbers of homeless were high. Some victims of bombing raids ended up living in tunnels or on the street. Little welfare assistance was offered to them and they received at best only small sums of money as compensation.

Food supplies quickly became a crucial issue. Rationing was introduced gradually.[12] Some rationing preceded the actual war: sugar was rationed from February 1940. From late 1940, edible oils and fats were rationed, then pasta and rice. At the same time bakers were ordered to adulterate wheaten bread with maize flour and, in October 1941, bread itself was rationed. Initially meat (which the poor ate only rarely anyway) was not rationed but allowed to be sold only a few days a week. Prices of non-rationed goods quickly rose and the rationing itself functioned poorly because the state proved unable to impose its will on food producers. Many peasants (often with the tacit approval of local officials) evaded bringing produce to the *ammassi* (government stockpiles). The simple act of procuring enough food for themselves and their families became a difficult, time-consuming activity for women. Even buying rationed goods, which were increasingly inadequate as the daily rations of various foodstuffs were gradually reduced (by 1943, in some areas, they offered a mere 1,000 calories a day), meant endless queuing.

Everyone had to resort to the black market and the hunt for food made this a period of frequent travel. Initially, buying on the black market might just mean an agreement with a local shopkeeper to get extra supplies of certain goods, but eventually many urban women began to undertake regular trips, on foot, by bicycle or by train, to the surrounding countryside with bags and suitcases to fill with any food they could find. Peasant women too began to move around a great deal, selling food. Some urban women themselves became small traders, buying in quantity and selling goods on.

As many historians have noted, this situation temporarily reversed the balance between rural and urban communities. Peasant women, for the first time, had the satisfaction of eating better than urban dwellers. They were also able to charge high prices as food became scarce and inflation an increasing problem. Peasant women were also used to managing with less, with a lifetime of experience in eking out scanty provisions. Ration books, for example, allowed them to obtain more sugar than they normally consumed and this could be sold or bartered. Often, however, the black market favoured the rich since almost anything was available, even extra ration books, for those who could afford it. For most civilians, particularly from the second winter of the war onwards, this was a time of hunger. The quality of food, too, declined and for many Italians the symbol of the privation of the time was the wartime 'black bread', made with adulterated flours of various kinds. The question of food led some women to stage open, group protests.

Bombing drove many out of the cities. The experience of evacuation varied greatly. Overall, there was rarely any kind of official organisation of evacuation and most Italians had to fend for themselves. For some it was a welcome period of peace away from the terrors of urban air-raids. For the rich it could be fairly easy, particularly if they owned a country residence. One wealthy woman, for example, recalled: 'After the bombings of early April (1943) we left our house in Palermo and went to our farm, together with the maids and the governess. We went by train, because the cars had been requisitioned. . . . All the jewellery was in a little suitcase . . .'[13] For most it was more difficult. As the bombardments intensified, many moved to just outside large cities and undertook a difficult daily commute to work. In some cases 'evacuation' was a terrible experience, little more than a disorderly, desperate flight. On 2 December 1942, in what amounted to an admission that the regime could not protect them, Mussolini told Italians to evacuate the cities. This massively accelerated the disorganised exodus from urban areas. As one despairing Florentine woman wrote in a letter, four days after the speech: 'What can I do? Everyone's running away: abandoned, empty houses after Mussolini's speech which has just frightened people . . . all you see in the street is removals and everyone is in turmoil.'[14] Some rural communities did well out of the crisis by charging exorbitant rents to desperate evacuees, but for others it put further strain on slender resources as members of their community who had migrated to urban areas returned home to relative safety and improved food supplies. Huge numbers evacuated. By 1 July 1943, nearly half the population of Turin had abandoned the city, about a third of whom had become daily commuters. Quitting the city was a sensible option since by the end of 1943 Turin only had space in its air-raid shelters for less than 200,000 people, with inevitable consequences. In a single night (13 July 1943), 402 died and 600 were injured here.[15]

By the third winter of the war, fuel supplies were running low and many homes were extremely cold. News from the battlefront was far from reassuring. Public opinion became increasingly critical of the government in this period, with many blaming the Duce personally for their suffering. Things were, however, about to get considerably worse.

1943–45 – the Resistance

Once Allied troops landed in Sicily (10 July 1943), the days of Mussolini's regime were numbered. On 25 July a coup d'état ended his twenty-year rule. For the next forty-five days many believed the war was over and came out to celebrate. Despite continuing repression of various forms of dissent, eventually many anti-fascists, including leading communists like Camilla Ravera, deprived of her freedom since 1930 and, in 1943, imprisoned on the island of Ventotene, were released.

The euphoria was, however, shortlived. The new government, under Badoglio, failed to surrender to the Allies, instead negotiating for too long. By 8 September 1943, northern and central Italy were under German occupation and soon Mussolini returned as head of a puppet government – the RSI (Italian Social Republic). The front line of the war then crept slowly northwards. It was hard from this point on for Italian women to escape the real horrors of war, for it came close to, or even inside, many homes. In the areas under Nazi occupation, the situation was grim. This part of Italy became locked in a bloody civil war between those who remained loyal to Mussolini (the so-called *repubblichini* – supporters of the RSI), and those who rallied to the Resistance.

There is a fascinating historiography on the role of women in the Italian Resistance, enriched by the collection of innumerable oral testimonies and the use of various other forms of memoir. Many of the stories collected are both moving and inspiring. Some include tales of great bravery in the face of terrible danger. It is also a very ample historiography: the books and articles on women's role in the Resistance far outnumber those written about women's other wartime roles.[16] Indeed, of all the topics covered in this entire book this is the one that has been most intensively studied by historians. The reason for this is the importance of the Resistance as a political and cultural phenomenon in the post-war period, seen as bestowing political legitimacy on the post-war republic, a phenomenon capable of restoring Italy's honour and cleansing it of its Fascist past. Women, of course, wanted to share in the citizenship this could confer. Moreover, the Resistance has been often presented not just as demarcating fascism from democracy, but as ushering in a new era of greater emancipation which female partisans earned for post-war women. Of course, as the next two chapters will show, there were many limitations to the 'emancipation', of women after the war, although some things undoubtedly did get better.

Although for obvious reasons reliable figures do not exist, it is clear that very large numbers of women took part in some way or another in the Resistance (albeit still a minority of all Italian women). Some estimates put the numbers involved as high as two million. Despite this, much early Resistance historiography portrayed it essentially as a male, armed movement. This was facilitated by the fact that many ex-partisan women were either too modest or soon became afraid to come forward to claim recognition. The experience of the communist partisan Tersilla Fenoglio (code-name 'Trottolina') after the 'Liberation' was not untypical. She remembered: 'I didn't take part in the parade. I was cheering from the side. I saw my commander go by, then Mauri, then all Mauri's units with the women they had there. Yes, they were there. Mamma mia, thank goodness I wasn't. People were saying they were whores. . . . The comrades did the right thing to not include us. They were right.'[17] Others were simply ridiculed, as the Resistance came to be celebrated in the early post-war period as a male event.

Whether recognised officially or not, research has demonstrated that many women were involved. Women from all age groups and all social classes took part and women were present in the work of every political grouping within the Resistance throughout occupied Italy. They included factory workers, students, clerks, housewives and peasants. Some were women without any previous political tradition or indeed even women who had previously been members of Fascist organisations. At the other extreme were the courageous few who had remained active as anti-fascists during the regime. Lina Merlin, for example, an important political figure in the post-war period, became a partisan after years of underground militancy for the Socialist Party, including a period in *confino politico*.[18] Many more, although they had not been politically active, came from anti-fascist families, often presenting themselves when

Illustration 6   Partisan women in Reggio Emilia.
(Reproduced courtesy of Istoreco, Reggio Emilia.)

interviewed as 'born' communist or socialist. Textile worker Maria Truffo (born 1905 in Turin), for example, said that she was a 'socialist from birth . . . I knew that (my father) had always celebrated the first of May and I did too'.[19] For others, the partisan choice stemmed from deeply held religious beliefs.

Although whole families could be anti-fascist, the way men and women of the same family participated in the Resistance differed greatly, for roles were almost always gendered. The numbers of women who shouldered arms to participate in the actual fighting were fairly small, although they did exist. One somewhat unusual partisan band in Emilia Romagna, for example, had 80 women among its 200 members, headed by a Bolognese furrier Novella Albertazzi (code-named 'Wanda'). Her activities included, on one occasion in 1944, leading the women of her unit in a major battle.[20] Most partisan women, however, engaged in rather different types of activity.

For many, their first Resistance activity was giving shelter and clothing to deserting soldiers on 8 September 1943, often dressing them in their own sons' civilian garments, in what Anna Bravo has called a 'mass *maternage*'.[21] But they had many other roles too. Some provided safe haven for Jews, partisans or Allied servicemen who had been shot down. Many became spies or messengers, a role they often did better than men as they tended to arouse less suspicion from Germans and *repubblichini* and were more likely to be able to pass roadblocks without being thoroughly searched. Indeed, one of the most widespread roles was that of the *staffetta* (courier), who carried messages hidden inside bicycle tyres or under piles of shopping from one partisan band to another, or delivered propaganda materials or newspapers. Others carried more frightening loads, like Laura Quattrini who transported a bundle of explosives to a bridge near her village just outside Rome that was to be blown up as a German convoy passed over it. She recalled: 'I remember how heavy it was: even so, I put it in a large basin that I normally used for dirty washing and carried it on my head to a hiding place where the partisans were to get it ready.'[22] Many women nursed the sick and wounded, collected funds or knitted garments for units camped out in mountain areas. Others, like Agnese, the rotund, maternal washerwoman protagonist of Renata Viganò's novel *Agnese va a morire* (1949), one of the most famous fictional portrayals of women in the Italian Resistance, were involved in the essential work of supplying partisan bands with food and clothing. Women also typed clandestine leaflets and articles for the underground Resistance press and took part in protests, often at the forefront of demonstrations about the lack of food, which broke out in various parts of Italy from early in the war. Many women were involved in the mass popular uprising (the 'four days') against the Nazi occupiers in Naples (28 September to 1 October 1943) and in the huge strikes in northern factories from March 1943 onwards. From November 1943 some of these activities, particularly the collection of food and money and the making of clothing, were carried out in special groups, the Gruppi di Difesa della Donna e per l'Assistenza ai Combattenti della Libertà (GDD – Women's Groups for Defence and for Assistance to the Freedom Fighters), which brought together women of various political persuasions or indeed of none.

In spite of the secondary importance many Resistance historians have ascribed to such roles, dismissed as unimportant compared with the activities of the (almost all male) armed fighters, it is clear that without them partisan bands would have been unable to operate. Thus the idea, put forward in early writing on this topic, that women essentially only 'contributed' to the (male) Resistance, is clearly problematic for, as feminist historians have argued since the 1970s, women themselves were clearly an integral part of the Resistance itself. Although few actually fought, many did essential and dangerous work for the Resistance cause. More recently some historians have gone further than this to argue that the traditional categories of what should be counted as 'Resistance' activity need to be rethought. Some, for example, have stressed the particular role of women in symbolic acts of defiance such as cleansing and burying the bodies of slain partisans against German orders.[23] Acts of this type, often previously dismissed as purely humanitarian, they argue, should be seen as political in their own right, as a defence of fundamental human values faced with the barbarism of war. Many now invoke the notion of 'civilian resistance'. This redefines 'resistance' to include autonomous actions of civilians which were orientated towards explicitly civilian goals, thereby encompassing actions which were neither fighting in an armed band nor assisting one, but rather aimed at keeping together the fabric of civilised society, defending basic freedoms, and not submitting to the enemy, either physically or mentally, in the situation of occupation. Civilian resistance, moreover, can imply a resistance against the concept of war itself. Many (although not all) of such acts of 'civilian resistance' were female activities.[24]

Many historians writing about women in the Resistance have tackled the question of women's motivations. Political motivations were important for some women but for others (as was, of course, also true of many male partisans) this was not the primary reason for their involvement. Women's motivations varied and included humanitarian or pacifist feelings, revulsion at the horrors of war, religious beliefs, political ideals, patriotic feelings faced with a foreign invader, family or other personal loyalties, a desire for some sort of personal 'emancipation' or simply the spirit of adventure. Despite this, the testimonies of many (although far from all) of those involved tended to invoke maternal feelings as a core reason for their participation in the Resistance. As Anna Bravo has argued, there were good reasons why some chose to have recourse to the 'maternal register' in recounting what they had done, as the maternal image is full of complex, contradictory meanings. Clearly it echoes Catholic imagery but, she argues, it was also the strongest female image on which women could draw and, indeed, the only socially acceptable one in which they could be stronger than men. It was also reassuringly asexual.[25]

1943–45 – daily life under Nazi occupation

Of course, far from all women in the German-occupied North became partisans. The majority just concentrated on trying to survive as best they could, forming part of what some historians term the 'grey zone' of those who did not make clear-cut political choices. They tried to avoid trouble, even, where necessary, at times helping both sides. The failure to take sides, however, was not always sufficient to ensure safety. Hunger, the black market and the endless daily hunt for food continued. Bombing and the gradual northward advance of the front line meant that many were forced to flee their homes. The sheer numbers of those in flight made the situation increasingly chaotic and dangerous. Some managed to secure a space indoors but others took refuge, sometimes for months on end, in mountain huts, barns, tunnels, caves, or even lived outdoors without any shelter at all. For many it was a traumatic, terrible experience.

The death toll was very high in this period of the war: an estimated 50,000 civilians perished in the raids which took place in some areas by day and by night.[26] Apart from those who died in air-raids or directly from the violence of the period, many women and children succumbed to disease due to the cumulative effects of years of poor diet, cold and high levels of stress.

Living in occupied territories, moreover, exposed many women to violent, dangerous situations. There was a great deal of contact between the occupiers and Italian civilians. The occupying troops often searched houses looking for partisans, deserters, men to conscript as forced labour, Jews, or just food. Some women died in the terrible series of massacres of civilians carried out as reprisals for partisan attacks. There were, for example, hundreds of women among the victims of the huge massacre by Germans and *repubblichini* in and near the village of Marzabotto in September 1944. In many other massacres mainly men died and women became the witnesses and sole survivors of incomprehensible and terrible events where their neighbours and relatives were slaughtered en masse.[27] For Jewish women the situation was particularly dramatic as this is when the Holocaust came to Italy: Jews were rounded up and deported to Nazi concentration camps. Under Nazi occupation, either Fascist allegiances or particular patriotism, both criteria which had been enough to exempt Jews from the Italian 'race laws' of 1938, could no longer protect them. One victim, for example, was Aurelia Josz, Milanese schoolteacher and founder of the Sant'Alessio school in Rome, where technical leaders had been trained for the Fascist Massaie Rurali. In 1944, aged 75, she was deported and died in Auschwitz.[28]

A not inconsiderable number of girls and women in the occupied areas suffered the horror and shame of rape although little, to date, has been written about this topic due to the inherent difficulties faced by historians investigating such matters. Unknown, but probably quite large, numbers were raped by German troops or *repubblichini* during the occupation, particularly in areas near the front lines.[29] Partisan women, too, were sometimes raped. Rosanna Rolando ('Alba Rossa'), a worker in a tobacco-processing factory, for example, was raped by four men and repeatedly beaten during her interrogation by *repubblichini* after her arrest in January 1945.[30]

South of the front line: under Allied occupation

Even in the zone occupied by the Allies, life continued to be very harsh for women.[31] The terrors of the civil war and bombing were over but the terrible scarcity of food continued. The Allied authorities proved themselves inept at ensuring the population had enough to eat and unable to control galloping inflation. By the spring of 1944, the allowance of rationed foodstuffs per capita was considerably lower than even the poor level in the German-occupied North.[32] In this period some Italian civilians literally starved to death. Only by recourse to the black market was it possible to survive and here prices spiralled rapidly out of control. Huge quantities of American goods found their way onto the black market. All this meant that, although initially many Italians greeted the 'liberators' with joy, soon there was disillusionment. Unrest, in the shape of food protests, erupted.

Only the occupying GIs ate and lived well and their spending further stoked inflation. Italians who ate best in this period were those who obtained employment with the invading forces or found other ways of separating GIs from their money and food. Many women, including even quite young girls, resorted to prostitution, as the only way to survive. Petty criminality, such as theft, became widespread.

For some women, the arrival of the Allied troops brought yet more horror. As one woman interviewed by Gabriella Gribaudi said: 'I have never celebrated the Liberation, because those are memories I won't ever forget. . . . What kind of liberation was that?'[33] She was one of thousands of women in a number of small villages to the south of Rome who, in 1944 in the aftermath of the Battle of Montecassino, were raped by *goums*, irregular North African soldiers fighting for the Free French. According to Gribaudi, some of the French soldiers viewed the Italians as a conquered people rather than one that they were 'liberating', and believed that it was acceptable to treat them badly. Certain French commanders, therefore, did little to control their troops.

The *goums* ran riot in the area, violently raping and sometimes killing women, slaughtering men who tried to defend their wives, daughters and neighbours, and looting as they went, including sacking churches. For many of the women affected, the physical and psychological effects of what had happened to them continued long after. Many were rejected by husbands or fiancés. Women of all ages were attacked including many elderly women and young girls. Even nuns and some men (probably hundreds) were raped. 'Angela C.' from the village of Esperia remembered:

> 'One stood by the door, a sub-machine gun in his hand. They all came in and took the women who didn't manage to escape. And they did everything, you know? . . . And the women were even beaten. Oh God, they were like animals. Worse than animals, five or six pounding at a single woman. They did it repeatedly, one after the other, and they were shrieking . . . many of the women died, all broken and bled dry, all smashed up or infected, the others were still alive. . . . The whole valley was full of weeping and wailing. . . . As they went through, it was hell. They didn't care about anything, even age. They even took old women and then even men, if there weren't enough women. They even took the priest'.[34]

This terrible series of atrocities became the subject of the novel *La Ciociara* (1957) by Alberto Moravia, which was subsequently made into a film starring

Sofia Loren (for which she received an Oscar in 1960) as a young mother raped together with her teenage daughter. As Gribaudi has noted, however, these fictional versions underplayed the sheer horror of the real events.[35]

Exactly how many women were raped will never be known: estimates vary widely. The difficulties of establishing exact numbers are considerable both because many of the victims were later too ashamed to come forward and also because other women who had not been raped attempted to claim financial compensation. Some argue that, in the areas around Cassino and Sora alone, over 60,000 women were raped and, of these, about 20 per cent were infected with venereal disease.[36] Other estimates give much lower numbers. The trail of *goum* violence continued as they advanced northwards. There were also a good number of rapes by (European) French troops. The French military historian Jean-Christophe Notin has claimed that the violence has been greatly exaggerated by the Italians,[37] although evidence from interviews and from both Allied and Italian documentation, examined by Gribaudi, gives ample proof that a large number of women were indeed violently raped.

Another group of women for whom the arrival of the Allies was not a happy event (but for quite different reasons) were those who remained loyal to Mussolini to the bitter end. For them, the Allies were invaders not liberators.

Collaborators and Fascists, 1943–45

A few women, driven by a fervent belief in the politics of the regime, fanatical patriotism or particularly strong loyalties to Mussolini, continued to actively defend Fascism after July 1943.[38] Certain of them even declared themselves ready to die for their Duce and the Fascist cause. Some joined the Gruppi Fascisti Repubblicani Femminili (GFRF – Fascist Republican Women's Groups), which emerged spontaneously after 8 September and then were officially 'founded' on 18 December 1943. Run from Brescia by a single National Inspectress, Licia Abruzzese (one of only four of the FF National Inspectresses to remain faithful to Mussolini in this period), the GFRF were effectively a continuation of the FF, with similar propaganda and welfare tasks (mainly, at this point, making parcels for the front and caring for refugees from the Allied zone).

More dramatically, some young women enrolled in the Servizio Ausiliario Femminile (SAF – Female Auxiliary Service – instituted 18 April 1944) to help defend the Republic of Salò.[39] Often featured in RSI propaganda, the SAF had a female general, Piera Gatteschi Fondelli, a 'Fascist of the first hour' and former leader of the Rome FF. A new, more militaristic, role for Fascist women had been foreshadowed by various articles in the party women's press in the late 1930s when some writers had begun to be increasingly enthusiastic about women's role in war,[40] but it was only now that Fascist women got the chance to actually try this out.

The SAF members were young middle- or lower middle-class women from Fascist backgrounds. They were mostly well educated (many were university students) and had grown up in the regime's youth organisations, usually doing plenty of sports. They were driven by a sense of betrayal at the events of 25 July and 8 September 1943 and a desire to help rebuild what they saw as Italy's lost 'honour'. As one volunteer, Rina Cioni, wrote in February 1944, in language that was typical of these die-hard Fascists: 'At last we'll be able to demonstrate that not all Italian women incite partisan hatred or encourage the worship of foreign countries, the black market and the quiet life. Motherland, here we are! . . . Sex is irrelevant! We are all ready to die, rather than go on living in shame and dishonour.'[41] Many of the auxiliaries were also indubitably drawn to the SAF by a sense of adventure.

Recruits had to follow a training course before starting. They were subject to normal military discipline as well as some special rules such as a ban on make-up, perfume, cigarettes, and on 'uncontrolled' mingling with male soldiers. They were all volunteers, albeit paid ones.

The RSI saw itself as a return to Fascism's early radical roots, but unlike female 'Fascists of the first hour', republican Fascists and the auxiliaries did not call for a political role for women. A good number of the auxiliaries did, however, long to be real soldiers, fighting and risking their lives for what they believed in. Fiamma Morini, for example, remembered: 'When we signed up, we wanted to go to war, we were prepared to shoot, to fight.'[42] They were destined to be disappointed. They certainly looked like soldiers: numerous photographs depict them marching on parade in uniform (albeit with skirts, not trousers). In practice, however, they had to resign themselves to support roles like nursing in military hospitals or clerical work such as telephony, filing, typing and so on and were only taught to fire guns for self-defence. Their role was not to fight but to free up men to fight.

It is clear, therefore, that some women did remain faithful to the regime in its dying years. Their numbers, however, were small: only a fraction of those who had belonged to the Fascist Party. By July 1944, about 40,000 women north of the front line had joined the GFRF. Even fewer became auxiliaries. By the end of the war, the SAF had 4,412 members and there were, at most, a few thousand other auxiliaries in various similar, more unofficial groupings, such as the women's section of the Decima Mas autonomous division.[43]

A few women went further, 'collaborating' in more ways than just welfare and clerical work. Some operated as spies and informants among the partisans or even behind Allied lines. In some of the more unofficial formations, auxiliaries were armed. A few of the female members of the Black Brigades participated directly, or were complicit in, acts of violence, such as round-ups of partisans and even torture. There were even a handful of women in the notorious Banda Koch.[44] Some women were to be found, too, fighting alongside men in the battle to defend Florence against the Allies.

After the Liberation, summary justice was meted out to many women who had been collaborators or auxiliaries or who had had (or were suspected of having had) affairs with German soldiers. Many had their heads shaved and 'M' (for Mussolini) inscribed on their foreheads with tar, or a sign hung round their necks. They were often then publicly paraded, their naked heads symbolising their shame. Many were imprisoned and some were beaten or raped by their captors.

The impact of war

The Second World War was a period of intense activity for many Italian women. The urgency of the situation enabled them to transgress the boundaries of 'respectable' feminine behaviour. The auxiliaries marched and a few bore arms. Much larger numbers of partisan women behaved in untraditional ways. The most extreme examples were those who worked with armed bands or even shot Germans but even the far more numerous couriers often had to travel alone, meet with members of the opposite sex, and go about after nightfall. For some women, the novelty of what they did was even greater. One of the most dramatic examples was the Milanese music teacher Gisella Floreanini. Floreanini held office as a Minister in the provisional government of the short-lived Republic of Ossola, an area of mountain territory close to Switzerland temporarily liberated by the partisans and run as an independent republic from 10 October to 2 November 1944.

But even for 'ordinary' women, this was a time of feverish activity. The urgency of the need to find food made traditional ideas of where and when women could go out alone hard to maintain. For many this was the first time they had to deal with state or municipal bureaucracies or, more generally, make decisions for themselves and their children in the absence of the head of family. Initially this meant doing things like managing the household budget or dealing with children's teachers. By the later part of the war it could mean taking big decisions like deciding whether to flee to what was perceived as a safer part of Italy or deciding between political adhesions of various kinds. In this period, the borders between the public sphere and the private sphere became unusually fluid.

This period of intense female activity contrasted with the fact that this was a time of inertia for many Italian men. Huge numbers of Italian soldiers became prisoners of war (POWs): 600,000 were held by the Western Allies, 50,000 by the Russians and, after September 1943, 650,000 by the Germans. Smaller numbers were imprisoned by the RSI. Many of these, particularly those fighting in Africa, were captured early in the war and spent years in captivity. The experience of these men varied greatly, but for many it was a time of passively living in limbo, just waiting for the war to end.[45] During the German occupation, moreover, many men, particularly in urban areas, hid indoors, for fear of German round-ups. Even when men were at home, therefore, in a reversal of the pre-war situation, it was often women who dealt with the outside world.

For some Italians, therefore, gender roles were turned upside down in this period. It was also a period which produced some genuine female heroines. It is important, however, not to romanticise this period, as some of the more hagiographic accounts of women's deeds in the Resistance tend to. For many women this was a terrible time. It was a period in which they experienced a total disintegration of the world they knew. Many faced extremes of fear and hunger and the threat of violence on a daily basis. Many endured the lacerating pain of bereavement, often repeatedly. The war widowed 125,763 women[46] and many more lost sons, close friends, relatives and neighbours. Large numbers of civilians themselves died. The level of confusion and uncertainty was so great that, as has emerged from many oral testimonies, during the later part of the war, many even felt uncertain about whose side Italy was supposed to be on (and consequently who exactly 'the enemy' was). This confusion was compounded by the fact that even the partisans could seem as threatening as the German occupiers if their actions provoked reprisals against civilians.

The legacy of this terrible period of war in terms of the yardstick of 'emancipation' is hard to evaluate. The war swept away the repressive Fascist regime forever and, at its end, women gained the right to vote (although, as Chapter 8 will show, other important legal reforms took longer). Women's role in the Resistance, in particular, became important as a symbol of women's strength and ability to take an active role in the public sphere. However, there were many limits to the emancipation it brought. Anna Bravo's findings on the pervasiveness of the 'maternal register' in how women recounted their wartime roles in the Resistance, for example, have led her to be pessimistic about the impact of wars on gender roles.[47] Indeed, although this was a period when women were very active in many new ways and demonstrated great strength and resilience in extreme adversity, much of this change was, as in many wars, temporary. The Resistance soon began to be celebrated as essentially something men had done, as a heroic armed movement which could restore the honour of the Italian nation (and indeed, although this was not so clearly admitted, the image of Italian masculinity, severely dented by military defeat and mass imprisonment). Many female ex-partisans were too modest or afraid to step forward to claim their place in history, or simply found that there was no place for what they themselves had done in the official celebratory discourse of the time. In the immediate post-war period, many, particularly men returning from the horrors of war on various fronts or gradually released from POW camps around the world, craved a return to 'normality' in the domestic sphere. As at the end of the previous world war, many women who had taken over 'male employment roles' lost their jobs.

'Normality' itself, however, was about to change, for Italy was on the brink of a great upheaval of a very different kind. In many respects a far greater and more enduring transformation of women's lives was to be brought by the huge economic and social changes of the immediate post-war period, the years of the economic miracle.

7
Moving into Town: New Social and Economic Roles, 1945–67

Peace, at last, returned in 1945, bringing with it a new democratic Republic. The early post-war years, however, saw yet more hardship and hunger. Homes and economic infrastructure needed to be rebuilt and many women had to come to terms with bereavement or deal with traumatised or injured family members. Many had to adjust to the return of men after a period in which they had become used to acting independently. Some lost wartime employment. Those who had been raped or who had resorted to prostitution during the war faced particularly difficult problems. Even after the initial reconstruction was complete, huge social and economic problems remained. As a parliamentary enquiry at the beginning of the 1950s showed, many Italians lived in great poverty: 11.7 per cent of families were housed in shacks, attics, cellars or even caves, and were too poor to afford sugar or meat; 11.6 per cent were in very overcrowded dwellings (with at least three persons per room) and ate very poorly; 65.7 per cent were less impoverished but had, on average, two persons per room and spent more than half their income on food.[1] Only a minority of homes benefited from modern conveniences.

Soon all this was to change, for the 1950s and 1960s, particularly 1958–63, saw the 'economic miracle', a period of extremely rapid growth bringing with it huge cultural and social shifts, changes that some European nations took over a century to complete. These years, as Guido Crainz has argued, saw a transformation of how Italians 'produced and consumed, thought and dreamed, lived the present and planned for the future'.[2] Italy, of course, was not the only European nation to experience growth in this period but the backwardness of its economy at the start and the rapidity of change made its experience a particularly dramatic one.

For many, this was a time of great optimism, a period when Italy rose from the ashes of Fascism and the terror and deprivations of war to join the developed world. Millions finally escaped a life where hunger was normal and gained access to material goods and opportunities undreamed of by their parents. Italy became a world of widening horizons: the poor, instead of merely surviving, could now aspire to huge material improvement. Dramatic social mobility and affluence suddenly seemed real and possible. All this change, perhaps inevitably, also made this a period of much moral anxiety.

In the 1950s and 1960s Italians were on the move. There was a huge migratory movement mainly from rural to urban areas and from south to north. Internal migration was not, of course, new but the sheer scale of it was. Between 1955 and 1970 almost 25 million Italians transferred their residence to a different administrative district. Some moved to the nearest town, others headed to northern industrial areas. During the peak of the miracle about one and a half million Italians migrated internally each year. There was also a renewed wave of emigration abroad (380,000 per annum in 1960–2). Many born into impoverished peasant households abandoned a largely subsistence rural lifestyle for a new American-style urban consumer culture. New modes of transport available to the masses appeared, initially scooters, then cars, and there was a vast increase in access to consumer leisure.

Economic growth did not, of course, eradicate mass poverty immediately and the social and economic upheaval was not without costs, particularly in the early years of the boom. Initially, many migrants faced low wages and poor living conditions and, indeed, a barely legal situation since the Fascist anti-migration laws were only repealed in 1961. As they flooded into industrialised areas many migrants had to squeeze into substandard, overcrowded housing, on dismal estates that mushroomed around large cities and which initially often lacked even basic services. Many, particularly Southerners, faced racist hostility from the local population. In the 1960s, however, wages rose and it was in this decade that the wealth of the economic miracle began to radically raise the standard of living of the mass of the population. Although this period of unprecedented economic growth transformed the ideas and aspirations of a whole generation, Italy and Italians were not, of course, remade overnight. The new society produced by the miracle was a mixture of tradition and modernity, where old ideas jostled with the new.

The pioneering generation of feminist historians in the 1970s and 1980s mainly showed little interest in these post-war decades, perceived as a boring gap between the excitements of the Resistance and the resurgence of second-wave feminism. It was, many felt, an era of dreary, unemancipated housewives, tied to home and family. It was also the era of the mothers of the 1970s feminists, the generation against which the feminists rebelled. More recent historiography has demonstrated that this was in fact a time of considerable change for women, particularly younger women. In this period, however, gender hierarchies remained essentially intact, albeit not unchanged.

The decline of the patriarchal peasant family

One of the most radical social transformations of this period was the break-up of the patriarchal peasant family, including the vast sharecropping households typical of central Italy. Once those born into such families migrated into urban areas they tended to set up small nuclear families. Indeed, the nuclear family became the norm for all social classes. Nonetheless, the idea of the extended family did not totally vanish as many of the new family units continued to rely on extended kin networks for emotional and material support, even if they no longer physically lived together.

This decline of the hierarchical peasant family had a huge impact on the lives of women. The rural–urban shift could bring a real liberation, not just from hunger, poverty and backbreaking workloads, but from demeaning customs and difficult family relationships, including freeing women from the dictatorial power of the female head of the household, the *reggitrice*. Consequently, young rural women in this period were often keen to marry a man who was not a peasant. As one Piedmontese woman put this, 'just to get away, plenty of women would have married a bear'.[3] In this, many were encouraged by their mothers, who urged their daughters to marry out of the peasant life in the hope that they would not suffer as they themselves had done. One peasant woman from the Vicenza area, for example, stated this in blunt terms when she said of her daughters that: 'I'd have preferred them to die than have to go and live with a mother-in-law.'[4]

Escaping the peasant world increased a woman's chances of finding a more respectful man but it was still unlikely that he would treat her as a real equal. Although the reconfiguration of gender roles in these years did include changes for men and masculinity, gender inequality continued to be seen as the norm. The old customs of the rigidly patriarchal peasant family now seemed increasingly anachronistic, something to be abandoned by a new generation of 'modern men', a generation who treated women with somewhat greater respect and allowed them more access to the public sphere, but men did not renounce their power. Indeed, many continued to attempt to defend masculine privilege against what they saw as an increasing female presence in the public sphere and greater 'emancipation'.[5]

The media, clothing and the body

The mass media, for the first time, reached all sections of the population. Television broadcasting began in 1954, cinema-going became more widespread and the numbers and circulations of magazines rose rapidly. This explosion of broadcasting and publishing brought visions of wealth and success to the masses, feeding their dreams and aspirations. By the late 1940s an estimated 10 million women read weekly magazines, including the highly popular *fotoromanzi*, comics which told serialised stories through pictures (initially drawings, then photographs), opening the world of print media to even the barely literate. Some acquired basic literacy through reading them. Others just looked at the pictures while the text was read aloud.

The media paid increasing attention to the female body. New role models for women, particularly Hollywood films, with their images of abundance and commercialised, glamorised images of women (including pin-ups like Betty Grable and Rita Hayworth), flooded into Italy straight after the war, hot on the heels of the occupying GIs. Despite various attempts to counter this model with a more 'Italian', less sexualised, style of beauty, the American images were popular.[6] Hollywood films also showed women smoking, wearing trousers and driving cars, all images that illustrated potential new roles far distant from the lives of many Italian women.

Cars, however, the ultimate symbol of the new prosperity, were claimed by men as their own. Indeed, many of the new images of masculinity in the media were associated with technology. No longer the potential soldiers of Fascist propaganda, men, in the publicity of the post-war decades, were portrayed as dynamic and ambitious, conquering the workplace or the road instead of the battlefield.[7]

Beauty contests were a feature of this period and attracted numerous contestants with their lure of fame and social mobility. The appeal of these contests and of the female film stars of the period was great for young women, fuelling their dreams and aspirations.[8] Women were encouraged more and more to play with their appearance. Make-up became acceptable for all classes. Women also began to wear less and less clothing, the most extreme examples being the bikini and the miniskirt, garments that would have been unthinkable only a short time previously. Initially, however, in Italy as elsewhere in the Western world, the early post-war years saw the 'New Look', the ultra-feminine backlash against the uniformed women of the war. After this, gradually clothes became more comfortable and practical and also more democratic. There was far less dressing to define class status, particularly among the young. Trousers, which previously had mostly been worn only by upper-class women, increasingly became acceptable female garb. As 'D' (born in 1940) remembered:

> 'Before, we always wore skirts and on a scooter you sat side-saddle and you had to keep your legs tight together, but your skirt rode up anyway and, as you went by, they whistled and blew kisses. Then, in 1960, I got a cousin to lend me his jeans and, patched up somehow or other, at last I could ride a Vespa as God intended. All of this was against the wishes of my scandalised mother, but trousers were a liberation, really convenient.[9]

Youth and education

'D' and her trouser rebellion are symptomatic of the fact that adolescents were becoming a distinct category in this period. In Italy, as elsewhere in the West, this was the period when teenagers of both sexes first began to establish themselves as an identifiable social group, separate from the adult world. Many enthusiastically embraced the rough, materialistic hedonism of the boom, although their consumption aspirations were different from those of adults. They wanted not washing machines, but scooters and transistor radios, juke boxes, rock music and jeans. They wanted, in short, to enjoy themselves. This new distinctive youth culture was not yet such a clear-cut phenomenon as it was to become by the late 1960s, nor did this generation find its own ideology as the next did. It was, nevertheless, there.[10]

It was somewhat more difficult for girls to see themselves as separate from their families than for boys. However, letters to advice columns suggest that many young women of the period did wish to live their lives differently from their parents. They dreamed of new wealth, of glamorous jobs and of travel.

Illustration 7   Young woman on a Lambretta scooter (1950s).
(Reproduced courtesy of Fototeca Storica Nazionale Ando Gilardi.)

For many, the cinema was an important place of sociability and the images on the screen helped fan their desire for a new, different life. Many wanted to work and this helps explain the rise in female employment that took place later, in the 1970s, when this generation came of age. Moreover, according to Simonetta Piccone Stella, many also aspired to a society with greater equality between the sexes.[11]

This period saw great advances in the levels of female education. The new prosperity meant that many Italians had steady incomes for the first time. Instead of simply surviving they could now plan for the future. These plans often included an increased interest in investing in the education of daughters.

With more girls staying on at school, illiteracy continued to fall. In 1951, 15.2 per cent of females were officially classified as illiterate compared with 10.5 per cent of males. By 1981 these figures had dropped to 3.8 per cent and 2.2 per cent respectively. Numbers of girls in secondary and higher education increased dramatically. This was true even before the reforms of 1962 (which created a unified middle school and raised the school-leaving age from 11 to 14). Comparing the academic years of 1955–6 and 1962–3, the number of girls in middle schools rose from 366,175 to 683,221, in secondary schools from 222,324 to 350,788 and in universities from 38,313 to 68,293. Numbers actually graduating from universities were much lower but this was also true of male students. Of course, numbers of boys in education increased too but, by the early 1970s, the gender gap was narrowing. The proportion of girls in middle schools rose from 39.9 per cent in 1948–9 to 47 per cent by 1972–3 and in upper secondary education from 37.3 per cent to 42.4 per cent. In higher education, the percentage rose from 26.3 in 1951, to 27.6 in 1961 and 37.5 in 1971. Regional differences persisted at school level but these gradually became less marked. In universities, however, there were no great regional disparities. Southern women were just as likely (or unlikely) to graduate as northerners.

The quality of girls' school experience changed too. Increasing numbers of girls attended mixed schools and, no longer anomalous pioneers, began to fit in better. The very formal relationships girls had previously had with male pupils in mixed secondary schools began to change. Friendships became possible. Many girls welcomed this novel, 'modern' aspect of life, so different from their mothers' experience. As one schoolgirl enthused: 'it's a positive aspect of modern youth, as a few years ago the idea of a relationship between boys and girls was unthinkable'.[12]

Improved education gave girls confidence and opened up new worlds to them. Although much of this only came to a head in the 1970s, it meant that a shift was already happening in the two previous decades. Most of the feminists of the 1970s had been at school in this period, enjoying a level of education far higher than that of their mothers.

Employment

Educational gains did not immediately create a boom in female employment. Unlike in some other Western economies where women's employment rose continuously in the post-war years, Italian rates stagnated until the early 1970s. During the 1950s and 1960s only about a third of Italian women were officially recorded as economically active. In 1950, 32 per cent of Italian women aged 15–64 were employed and this figure was virtually unchanged at 33.5 per cent in 1970. The comparable figures for the UK were 40.7 per cent in 1950 rising to 50.7 per cent in 1970; for Germany they were 44.3 per cent and 48.1 per cent; for Sweden 35.1 per cent and 59.1 per cent; and for France 49.5 per cent and 48.3 per cent.[13]

Perceptions of what was happening, however, often differed from reality and many commentators at the time referred to women's increasing role in employment. This was doubtless because, although actual numbers did not rise, many women were doing more visible types of work. Secretaries, factory workers and shop assistants were more noticeable than peasants, whose labour was often invisible. The main trends were a rapid fall in female employment in agriculture and a modest rise in other sectors, particularly clerical and service jobs. Census statistics (only a rough guide, of course) show numbers in agriculture falling from 2,036,024 in 1951 to 1,498,800 in 1961. In the same years, those in manufacturing rose slightly from 1,354,696 to 1,489,493, those in commerce from 438,052 to 607,510, those in 'services' from 681,124 to 725,380 and in public administration from 303,061 to 405,249. Overall numbers of 'economically active women' remained stable at 4,913,853 in 1951 and 4,864,131 in 1961.[14]

Women abandoned the land more slowly than men. The early and mid-1950s briefly saw a new generation of 'white widows'. Some resembled the 'white widows' of their grandmothers' day, their husbands abroad in places like Germany or even Australia. Others were part of the process of internal chain migration whereby peasant men set off alone to northern cities and women stayed behind, tilling the fields to ensure the survival of the family. As Amalia Signorelli has argued, women's farm-work in this period was essential to economic growth. Women provided flexible labour, crucial to smoothing the process of migration. Their hard work on the land and pragmatic willingness to take over male work roles in farming (in contrast to men, who resisted at all costs doing anything considered 'women's work') were vital in a period of low male industrial earnings. Unlike some scholars who have seen these women as the repository of old values, an archaic force defending peasant values against the innovations of the modern world, Signorelli argues that many rural women did embrace modernity: they were often positive about new ideas, including the prospect of factory work or even overseas emigration.[15]

By the late 1950s, some of these women themselves were migrating to industrial areas to join fathers or husbands. At first, the labour market was tightening, so jobs were available for some of them. Although older migrant women often did not work once they arrived in town, younger women found employment in factories, shops and services, often with low pay and poor conditions. At the height of the boom, between 1958 and 1963, according to official statistics female employment in agriculture fell from 35.6 per cent to 27.9 per cent whilst rising from 29.3 to 39.3 per cent in industry and from 33.1 to 41.3 per cent in services.[16]

After this, women's employment declined. During the 1960s, official statistics show about a million women leaving the labour force. This was partly because work became harder to find. The exodus from the land continued but industry was becoming more uncompetitive as male wages rose, and, as a result, some women were expelled from the labour market, particularly as the principle of equal pay, agreed in 1960, made employing them less attractive. Certain industries began a process of restructuring that led to female redundancies.[17] At the same time, improved male earnings enabled more women to become full-time housewives as their husbands now commanded a 'family wage'. The pattern increasingly became that women worked when they were young, then left the labour market after the birth of their children, after which they found it hard to return. It is worth noting, nonetheless, that even in this decade, it is likely that many 'housewives' did at least some hidden work, such as outwork or other forms of intermittent or part-time employment, often off-the-books, that failed to appear on census forms.

At least some of the decline was positive as it was due to greater numbers in full-time education. This, in turn, helped increase numbers in the professions, commerce and services. The percentage of women among those graduating in medicine rose, for example, from 3 per cent in 1951, to 10.3 per cent in 1960 and 12.65 per cent in 1968.[18] Women also improved their position in university teaching. In 1951, 9.8 per cent of university lecturers were female but by 1971 the figure was 21.3 per cent. In most professions, nonetheless, women still faced a good deal of prejudice and they were very much in the minority. Many impediments remained, moreover, to their promotion. Very few lecturers, for example, reached the top grade of *ordinario* and only a third of head teachers were female. In the civil service, women remained largely in the lower grades.

Teaching was still the main female profession. In 1951, about half of middle school teachers were female and over 70 per cent of primary teachers. By 1971, 63.7 per cent of middle school teachers, nearly half of all secondary teachers and nearly 80 per cent of primary teachers were female.[19] Many middle-class and lower middle-class parents continued to encourage their daughters to take up teaching as this was deemed suitable, respectable work. Moreover, as one woman interviewed in the late 1960s said: 'Teaching is the career that is most easily combined with a family, for women, because it doesn't take up the whole day.'[20]

This period also saw the emergence of new, glamorised all-female employment opportunities that emphasised sex appeal, such as air hostess, model, beautician, television hostess and travel guide, jobs to which many young women, their dreams shaped by films and glossy magazines, aspired. The idea of becoming a film actress, in particular, with its lure of sudden wealth and instant fame became the ambition of many girls. Such glamour jobs did of course help reinforce the idea that women only worked when they were young and single. They were also jobs for which they did not have to compete with men. These new glamour professions were the first jobs in which women did not have to pretend to have no body, to be asexual, which perhaps helps explain their popularity with the young.

Many women, however, were still in 'traditional' jobs at the end of the miracle. In 1951 there were nearly 400,000 servants working in Italy, the vast majority of them female, and the number remained little changed in 1961. By 1971, as domestic technology took over, numbers had dropped but were still just over 200,000.[21] Even for those in more 'modern' jobs, moreover, work was not always particularly emancipating. Most working women earned low pay, held subordinate positions in the workplace and, until marriage, lived with their parents. Even young women employed in the burgeoning retail sector often found the work tougher, more boring and less glamorous than they had expected.

Such complaints, of course, were not confined to Italian women and do not help explain the comparatively low levels of female employment here. More relevant was the scarcity of part-time work, which made it harder to combine employment and maternity than in some other countries. Admittedly, improved maternity legislation had been introduced in 1950, championed by the communist deputy Teresa Noce, which extended maternity leave for many categories of workers (albeit excluding outworkers and sharecroppers) and prohibited the dismissal of women for a year after a child was born. This legislation was valuable to those able to benefit from it but in practice was far from a clear success for it discouraged employers from employing married women. Far from untypical was the situation reported in the communist newspaper *Unità* in 1958: 'When the 400 women workers at Piaggio were taken on they had to agree to resign if they got married. That way the employer is saved the bother of the annoying maternity legislation.'[22] Even if work was available, moreover, extra-domestic employment did not always make economic sense for mothers. Unlike on the land, where infants could be left with other household members, many urban mothers had to pay for childcare and most earned too little to make this worthwhile. Another important factor was the relatively slow growth of the service sector due to the deficiencies of the Italian welfare state. For many women, moreover, the welfare state was far less liberating than in some other European countries. In Italy's inefficient, bureaucratic and often corrupt system, getting access to services was time-consuming, involving much form-filling and queuing, tasks that usually fell to women, making it harder, rather than easier, for them to work.

Finally, it is clear that supply factors were also important. Although some women were forced to stop working by the factors just outlined, others quite simply preferred not to do so. For many, particularly those from peasant backgrounds, the option of dedicating themselves to caring properly for their family and home could seem a conquest, a chance to be a proper mother, something that had largely only been possible for wealthy women in previous generations. This was very much the era of the housewife.

The 'modern housewife' and the new consumerism

According to census statistics, housewives far outnumbered working women. In 1951 there were 12,517,193 housewives, rising to 12,697,171 in 1961. Only in 1971, when the downward trend in female employment began to turn, did numbers decline to 11,973,311.[23] This generally stationary situation should be seen as effectively a rise since the role of many classified as 'housewives' was very different from that of many of those counted as such in earlier censuses, which, as discussed in previous chapters, included many rural women who did farm-work. The 'modern' post-war housewife, by contrast, devoted herself more or less exclusively to a domestic role. Such figures, of course, existed in earlier decades but they had been primarily middle and upper class. Of course, some of these post-war 'housewives' were probably also doing outwork, but this was unlikely to affect how they primarily identified themselves. Occasional or part-time work done at home was not enough for a woman to consider herself a worker.

The job of a housewife was transformed by technology in this period. Millions of women whose mothers had hauled water from wells and washed laundry in rivers now had indoor taps, electricity and, eventually, labour-saving domestic appliances. There were also new American detergents instead of home-made soap or wood ash. Washing up liquid replaced bicarbonate of soda or, for the very poor, simple water. One of the jobs of the new 'modern housewife' was to purchase such goods for the family. Instead of making soap and other necessities, women increasingly shopped for them. This was particularly true of urban housewives but even women who remained on the land gradually began to use fewer home-made products.

Encouraged by the Americans, who saw the consumer society as the antidote to the spread of communism, consumption, promoted in a wave of advertising in the print and screen media, was presented to Italians as the very essence of modernity. Such advertisements and other representations of modernity conveyed highly gendered messages. In advertisements, in radio and television programmes, in the numerous home economics manuals produced in this period, and in the growing numbers of women's magazines, women were usually represented as housewives, and consumption as a core element of their new role in society. The fact that many advertising campaigns primarily targeted women was, in itself, something new. In the past it had often been men, not women, who had purchased things for households. The importance of women as consumers was reflected in the fact that during the boom the percentage of advertising in women's magazines soared. It became more expensive to advertise in them than in publications aimed at a mixed readership.[24]

For many women, the housewifely role was, indeed, what they wanted. Battered by the trauma of war, they yearned for peace and domestic comfort. Becoming a housewife could seem a step up, an emancipation from the slavery of work on the land. For millions still on the land, the urban housewife role became something to aspire to, a world of modernity, comfort and ease. Many young working-class girls, too, dreamed of being housewives in modern, well-equipped homes. A survey of 100,000 housewives, carried out by the Catholic organisation CIF (see Chapter 8) in 1949, showed that about 90 per cent were content to be housewives. Their dreams and aspirations were filled not with the emancipatory potential of employment (although most saw this as desirable for young women before marriage) but with material improvements like electricity and indoor plumbing.[25] This situation did, however, seem to change. A later survey of housewives, published in CIF's magazine *Cronache* in 1964, revealed a different picture. Many declared themselves dissatisfied with the limitations of their lives and aspired to more access to 'culture' and a greater role in the public sphere.[26] By this time, many of their daughters, moreover, had different ambitions. As one schoolgirl said, 'marriage isn't everything, nowadays girls try to make a life for themselves even without marriage'.[27]

Consumption patterns changed over time. Until 1958, consumer spending increased little because wages remained low. In this period, however, although few acquired large consumer durables, elements of the culture of consumerism came to Italy. Many began to buy cheaper items like cosmetics, off-the-peg clothing and magazines. Moreover, the pull of the consumer society was felt long before it was a reality. Millions aspired to fridges and cars and other elements of the 'American lifestyle' well before they could actually afford them.

Often women took a leadership role in the new consumption, seeing modern consumer goods as symbolising a break with the poverty and restricted lifestyle of the past.[28] Some peasants, however, found it hard to shake off deep-rooted traditions of parsimony and self-sufficiency. Recent migrants into Turin in the 1950s, for example, often continued to make their own clothes, jam and so on, and frequently the first item of household technology they acquired was a sewing machine. As one woman remembered, 'we're from a peasant background and having a hundred lire in the house or just ten made no difference because I couldn't make myself go and buy anything'.[29]

In the 1960s, consumption rose. Increasing numbers could now afford domestic technology like televisions, washing machines and fridges. Of course, at the time, most of these innovations were far from new inventions (the first domestic fridge had appeared in Chicago in 1913), but in Italy only a tiny elite had owned them. In theory, the new technology was potentially liberating for women, making domestic tasks easier and removing much drudgery. The oral history research of Maria Chiara Liguori, for example, suggests that some embraced the new material culture with enthusiasm. The new labour-saving devices had, of course, the greatest impact on poorer women, since the wealthy had not previously done much housework themselves. For them, machinery just replaced servants. For the poor, in contrast, the difference was huge. Acquiring the new amenities and technology could make them feel as if they had risen up the social scale. As 'B' (born 1932) said, of her first indoor bathroom, in 1957: 'It felt like being in a rich person's house. Even though I knew things like that existed, because I saw them when I worked in posh people's homes, I thought only they could have them.'[30]

The washing machine was particularly significant given that laundry had previously been the single most onerous domestic task.[31] Before mechanisation, the washing of large items like sheets had been a labour-intensive, laborious process that took days to complete. This work was always done by women. Peasant women had washed their own family's clothes (and sometimes also those of the landlord). In urban areas laundry was done by working-class women, by washerwomen or servants.

Of course, as various studies on the impact of domestic technology in other Western countries have shown, as technology improves, so do expectations.

Standards of cleanliness rise, creating just as much work for the housewife.[32] In Italy, as elsewhere, television and advertisements reinforced this idea, presenting the new consumer durables as emblems of domesticity, rather than something that could liberate women from the home. In such representations, women were promoted as both domestic and modern at the same time. They carried the message that the time freed up should be dedicated to the family, helping children with their homework and so on. Rarely did advertising show the use of domestic technology for working women.

A negative feature of the new labour-saving home was that it could effectively imprison women indoors. Previously, many household tasks had meant going out. Doing laundry, for example, had generally been a sociable activity where women gathered together on riverbanks or at communal pumps, offering opportunities for gossip and banter. Women also used to go out to fetch water and, in urban areas, to buy food daily. Even farmwomen in large family units often did agricultural and domestic tasks together. In the world of the new modern housewife, laundry became a private, solitary activity and fridges enabled less frequent shopping. Now life was more comfortable in the new nuclear family with inside bathrooms and washing machines but it was also more socially isolating: comfort came at a price.

This technology did not reach most Italian homes until the 1960s. In 1956 only 2.81 per cent of Italian families had a washing machine and 8.31 per cent a fridge. By 1965, however, 23 per cent owned washing machines, rising to 41.8 per cent by 1968. Fridges spread even more quickly (probably reflecting the fact that men, who continued to hold the pursestrings for major purchases, prioritised them over relieving the burden of laundry). By 1965, 55 per cent of Italian households had fridges and this had risen to 71.9 per cent in 1968.[33]

Changes in the private sphere: demography and sexuality

Because the post-war years were a time of change they were also years of anxiety. Politicians, churchmen, social commentators and doctors all expressed worries of various kinds. There were fears about the erosion of the family, the loss of parental authority over children, 'juvenile delinquency', the confusion of classes, the loss of moral and spiritual values in a period of unbridled materialism, and the spectre of the Americanisation of society. In fact, the social fabric mainly held together well until the late 1960s. Women played a role in this, keeping families together at a time of change, in a period when husbands and children spent much time outside the home, at work and school.

One aspect of this stress on the importance of the family was, once again, a renewed emphasis on women's maternal role. Indeed, some began to blame mothers for the ills of Italian society. This was the time, according to Marina D'Amelia, that the 'invented tradition' of *mammismo* (see Chapter 1) appeared, the term being coined in 1952 at a time when some Italian intellectuals were trying to explain the disastrous state of their nation and its recent past.[34]

Family law was not reformed: the 1942 Civil Code remained in force, keeping wives in a very unequal legal position. In this, the state was flanked by the Church, which continued to uphold the authority of husbands. Even in the late 1950s, Catholic magazines still condoned men who beat their wives.[35] Beliefs about the inferiority of women continued to pervade Italian society. Court judgements reinforced the idea that the male head of family was in charge of his wife, with the right even to read her private correspondence or to prevent her from going out to work.[36] Change did occur gradually. Whilst in 1961, the Constitutional Court upheld the idea that female adultery should be punished more harshly than male adultery, in 1968 a new sentence declared this idea out of date.[37] It was in these decades, too, that the legal system began to cease to condone domestic violence.

Although, as was discussed above, the shape and internal dynamics of many families changed greatly with the rural–urban shift, the institutions of marriage and the family remained strong and, indeed, the average age at marriage fell slightly in this period. The idea of 'companionate marriage', founded on love, spread to all social strata. Even in the 1950s, however, economic factors could still play a role. Dowries persisted and this gave parents a good deal of influence on marital choices. Other methods were also used. One lonely twenty-year-old wrote that, to stop her marrying her disabled boyfriend, her parents, 'hit me, they've punished me in every possible and imaginable way. . . . As a last attempt, they keep me locked up in the house, so I can't see him.'[38] Recent migrant parents were often particularly interventionist if they wanted their daughters to marry someone from their village of origin, as a way of holding on to networks, influence or landholdings.

Many did end up unhappily married. Although divorce was still not legal, increasing numbers of couples separated unofficially. Antonio Sansone, who unsuccessfully proposed divorce legislation in the 1950s, estimated that about 600,000 Italians had taken this step, many of whom had created new *de facto* families. This situation, of course, was problematic as any resulting children were illegitimate.[39] Divorce was given much publicity by Pietro Germi's light-hearted and highly successful film *Divorzio all'italiana*, released in 1961, in which the main character, Baron Cefalù, 'divorces' his wife by shooting her and passing the murder off as an honour killing. From 1965 onwards, a rise in legally sanctioned marital separations began, increasingly for 'consensual' reasons rather than because one partner accused the other of wrongdoing. Some Italians, it is clear, were becoming less inclined to just put up with bad marriages, whatever the Church's view.[40] The question of birth control also showed resistance to Church teachings.

Most of the Fascist pro-natalist legislation was quickly repealed, some even before the ending of the war. ONMI, however, reopened for business essentially unreformed in 1946, providing assistance to women who were not in state insurance schemes and could not afford private treatment. The trend towards the increasing medicalisation of childbirth, begun under Fascism, continued. In many parts of Italy, the old figure of the local midwife, working independently, delivering babies at home (albeit with official training since the 1930s), gradually vanished as increasing numbers of women had hospital births. This trend was not universal, however. In rural areas there were still many home-births, attended by a midwife or even only female relatives and sometimes cared for by a mixture of traditional and modern medicine. In 1971, about 50 per cent of Italian women still had home-births, due to insufficient maternity beds.[41] Nonetheless, a combination of better housing, food and medical care greatly reduced infant mortality rates. Whereas 66.6 per thousand infants died in their first year of life in 1951, only 28.5 per thousand did so twenty years later.

In addition to ONMI, a few other elements of the Fascist demographic legislation were retained such as family allowances. More problematically, Article 553 of the penal code, which prohibited spreading contraceptive information, remained in force until 1971. Abortion too was still illegal. Once the Pill appeared (available in the US from 1960) it could not be prescribed for contraceptive purposes in Italy. The only legal contraceptive was the condom, albeit still presented as protection against venereal disease. Some, rather isolated, voices did speak out against this situation: in 1953, AIED (Associazione Italiana per l'Educazione Demografica – Italian Association for Demographic Education) was founded, which braved police repression to argue publicly for birth control. Many professional demographers, moreover, began to speak of the links between overpopulation and poverty and the need for the birth rate to fall as life expectancy grew. This academic debate did not, however, lead to government policies to reduce the birth rate.[42]

Nonetheless, the decline in family size continued. It fell, albeit rallying a little in the late 1950s and early 1960s, from an average of 3.97 persons in 1951 to 3.38 by 1971.[43] Regional differences persisted, although the downward trend was to be found everywhere. In the South and Islands, families contracted from 4.2 persons in 1951 to 3.7 twenty years later. In this period, the vast majority of women got married and most had their children in their mid- or late twenties. Few gave birth over the age of 35. Because female life expectancy rose from 67.5 in 1951 to 75 by 1971 (compared with 63.9 to 69 for men) and because women aged over 35 usually only worked for about 8–12 years during the rest of their lives, there were increasing numbers of middle-aged and elderly women without either employment or childcare responsibilities.[44]

In 1951, the Pope, somewhat contradictorily, declared the rhythm method acceptable although the Church continued to vehemently oppose other forms of birth control. There was a gap, however, between official discourse about sexuality, still largely governed by Church morality and the honour code, and the attitude of many Italians. Most Italian couples, Catholics and non-Catholics alike, limited the size of their families. Father Alfredo Boschi, in his popular guide to sexual morality for confessors and priests, which was widely read by doctors, admitted that birth control was so common that priests 'felt a sense of helplessness, as for a battle inevitably lost'.[45] Some carefully worded surveys in the early 1950s confirmed this picture, showing that many Italian women considered a small family good. Not only did most approve of birth control, many admitted using it. As one respondent put this in 1953, 'two children are enough. Its better to commit a sin than have children who'll end up unemployed. There's poverty and a housing shortage. Having lots of children is a crime.'[46]

The low birth rate was seen as evidence of moral decay by Church authorities and medical practitioners (many of whom were, of course, themselves practising Catholics) alike, and they often blamed women. The recourse to birth control was often seen as due to the 'selfishness' of modern women. This, of course, was in denial of the fact that male co-operation was essential for the rhythm method, *coitus interruptus* and condoms, although not, of course, for abortion.[47]

Church pronouncements and police repression of AIED, however, could not totally stem the arrival of more information about sexuality, including the publication in 1950 and 1955 of Italian translations of the Kinsey Report. In 1959, this was joined by what was somewhat inaccurately dubbed the 'Italian Kinsey Report', Gabriella Parca's *Italian Women Confess*.[48] A publishing sensation when it first appeared, Parca's book was composed of extracts from 300 letters from women (mainly young working-class and peasant women), chosen from letters sent to the 'agony aunts' of two popular magazines. Unlike Kinsey she did not do actual interviews. Advice columns were very popular in this period, appearing mainly, although not exclusively, in women's magazines.[49] Parca's letters revealed the gap between official portrayals of women as serene wives and mothers and the everyday lives of many young women, often marked by unhappiness, frustration and loneliness. As Parca herself summarised in the introduction to the book, the image that it painted was of, 'women who were obsessed by the problem of sex, impulsive but inhibited by prejudices, generally dissatisfied with their lives, but incapable of making the smallest attempt to change'.[50]

Many of the problems described in Parca's letters stemmed from the fact that, although approved sexuality for women was still located within marriage or, at most, as a prelude to marriage ('pre-marital relations'), this was a period of transition. Although older customs survived, society now offered new ways for girls and boys to meet. Women were moving around more (taking trams to work, for example) and girls and boys mingled at school, at dances, at parties, at the cinema and on holiday. Unmarried girls were increasingly allowed to go out in the evenings, something that had been most unusual previously. One survey in 1958, for example, even claimed that, in the North, many girls were allowed out in the evenings by the age of 16 and that Southern urban girls were permitted a certain amount of freedom by 18 (although, according to Simonetta Piccone Stella, these findings may have been somewhat optimistic[51]).

Such new freedoms could be problematic. Boys often put pressure on their girlfriends to have sex. Girls who complied could lose their reputations and their chances on the marriage market. An unsullied reputation was still important, more important in some cases than actual virginity, and a woman's marriage chances could be damaged by an unfounded accusation, making great care necessary. Pregnancy too was a risk without effective contraception. In certain respects, the sexual double standard had never been more difficult for girls and women. The problems encountered by young women whose boyfriends demanded sex as the *prova d'amore* (proof of love) was a pervasive theme in Parca's postbag. 'Pitiless' from Turin, for example, echoed many other stories when she wrote that, 'after various personal experiences,

I'm convinced that today no young man expects to marry without demanding from his fiancée "the proof of true love" or worse "to be sure that she can make him happy"'. It is doubtful, however, that many would have agreed with her proposed solution of: 'I'd like to go back to olden times when girls got married without even knowing their fiancé'.[52]

Many young couples in this period probably did engage in various forms of sexual activity even if often not actual penetrative sex. Setting boundaries for this, however, was a delicate terrain given girls' almost total lack of sex education. Even intimate touching short of full sex could compromise a girl's reputation.[53] The melodrama of some of Parca's letters, with their talk of suicide, fleeing to convents and so on, clearly reflected the favoured reading matter of the authors but their anxieties were far from unfounded in a society where marriage and motherhood were still seen as women's primary aim.

The stakes were particularly high in parts of the South. The South was not, of course, unchanging in this period but many communities were still governed by the honour system and honour killings still occurred. Even in the 1960s, a seduced and abandoned woman might have to murder the man responsible (or have a relative do it for her) in order to restore her standing in the community. Sometimes it was women who took action. One particularly dramatic example was a woman from Agrigento who killed her daughter's seducer. She said, in an interview with Lieta Harrison: 'To wipe out the dishonour, to be respected again, there was only one thing to do: kill! And I killed. The shame had been public, and the reparation had to be public too . . . I killed him at midday in the village piazza.'[54] Adultery too could be risky for women. As a Sicilian man explained: 'If a man doesn't wash his honour in his wife's blood, he's the dishonoured one.'[55]

'Dishonoured' women who remained unavenged were often thrown out of the parental home or shunned by the local community. They were generally seen as 'fair game' by men. Typical was the attitude of one man who, when asked how he would behave towards an unmarried mother in the workplace, said: 'Of course I'd like an unmarried mother among my employees – one thing leads to another, you know. But my wife is so jealous.'[56] Sometimes 'dishonoured women' did manage to marry but usually had to content themselves with poorer, older or somehow less desirable men. Even in the North, a woman was supposed to sleep with only one man, the man she married. No such importance was placed on male chastity or fidelity.

It was still considered normal for rape victims to marry the rapist in order to regain their 'honour'. However, in 1966, the Sicilian teenager Franca Viola made front-page news (and later inspired a film) by having the temerity to refuse a 'reparatory marriage'. Her bravery (and her father's unfailing support) paid off. Her attacker was tried and given 11 years imprisonment. She herself still managed to marry her fiancé. This very well-known case was important in publicising the iniquities of the honour system.

The legal system could help a 'wronged' woman. A man who seduced and then abandoned a woman, for example, could be ordered by a court to recompense her financially. As late as 1968, 'E.A.' went to court to demand damages from the estate of a man with whom she had had a relationship for 15 years.

During this time she had granted him (in the words of the court) 'libidinous services' and then her virginity. He died before fulfilling his promise to marry her, leaving her nothing in his will. The court awarded her ten million lire (a considerable sum) from his estate.[57] Cases like this are emblematic of the fact that, although extra-marital sex was not uncommon in this period, it generally took place in a context of expected marriage. It was, therefore, mainly seen, by women at least, as part of the lead-up to a formal engagement.

Attitudes to sex and marriage help underscore the complex, contradictory nature of this period and the fact that the changes which were taking place, although in many ways reflecting wider changes in the Western world, continued to be marked by the specific situation in Italy. The figure of the Italian housewife in this period, for example, was far from just a replica of the American model so famously described by Betty Friedan in *The Feminine Mystique*. Italy did not have the baby boom that America did (only a slight increase in births) and Italians in this period were moving into small urban apartments in close proximity to others, not out to suburban houses with their socially isolating domestic privacy.[58] We still lack proper research on the lives of middle- and upper-class women in this period, but the absence of a collapse in female participation in jobs like teaching and clerical work suggests that there was no specific trend towards greater domesticity for this particular category of women.

The situation for Italian women in this period was, therefore, both similar to and different from what was happening in some other countries. The sheer speed of the transition, of course, made this in many ways inevitable. Many Italians displayed enthusiasm for the benefits of modernity and consumerism, whilst at the same time wishing to retain elements of what they saw as Italian lifestyles (which often included what they understood as 'Italian' gender roles). The 1960s, in particular, when these changes really took off, were, as Luisa Passerini has argued, 'an extraordinary mix of new and old'.[59] Uncertainty about the nature of the changes Italy was experiencing also affected many opinion-makers and politicians of the period. Both the major political forces of the day, Communists and Catholics, had reservations about the benefits of a consumer society. Both, moreover, made great efforts to recruit women to their cause, now that they, at last, were part of the electorate.

8

Women's Politics in the Shadow of the Cold War, 1945–67

In the post-war years, during the height of the Cold War with its stark, polarised politics, Italian women failed to rebuild autonomous political organisations, instead operating politically mainly under party banners. Although one looked to the Vatican and the other to Moscow, there were many similarities in the approach of the two main parties, the Christian Democrat Party (DC) and the Communist Party (PCI), to the mobilisation of women and to ideas about gender. Both embraced female suffrage and created mass women's organisations. Both emphasised women's maternal role, had quite 'traditional' ideas about the private sphere and presented themselves as defenders of the family. They did, of course, differ on some questions but there was enough common ground for women from both parties to work together on legislative reform. The extent of their co-operation, however, was limited by the rapid collapse of Resistance cross-party unity.

Unprecedented political opportunities opened up to women in this period, offering them a real 'political apprenticeship' after two decades of dictatorship. Of course, under Fascism women had participated politically but now, for the first time, women could, at least in theory, walk the corridors of power as equals with men. This was a period, however, of many contradictions where political discourse oscillated between emancipationist rhetoric and evocations of women's domestic and maternal destiny.

The role of the family and the identification of women primarily with it remained strong in this period. In some respects this was problematic for women's role in the political sphere. Women, for example, were urged to vote to defend the family, not their own interests. The family, however, could also be a site of political socialisation. During the *ventennio*, anti-fascist politics had gone underground into the private sphere and, although family commitments could hinder women's political activism, for many it was their family background that had nurtured their political ideals. Many post-war activists had grown up in anti-fascist families. Political identities, moreover, often reinforced

129

family identification. In this period of strong political sub-cultures, party membership was often an all-embracing social identity, shared by whole families or even whole communities.

Whilst some fathers, brothers and husbands were inspirational and encouraging, many men remained ambivalent or even hostile to women's political involvement. In political parties, women continued to be sidelined and relegated to peripheral activities like welfare whilst male politicians dealt with what they saw as more important, more 'political', concerns. Male politicians could no longer, however, completely ignore them, for now women could vote and stand for political office. Although few were actually elected, those that were did successfully push through important legislative reforms. Theirs was not an easy task. In the first parliamentary speech made by a woman deputy, Angela Cingolani Guidi (DC) voiced this problem: 'We've heard many nice things said about us but in reality there's been little concrete evidence of trust in terms of appointments to public office.'[1] Such trust took a long time to emerge. Italy did not have a female cabinet minister until 1976, although women did hold junior ministerial posts before then, the first being Cingolani Guidi herself, appointed in 1952 as under-secretary for industry and commerce.[2]

The war and Resistance helped legitimise women's place in politics and some of the strengths, weaknesses and contradictions of women's post-war political role stemmed from the politics of the Resistance. During the Resistance, women had taken on new, active roles but mostly (albeit not exclusively) in a gender-specific manner. Many male partisans had viewed them with distrust or ambivalence. If the women in the Resistance were often seen, and indeed saw themselves, as carrying out a 'mass *maternage*', then it is not surprising that political discourse of this period frequently referred to women's maternal role. In the Resistance, moreover, women had 'emancipated' themselves by working in unity with men, fighting for a greater (supposedly ungendered) cause. This pattern continued after the war.

Other legacies were important too. The memory of pre-fascist liberal feminism was gone by this time, swept aside by Fascist dismissals of it as 'un-Italian' and by the Left branding it as 'bourgeois'. Many political leaders had, however, witnessed the Fascist Party's successful mass mobilisation of women and this idea was adapted to new political causes. Now, once again, many women joined all-female mass organisations linked to a political party (although, it must be stressed, the similarities with Fascism lay more in the pattern of mobilisation than in the causes women were mobilised for).

The new feminist historiography, born in the 1970s, initially showed little interest in these post-war organisations whose politics seemed timid and old-fashioned. More recently, however, historians have begun to examine them afresh. Many now argue that, despite their limitations, they did create political spaces for women and laid important foundations for the politics of the 1970s.

The Church and Christian Democracy

The Church was still a powerful force in this period, reinforced by its capillary network of lay organisations, its links with the ruling political party and the incorporation of the Lateran Pacts into the new Constitution. Catholicism remained a formidable opponent of gender equality and continued to emphasise women's maternal destiny, female 'purity' and domesticity. As Pius XII stated in October 1945 (albeit whilst also urging women to go out and vote):

> Every woman's destiny is motherhood . . . as such, women can only see and fully understand all the problems of human life through the family. . . . Equal rights with men have, by making women abandon the home where they were queens, subjected them to the same burden of work . . . dazed by the agitated world they live in, dazzled by the tinsel of false luxury, [women who work outside the home] become greedy for suspicious pleasures.[3]

The Vatican was particularly alarmed by manifestations of modernity that implied freer attitudes to sexuality. Catholic ideas of beauty emphasised spiritual, inner beauty, not bodily attributes. The Church attacked cosmetics, beauty contests and American films with their sexualised images. Maria Goretti (1890–1902), a young peasant girl who died defending her virginity against a rapist, was canonised in 1950, a poignant symbol of female purity and chastity for unsettling times. The Church also worried about trends like the proliferation of agony aunt columns, which threatened its monopoly of confession (although the Catholic magazine *Famiglia cristiana* did have its own column, with answers provided by a priest).

Catholic attitudes were not, however, immutable. In the 1950s even *Famiglia cristiana* began to talk, for the first time, of women's happiness as a desirable aim and advised husbands to display compassion and understanding towards their wives, although such happiness was to be sought within the family, not in the world of work.[4] But gradually Church acceptance of even this increased. In 1960, John XXIII declared that there were 'two centres of attraction, two core elements of women's lives: family and work'.[5] The Ecumenical Council Vatican II (1962–5) expressed support for legal equality for women and encouraged them to play a role in promoting Catholicism. This landmark meeting did not, however, substantially modify the Church's position on gender relations and restated the idea that women's primary role was maternity.

The Church's political ally, the Christian Democratic Party, was less rigid. Although it continued to see women essentially as wives and mothers, it was more open to change. It embraced American culture more freely and encouraged escapist entertainment, even beauty contests. Hollywood films were preferred to the social realities of neo-realism. From the start, however, Christian Democrats often focused as much on female duties as rights.

The Left: Communists and Socialists

The PCI, in contrast, spoke frequently of rights and officially supported 'women's emancipation'. Otherwise, their ideas presented only a limited challenge to Catholic views. Communists still saw emancipation as essentially an economic question and were reluctant to address issues like inequality within marriage, sexuality and divorce. This approach was partly due to the fact that the PCI was attempting to woo Catholic voters but also stemmed from the influence of Catholic cultural traditions on party militants, many of whom quite simply did not believe in gender equality. Thus, for much of this period, the only substantial difference between Catholic and Communist positions on gender relations was the Communists' stress on the importance of waged labour.

The PCI constantly reiterated its support for the institution of the family. The ideal communist woman was a party member and worker but also a good wife and mother. This dual role was presented as unproblematic. The family was portrayed as a place of refuge in a harsh capitalist world and women's oppression as a product of fascism or capitalism, not male power. The Communists did campaign for state welfare provisions like nurseries and better health care to assist women in their role as wives and mothers, but never challenged the primacy of this role. Even their support for women's work was not unwavering, particularly in the early post-war years of high unemployment.

As Sandro Bellassai has argued, Communists tried to present an ideal of masculinity (heavily influenced by workerist ideas) which was, nonetheless, supportive to women. Their approach, however, reflected male insecurity faced with the social changes of the time and many aspects of traditional masculinity were never really challenged. The party, for example, often condoned the sexual double standard, seeing an active sex life as essential for men. PCI representations of masculinity oscillated between traditional peasant patriarchal culture and attempts to embrace modernisation by constructing the ideal of a good modernity, contrasted with the decadent modernity of capitalism and America.[6]

The PCI shied away from questions like divorce and the supposedly American idea of birth control. Like the Church, it had a pedagogic approach to morality, attempting to educate its activists in suitable moral behaviour. In schools for party activists, otherwise important in widening the horizons of PCI women, students were lectured on moral issues. Unconventional sexual behaviour was branded as 'petty bourgeois'.[7] The communist press tried to offset anxieties about too much gender upset and the threat of 'masculine' Soviet women with reassuring images of women deputies with children in their arms or female Soviet parachutists doing laundry, and by publishing reports on Soviet women's love of lipstick and perfume.[8] Conversely, 'excessive emancipation', like smoking and wearing revealing clothes, was branded 'American' and unsuitable for Italy.

Initially, the attitude of the PSI to gender questions was not dissimilar to that of the PCI, although Socialist women opted not to organise in a separate section. Although some Socialists did speak of emancipation, others placed much emphasis on women's maternal mission. Even more than the Communists, they tended to deny the specificity of women's problems and called on women to fight together with men for a more equal society.[9] In the 1950s and 1960s, however, Socialist parliamentarians were important in promoting issues neglected by the PCI. These included the reform of prostitution law in 1958 and divorce bills in 1954, 1958 and 1965. Some Socialist deputies, moreover, provided political protection for AIED, the birth control campaign group.

The vote

Italian women voted for the first time in 1946.[10] The question is often posed whether they *won* suffrage or were merely *granted* it. In practice, both these statements are true. The issue arises from the fact that the suffrage legislation was passed during the war, at a time when open, public debate was impossible in much of Italy: the North was still in the throes of civil war. Thus universal suffrage arrived without pomp and fanfare and with little discussion. The measure was passed by the Bonomi government (an unelected body composed of representatives of the Resistance parties) on 1 February 1945. It enfranchised all adult women (except prostitutes working illegally outside brothels, although this was reversed in 1947). Due to an oversight, women's right to stand for office was added only in March 1946, just before the first local elections. In practice, however, this principle was already effective. In the (nominated) Consultative Assembly, the temporary parliament before the first general election, women occupied thirteen seats.

The extension of the franchise was decided almost as if it were obvious, something hardly worth debating. Bonomi's government passed the measure, 'unanimously, practically without discussion'.[11] As a result, for years it was ignored by historians as a 'non-event'. Even at the time, some derided women for getting the vote without making any effort. In fact, as earlier chapters have shown, women had fought long and hard for suffrage, nearly winning it in 1919. Although the memory of pre-Fascist suffrage politics had been virtually erased by this time, a few feminists were still alive and some now in government were old enough to remember their campaigns. In 1944, women representing the various anti-fascist parties tried to refresh their memories. They presented a letter to the National Liberation Committee and, in October, together with women from two pre-Fascist feminist organisations (FILDIS and Alleanza Pro-suffragio), set up a suffrage committee. During the three months of its existence, it lobbied the government, printed a pamphlet and organised a petition. The suffrage issue had also been raised by the GDD (the wartime Resistance women's groups). Far from all partisans, however, had supported it: only men voted in 'liberated zones'.[12]

It was primarily wartime changes that made female suffrage seem inevitable. Many ascribed (and this view is often reiterated today) the measure to women's role in the Resistance. To cite but one example of many, the former seamstress Rina Picolato (PCI), speaking in the Consultative Assembly, argued that women's presence in that assembly was 'a recognition of the part women played in the liberation of the country'.[13] This was indeed true: the role of partisan women was extremely important. In the Resistance, women had demonstrated their worth in unprecedented forms of activism. Many had been politicised by their experiences as well as gaining new confidence. A generally unspoken aspect of the relationship between the Resistance and suffrage was the idea that citizenship was linked to the bearing of arms.[14] However, to understand why the vote, which previously had been so difficult to achieve, was now obtained so easily, other factors need to be taken into account. These include the wider wartime role of women, including non-partisans on the home front, and the fact that most other parliamentary democracies now had female suffrage. Moreover (although this is more rarely mentioned),[15] the mass mobilisation of women during the *ventennio* undoubtedly helped establish the idea that women had a place in the political sphere.

Male opinion was divided. Some men dismissed female suffrage as unimportant, believing that women would vote as their husbands bid them. Others, conversely, felt uneasy because the secret ballot undermined their authority over their wives. Many considered women unready to vote, or thought they would not bother to do so. On this latter point they were proved utterly wrong. In 1946, 81 per cent of female voters (compared with 83 per cent of men) voted in the local elections and 89 per cent (and 89.2 per cent of men) in the general election.[16] In 1953, the female turnout was 94 per cent (93.5 per cent for men).[17] This astounding success was partly due to the energetic campaigns of political parties. Indeed, the first few elections were intense moments for women's political education. They were bombarded with information about how to vote, who to vote for, the importance of elections and so on. Party activists also assisted with practical aspects, such as obtaining an identity card.

Political leaders had pushed the measure through, in particular Palmiro Togliatti and Alcide De Gasperi, leaders of the PCI and DC respectively. Togliatti saw female suffrage as an integral part of the modernisation and renewal of Italy, stating, in 1945, that: 'Italian democracy needs women and women need democracy.'[18] Among the mass memberships of both their parties, however, many had reservations. Many on the Left (including many women) still harboured long-held fears that women would just follow the guidance of priests. Indeed, this was precisely the hope of many Christian Democrats, who believed that the female religious masses could help secure victory over the atheist forces of communism.

Their aim, therefore, was to ensure a high turnout of the new electorate. In October 1945, Pius XII told 1,500 leaders of the women's Catholic organisations assembled in Rome that, for women, voting was a duty, not a right. It was to be used to stem change, to defend the family and traditional values. 'Every woman, without exception, has, you must understand, the *duty*, the strict *duty*, to be present and to become active . . . in order to hold back the currents that threaten the home, fight against doctrines that undermine its foundations, and prepare, organise and bring about its restoration' (my italics).[19] In a departure from Church tradition, it was even suggested that, in this matter, women could disobey their husbands. Guidelines for electoral campaigning by GF organisers spoke of urging women to 'withstand, even in the family, anyone who has opposing ideas to ours (in this matter, there is no obligation to obey fathers, brothers or husbands)'.[20]

The advent of suffrage had huge symbolic importance for women. For many it was an emotional event. The author Maria Bellonci, for example, remembered that, on 2 June 1946, 'that evening, in a rough wooden hut, holding a pencil and two ballot-papers, I suddenly understood that I really was a citizen'.[21] Another woman said: 'Quite honestly, I am still moved today when I go and vote. Imagine what it felt like at the time! I think my hands trembled.'[22]

The vote also mobilised women to new kinds of activism, such as speaking at election hustings. One Tuscan woman recalled how, on the campaign trail in Sardinia in 1952, 'when I spoke, with the megaphone . . . in those cold, god-forsaken villages, full of silence . . . people were very curious, they came to listen, and to look. A woman speaking, that was quite something.'[23] Photographs of female voters and campaigners frequently appeared in the press. The impact of female suffrage on the political system is harder to judge. It has often been argued that it was crucial in sustaining the powerful position of the DC. Paola Gaiotti De Biase, however, has suggested that both the DC and the PCI drew electoral strength from the fact that they were the parties that paid most attention to women.[24]

The Constitution

Only 3.7 per cent of the deputies in the Constituent Assembly were female. Of the twenty-one women elected, nine were Communists, nine Christian Democrats, two Socialists and one from the populist Uomo Qualunque party.[25] Despite their small numbers, their presence was vital in ensuring the inclusion of important clauses for gender equality. On these issues, women from different parties often found common cause. As PCI deputy Nadia Spano recalled: 'There was solidarity between deputies from different parties: on many issues like maternity, family, women's work there was collaboration, understanding.'[26] The result of this cross-party co-operation was a Constitution that was strong on women's public-sphere rights but ambivalent about gender equality in the private sphere.

The Constitution promised equal rights and pay for working women and the right to vote and hold public office. Article 3 boldly declared that: 'All citizens have equal social status and are equal before the law, without regard to their sex, race, language, religion, political opinions, and personal or social conditions.' This was reinforced by a potentially useful sentence reading: 'It is the duty of the Republic to remove all economic and social obstacles that, by limiting the freedom and equality of citizens, prevent full individual development and the participation of all workers in the political, economic and social organisation of the country.' Article 48 was also unambiguous, stating that: 'All citizens, men or women, who have attained their majority are entitled to vote.' Article 51 read: 'All citizens, of either sex, are eligible for public office and for elective positions under equal conditions, according to the rules established by law.' The final part of this sentence was a substitute for the original phrasing of 'in conformity with their abilities, according to the rules established by law', which female deputies had objected to as a dangerous loophole. Their attempt, however, to ensure that Article 51 would allow women to become magistrates was unsuccessful.

Other relevant clauses were more ambiguous or reflected Catholic values. For example, the promise in Article 37 that: 'Working women are entitled to the same rights and, for equal jobs, the same pay as men,' was qualified by: 'Working conditions must enable women to fulfil their essential family role and ensure an adequate protection of mothers and children.' This latter phrase was the work of Christian Democrats like Maria Federici. The protection of maternity was not, of course, in itself a bad thing: potentially this clause paved the way for useful legislation for working mothers. However, the words 'essential family role' defined women's place as firmly within the private sphere, making their identity as citizens 'weak and precarious'.[27] Sociologist Chiara Saraceno has wryly commented that: 'Every time I read this article, I wonder if men have families too, or not.'[28] The debate on Article 37 in the Assembly demonstrated that some deputies did not want to encourage female employment at all. Others wanted women's domestic role to be presented as primary and employment as secondary.

The family was given an elevated status by Article 29, which defined it as, 'a natural association founded on marriage'. Many of those who helped draft the Constitution firmly believed in a clear gender hierarchy in the family. Thus, Article 29's statement that: 'Marriage entails moral and legal equality of the spouses', was qualified with a phrase that effectively negated it, 'within legally defined limits to protect the unity of the family.' Many deputies, in the debate on this article, insisted on the need for male authority in the family. The alternative, one argued, was 'terrifying anarchy'.[29] Nilde Jotti (PCI) pressed in vain for divorce, although the indissolubility of marriage was not mentioned in the Constitution, which was a victory of sorts.

These problems notwithstanding, the Constitution was a giant stride forward in gender equality. Only the political rights, however, were implemented immediately. For years, much of the Constitution remained a dead letter, a beautiful (if contradictory) statement of intent for which the enabling legislation had not been passed. It was forged in the heady early post-war days, when there was still space for lofty ideals, an atmosphere that soon evaporated. Many conflicting laws lingered on the statute books for years, partly because social structures and cultural beliefs were considerably less advanced than the ideals enshrined in this founding document. Even in the Assembly itself, views were often aired that showed the kind of opposition that needed to be overcome before women could win even formal equality. The Constitution did, nonetheless, create an important platform for future reform either through decisions of the Constitutional Court, which from the mid-1960s became more open to reforming gender-related legislation (like the 1968 ruling which declared unconstitutional the differential treatment of male and female adultery) or through parliament (see below).

Women and political organisations

In this period a good number of women were active politically. They could be found organising meetings, giving speeches, handing out leaflets, standing for election, participating in strikes and demonstrations, studying the politician's trade at party schools or busy with politicised welfare activities. Women joined a range of organisations including trade unions, co-operatives and political parties or new mass organisations linked to them. For some, joining such organisations was a minor part of their lives. For others, it became a core part of their identity, giving them a sense of worth and importance. PCI activist Angela L.,

Illustration 8 Woman reading a trade union newspaper.
(Reproduced courtesy of Fototeca Panizzi, Reggio Emilia.)

for example, wrote that, 'the Party has completely transformed me: from the obscure petty-bourgeois, sentimental clerical worker I used to be, it has made a fighter, it has given me a new personality'.[30]

Angela L. was from the communist heartland of Bologna but women all over Italy and from a range of social groups were politically active. Many joined unions, although women were still very much in the minority. The left-wing union CGIL in 1949, for example, had just over a million female members compared with seven million men. This reflected both levels of female employment and the unsupportive attitude of many male union members to women in the workplace.

Even some peasant women became politically active. They were deeply involved in the wave of rural unrest that swept across the South in 1944–7 and 1949. In some cases, such as the occupation of the Lacava estates near Matera, they led the crowd.[31] Some women from sharecropping households took part in protests in the immediate post-war period, encouraged by union organisers who broke down the public–private barrier by going directly into homes to drum up support. These sharecropper protests were laden with symbolism as they targeted the demeaning *regalie*, the 'gifts' of eggs, free laundering and so on that women had to offer the landlord, according to the terms of contracts negotiated by the male head of family. In this 'strike', the *regalie* were withheld and donated to hospitals and welfare organisations.

Sharecropping women could join various political organisations. These included the 'women's commissions' of the left-wing Federmezzadri union. The Coldiretti (the Catholic organisation for small farmers) also created a women's section, the Donne Rurali, founded in 1952. By June 1955, this latter organisation, which was quite clearly modelled on the Fascist Massaie Rurali, had 260,000 members.[32]

Catholics boasted a range of other organisations, including charities and the various wings of Azione Cattolica (AC – Catholic Action). AC continued to be a conservative, spiritually-orientated organisation strictly subordinate to the Church hierarchy, albeit taking an active role in spreading the faith. Large numbers of women belonged to it. In 1946, the GF had 884,992 members and UDACI 369,015. Membership peaked in 1956 with 1,265,499 in GF and 630,000 in UDACI although numbers then gradually declined (with 939,990 in GF by 1968), a trend that accelerated after 1969 when, as a result of new ideas arising from Vatican II, they were merged into mixed-sex groups.[33]

Some pre-fascist women's associations resurfaced, including the CNDI and the UFN. In the 1950s, for example, members of some of these organisations were involved in a committee established to promote equal pay and oppose discrimination in employment.[34] Overall, however, these relatively small groupings were totally overshadowed by political parties and their flanking organisations. Quite high numbers of women, far more than in Liberal Italy, joined parties. Both major parties were keen to recruit women as voters, although they often gave little priority to them, seeing 'work among women' as peripheral to the main concerns of party politics. The DC and the PCI both had special women's sections.

The women's wing of the DC, the Movimento Femminile (MF – Women's Movement) was founded in 1944, with, at its helm (until 1947), the extrovert and energetic Angela Cingolani Guidi, a veteran member of the Catholic women's organisations and long-time suffrage campaigner. Some in the DC opposed the idea of organising separately but she and others saw it as an effective way of preparing women for a full role in the party. Her view prevailed and the separate structure continued even after newer, younger leaders succeeded her.

With a seat on the party directorate and, from the mid-1950s, a legal office dedicated to preparing bills for the legislature, the MF was not without influence. It was not, however, particularly effective. Vera Dragoni, MF provincial delegate in Florence in the 1950s, bitterly condemned it as, 'a convenient structure, not functioning, very subordinate to the party, crammed with members but hardly any of them active'.[35] Such criticisms were not unfounded. Many of the members (253,000 in 1946, 462,381 in 1954, and 574,054 in 1963) were indeed paper members, automatically signed up by the head of household as a part of 'family membership'. Given the DC's clientelist nature, moreover, many joined primarily to obtain services and jobs. About 60 per cent of MF members came from the South and Islands. Three-quarters were housewives.[36]

The PCI also created women's sections, although only as local cells and not in a national organisation like the DC. In theory (but not in practice) this was a temporary strategy. Here too the idea of separate groups was controversial. Some, like Teresa Noce, opposed them, arguing that women should not be differentiated from men in the party. Others hoped the sections would encourage the participation of those intimidated by mixed meetings, particularly in the South. In practice, although some sections functioned well, many were inactive and ineffective. Nor did they exist everywhere in Italy (local federations were not compelled to establish them). The role of party women, too, was ambiguous. Some were very active. Others, lacking the confidence to participate in the properly political activities, sometimes ended up doing things like cooking food for the annual Festa dell'Unità.

For much of this post-war period roughly a third of PCI members were female. Numbers rose gradually from about 250,000 in late 1945 to peak at 575,168 in 1954, after which they declined, falling to 407,137 by 1963. Membership was strongest in the Centre and weakest in the South. Despite the party's focus on workers, in 1947–63, around 45–55 per cent were housewives, often wives of PCI members. Only a minority (15 per cent in 1954) were factory workers.[37] Family membership was a factor here too: some Communist men just signed their whole family up for the appropriate party section.

Although both parties tried to train women for leadership, there was a persistent shortage of leaders. As a result, those who did take on leadership positions, whether locally or nationally, often found themselves overloaded with multiple responsibilities in a range of organisations. These included unions, local government and the mass organisations UDI and CIF.

The Unione Donne Italiane (UDI) and the Centro Italiano Femminile (CIF)

The origins of UDI[38] lay in wartime politics, with the women's Resistance groups, the GDD. Although the GDD were created following a PCI party directive, rather than spontaneously founded by women, they did speak of women's rights, albeit emphasising male–female unity in struggle. In 1944 they defined their aims as: 'To organise women for the conquest of their rights as women and as Italians, in the context of the struggle of the whole people for the liberation of the nation.'[39] A typical organisation deriving from the 'Popular Front' approach to defeating fascism, they were open to all antifascist women. UDI, founded in 1944 in the 'liberated areas' as a peacetime version of the GDD (with which it was fused at the end of the war), attempted to continue this cross-party approach. Its initial members even included a few Christian Democrats, and, had the Cold War not broken out, it might have been able to fulfil its aim of uniting women of all (or no) political persuasions (although, from the start, Communists predominated). In the increasingly tense political climate of the time, however, Resistance unity politics was doomed and women from other parties left even before the war was over.

Until 1947, UDI operated relatively autonomously (albeit with strong, unofficial, links with the PCI) but then, as the Cold War intensified, became increasingly subordinate to the Left. Most of its leaders were high-ranking Communist or Socialist women and many *udine* also belonged to these parties. It soon became essentially a flanking organisation for the Left, particularly the PCI. Membership was highest in PCI strongholds like Tuscany and Emilia Romagna (42 per cent were from these areas in 1946 and 70 per cent by 1962).[40] Nationally UDI claimed a membership of 50,000 in April 1945, 401,391 in 1946, 425,875 in 1947 and 1,037,655 in 1950[41] although Casalini has demonstrated that discrepancies in the organisation's own figures suggest that they are only a rough guide.[42] Thereafter membership declined to, by 1964, 220,000.[43] From 1947, in an attempt to expand membership, UDI created specialised organisations for war widows and heads of families, for peasants, for housewives and for girls, as well as local associations like the 'Neapolitan Mothers'. By 1949 these had 243,000 members. This strategy was, however, abandoned in 1953, seen as harming UDI's national unity.

Togliatti saw UDI as a useful means of drawing all sectors of the female population to communism and, as such, essential to his strategy of making the PCI a mass party. But some male Communists were indifferent or hostile to it and even some of the women who ran it considered it a kind of exile from real party business. Indeed, many activists were reluctant to undertake 'work with women' of any kind. Others, however, saw it as offering an important political apprenticeship for women.

Initially, UDI's ideology was 'emancipation'. Its Statute, issued in 1946, called for: 'women's emancipation, the elimination of all discrimination, customs and living conditions that keep women in a state of moral, social, civil and cultural inferiority, and hinder the widening of the democratic basis of national society'.[44] At this point UDI campaigned for equal pay, nurseries, better working conditions and training, as well as a range of other provisions like rights for illegitimate children and better schools. In 1945 it even lobbied the government for a complete reform of the Civil Code. Due to the deepening political divide of the time, however, UDI became more conservative. By 1947, its congress convened under the slogan: 'Happy families, peace and work'. Emancipation had been sidelined. By the late 1940s, it was subordinated to PCI politics, essentially a transmission belt for party ideas. It shared the persecution of left-wing organisations in this period. Ida Cavallini, a young *udina* from Ravenna, for example, was arrested for handing out mimosa in 1948.[45]

During the late 1940s and the early 1950s UDI faithfully campaigned primarily for party campaigns, such as against the atom bomb (pacifism was seen as particularly appropriate for women), and helped fight elections. Even the way in which UDI women were mobilised was often questionable – for example, by appealing to their maternal feelings. During the 1950s, however, UDI gradually placed more emphasis on women's rights and from 1956, a watershed year for world communism, slightly loosened its ties with the PCI. In this new climate an UDI document of 1956 even spoke of the need to pay more attention to birth control and family law reform. It was increasingly recognised that simple legal equality was not enough. Particularly after Giuliana dal Pozzo became editor in 1956, UDI's magazine *Noi donne* frequently diverged from the official PCI line on matters connected to the private sphere, to the extent that some of its readers were scandalised and cancelled their subscriptions.[46] For example (beginning, in this case, in 1955), *Noi donne* published a series of pioneering articles discussing divorce and, in 1961, devoted a four-page spread to the film *Divorzio all'italiana*, at a time when the PCI, if not opposed to divorce, deemed it politically inexpedient to discuss it.[47] In the 1960s, *Noi donne* frequently aired the problems of 'modern marriage' and the need to reform family law. In 1964 UDI called for the repeal of the Fascist legislation on birth control and in the late 1960s, the national leadership began to advocate greater autonomy from the PCI and PSI.

Regardless of the strengths and weaknesses of its ideology, UDI membership could be an intense and important experience. For some the single-sex UDI meetings were the only political space where they felt really comfortable. UDI was the nearest thing that Italy had in this period to a mass feminist organisation. Its ideas may have seemed timid to the feminists in the following decade but in many ways they were very advanced for their day. Even once its membership had declined from the early large figures, it still involved many more women than pre-Fascist feminism had done and had a wider class base with many working-class and peasant members.

The emergence of UDI led Catholics to sponsor their own, rival, version, CIF (the Centro Italiano Femminile), founded in Rome also in 1944. Unlike UDI, which in theory was open to all non-Fascists, CIF welcomed only practising Catholics. Although initially CIF sometimes co-operated with UDI, one of its main aims was to channel women away from it.

CIF was distinct from the spiritually orientated AC (although AC leaders were involved in its foundation). AC prepared women for their supernatural destination whilst CIF prepared them for an active role in the earthly realm. Unlike AC, CIF was officially 'autonomous', not subordinate to the Church hierarchy. At all levels, however, from village to national, CIF committees had a 'religious consultant', a priest who advised them on religious matters, and CIF presidents were vetted by the Church authorities. Although not officially part of the DC, CIF had many links with it and party leaders of both sexes often addressed its conferences.

CIF was an umbrella body for 26 Catholic women's organisations (including UDACI, GF and various charitable, trade union and professional associations) affiliated to it. It also had individual members organised into groups for housewives, 'professionals' and youth. This unwieldy structure proved problematic. Particularly at first, it created tension with the AC women's organisations who wanted CIF to just provide them with services and representation, fearing that individual membership might give CIF a dominant position. The Vatican, however, supported individual membership as a means of spreading Catholic influence in society. AC also resented CIF's welfare activism, which threatened its own activities. This friction eventually led to the downfall of CIF's first president Maria Federici in 1950.[48]

Because of its structure it is difficult to gauge the size of CIF's membership, as this depended on the size of its component organisations.[49] During the 1948 elections, it claimed it could mobilise six million votes although, according to Cecilia Dau Novelli, the actual number was probably nearer four.[50] In 1949, a survey of CIF activities carried out by Federici showed that in some provinces membership was quite high. Milan, for example, reported 182,000 members, Trent 31,700 and Verona 30,500. Campobasso, however, had only 1,000. In most provinces the vast majority were affiliated, not individual members. Macerata, for example, had 85,000 federated members but only 8,500 individuals.[51]

Although CIF viewed women principally as wives and mothers and focused primarily on housewives, it did consistently advocate women's rights. This included employment rights like equal pay, the removal of legal restrictions on female employment and even the abolition of the marriage bar, although its preference was for the 'family wage' to enable women to choose a domestic role. During the economic miracle, its interest in working women rose and some CIF activists increasingly saw employment as potentially enriching women's lives although, as before, the family came first. The aim was to enable women to work without neglecting their families.

During the miracle, creeping secularisation made CIF's task difficult. Like other Catholic organisations, it struggled faced with the deep social changes of the time, the consumer society and, eventually, feminism. In 1970, it tried to revive its fortunes with a new structure, becoming an association rather than a federation, but by now it was outdated, overtaken by social and political change and with a dwindling membership.

UDI and CIF both tried to prepare women for an active role in society and politics. They 'educated women for democracy', which included encouraging them to vote, since many feared that they would be too fearful or ill-informed to do so. Initially, in theory, neither organisation directed women to vote for a particular party but simply urged them to exercise their democratic right/duty (although CIF activists did ask women to use their vote to defend Christianity). By the time of the dramatic 1948 election, however, CIF campaigned openly for the DC, and UDI for the Left. Much electioneering was done by specially trained 'propagandists' who toured energetically around towns and villages giving talks and holding meetings. In both organisations, education for democracy was understood to go beyond simple voting to help forge an active form of citizenship where women took responsibility through welfare, lobbying for reform and so on.[52] Both UDI and CIF also campaigned for legislative change. UDI members, for example, collected signatures for petitions and participated in innumerable demonstrations and protests for pensions for housewives, better maternity leave, the abolition of the Serpieri Coefficient (see below) and so on. CIF carried out a good deal of research in the form of surveys and participated in morality campaigns, including efforts to 'redeem' prostitutes.

Both organisations did a great deal of welfare work, particularly during the reconstruction years when they assisted refugees, returning soldiers, orphans and the homeless and even became involved in food rationing. They ran children's summer camps, canteens and nursery schools. UDI welfare was often focused on putting pressure on local authorities or the state to provide facilities like nursery schools and this led some UDI women to themselves become involved in local government. Even after the emergencies of the immediate post-war period were over, welfare continued to be a core activity of both organisations. Initiatives included extensive adult education programmes, ranging from practical subjects like adult literacy and typing to lectures on how the political system worked. CIF also specialised in 'moral lessons' and domestic science and farming courses for peasant women (even as late as the 1960s).

Welfare, of course, had been part of women's politics for a long time, including under Fascism, and as such, this could be seen as an element of continuity with the past. Under Fascism, however, despite its rhetoric about 'modern' approaches to welfare, party welfare had been class-based and patronising. In contrast, many UDI welfare activists were themselves from working-class or peasant backgrounds and UDI saw its welfare work as embodying what Dianella Gagliani has termed 'anti-patronage', a practical and empowering form of politics, offering solidarity, not paternalism, to the needy.[53] Refugee children, for example, were placed in ordinary families, not institutions. Parents were encouraged to lobby for improvements to schools and so on. Nonetheless, in one respect the post-war political forces used welfare in a very similar way to the PNF, namely to consolidate their roots in society.

CIF's approach to welfare was, of course, shaped by Catholic ideas. Welfare fulfilled the Christian duty to assist the poor but it was, at the same time, a means of spreading the influence of Catholicism in society. It also reflected CIF's somewhat ambivalent approach to women's extra-domestic role. In 1945, for example, it rejected a proposal from the trade union federation CGIL to increase the number of nurseries and factory canteens as these robbed women of the joy of performing these tasks themselves for their families.[54] Although less committed to the idea of state welfare than the Left, CIF's links to the ruling party secured it considerable public funding. In 1948, for example, it obtained 300 million lire whereas all the Left organisations combined received only 60 million.[55]

Both organisations produced magazines. UDI's lively *Noi donne* was aimed at a wide readership, its contents ranging from political news to film reviews. Circulation was 300,000 by 1953. CIF's *Bollettino*, in contrast, offered primarily organisational information for activists (although it did begin to include serialised novels, photos and so on when it was renamed *Cronache* in 1952) since there were already other Catholic magazines for women, notably *Famiglia cristiana*. In 1953, CIF launched a new magazine, *Stella*, as an alternative to what it saw as the immoral glossies of the day, hoping to reach out to a wider readership, but this soon collapsed.

Both UDI and CIF organised numerous festive occasions and recreational activities including dances (UDI only), children's parties, craft exhibitions, fairs, outings, pilgrimages and so on. Each organisation also had annual celebrations to help promote and reinforce their identities, typical of the Italian political subcultures of the time. These annual days were a focus of considerable activity. International Women's Day (8 March) was the moment when UDI became most visible to the wider public, with exhibitions, demonstrations, talks, choreographed parades and other events, everything festooned with yellow mimosa blossoms, the symbol of the day. CIF's annual festivities had a more religious flavour, focusing on the feast day of the patron saint of Italy, Catherine of Siena (a fitting choice for an organisation concerned with women's role in the public sphere), and then, from the early 1950s, the 'Giornata della Donna Cristiana'.[56]

CIF and UDI were rivals, in competition with each other (indeed, at local level, some of their activism was fuelled by a desire to outdo each other) and in some respects their ideas differed. This can be seen, for example, in their approaches to welfare. In other ways, however, they were mirror images of each other. Both tried to educate women politically and both were democratically run. Both, despite their limitations, were forces for modernisation.[57] Both offered spaces for women to engage in political activism and build confidence without too much male interference. They also offered numerous social opportunities (including plenty of essentially recreational activities) in a period when many led domesticated and sometimes fairly isolated lives. Whilst neither was really 'autonomous' in the full sense of the word, they were, nonetheless, far more so than the women's party sections. Both, moreover, mobilised plenty of much needed support for the efforts of women parliamentary deputies to push through important legal reforms.

Elected politicians

Very few women were elected to parliament. Most, as Table 1 shows, were in the Chamber of Deputies: only tiny numbers reached the Senate. This situation partly reflected women's own reluctance to stand for election. Only exceptional women had the confidence to survive in the very male parliamentary world in an era where discourse about the primacy of maternity made them seem anomalous. They had to be able to shrug off the often belittling comments of the press. Consequently, to many 'ordinary' Italian women, it was difficult to see such unusual figures as role models to emulate.[58] The parties, moreover, selected few female candidates. The best in this respect was consistently the PCI, partly because it tended to field candidates who had proved their worth with long party service, in local government for example. By contrast, the faction-ridden DC, where clientelist networks were so important, often chose outsiders, a more difficult terrain for women to compete on. In all parties, moreover, far from all men welcomed female candidates. Women who were selected often had to face the hostility of disgruntled male rivals. A week before winning her seat in the Constituent Assembly, the young socialist Bruna Bianchi, for example, was urged to sign a resignation letter, drafted by some

TABLE 1   Women in Parliament, 1946–79

	1946	**1948**	**1953**	**1958**	**1963**	**1968**	**1972**	**1976**	**1979**
% of women in the Chamber of Deputies	3.8	7.8	5.7	4.1	4.6	2.8	4.1	8.5	8.2
% of women in the Senate	n/a	0.9	0.4	0.8	1.9	3.4	1.8	3.4	3.4

Sources: M. Guadagnini, 'Le donne nel Parlamento italiano dal 1948 a oggi', *Quaderni di sociologia*, 33 (1987): 130–57, p. 153; K. Beckwith, 'Women and Parliamentary Politics in Italy, 1946–1979', in H. Penniman (ed.), *Italy at the Polls, 1979* (London, 1981), p. 242.

men in her local federation, in which she offered to stand aside to make way for a male candidate. Bianchi, a university graduate despite being the daughter of a village blacksmith, stood her ground and was elected.[59] The scarcity of women in positions of power was not, however, just due to misogyny. Often women themselves were reluctant to vote for other women, thinking that men could do the job better.

During the early years of the new parliament, fielding a woman was a novelty that could potentially attract votes. After this, until 1972, few new female faces appeared. Many deputies were women who had won their political spurs as clandestine anti-Fascists or partisans. As Nilde Jotti commented, the Resistance was 'the greatest school for politics that could exist'[60] but this particular school was not, of course, open to younger women; 70.5 per cent of the Communist women in the first legislature (elected in 1948) had been active in the Resistance (although this was true of only 12.5 per cent of the DC female deputies, many of whom, instead, had a background of AC activism).[61] Numbers of female deputies rose and fell in successive legislatures but it was not until the 1970s that they really grew.

Similar problems in local government prevented a real increase in female councillors. In the first local elections (1946), 2,000 women were elected, a big achievement but only a small percentage of councillors nationwide. After this, women remained in the minority as the structures were hardly welcoming and there was still much prejudice. Angela Verzelli's research on female councillors in Bologna, for example, found that many left because they had such negative experiences of working in structures not open to their interests, where they felt they could achieve little. Instead they chose to be active on a more local level, campaigning around more concrete, practical issues.[62]

The pioneering female parliamentarians found themselves in an ambiguous position. It seemed unclear whether they had been elected to represent all Italians or simply to defend women's interests. The same question was not posed about male politicians for it was assumed, often wrongly, that they spoke for all. In practice, women did intervene on all sorts of topics, but needed courage to do so. When for the first time a woman spoke on a non-'women's issue' (Marisa Cinciari Rodano from the PCI), her speech on foreign policy was met with some hostility. Some journalists left the room in disgust, without even waiting to hear what she had to say, whispering to each other about the house-work she was neglecting.[63]

Legislative change

In spite of their effectively marginal position, these female deputies delivered some important legislative improvements. Molly Tambor has aptly dubbed them 'women's rights constitutionalists', because their rationale for reform was often based on the fact that legislation still contradicted the Constitution, 'thereby bypassing arguments with conservative or antifeminist thinkers about the morality or ethics of the women's rights laws they proposed'.[64] On many bills women from different parties supported each other. This was true, for example, of the first major piece of legislation of specific importance to women, improved maternity protection for workers, introduced in 1950. Although the bill's main architect was Teresa Noce (PCI), Maria Federici (DC) helped ensure that it gained enough support in parliament.

Much legislation was passed in a cluster in the late 1950s and early 1960s, during the height of the economic miracle, beginning with the 1956 Act which enabled women to take new roles in the Assize and Juvenile Courts. Although a minor reform, this represented a first step towards the implementation of Article 51 of the Constitution. Far more widely debated was the reform of prostitution legislation.

The 'Merlin law' of 1958 was named after the socialist senator and former primary teacher Lina (Angelina) Merlin who bravely championed it over a decade. The law banned brothels as well as the registration and inspection of prostitutes. It criminalised pimping, the trafficking of women and soliciting, but not prostitution itself. The law also promised the foundation of state reformatories to assist prostitutes who wished to abandon the trade, and was to be policed by a new all-female police corps. These latter provisions, however, were never properly implemented.

During the passing of this legislation the terms of the debate were much the same as they had been over the last century. 'Regulationists' argued that brothels, controlled by police and doctors, protected public health and that prostitution prevented adultery by creating an outlet for men's sexual drives. Cucco, a neo-fascist deputy, even asserted, referring to the 'needs' of young men, that it was common knowledge that: 'at a certain age, sexual abstinence can often lead to a form of real intoxication of the organism'.[65] 'Abolitionists', conversely, said that men should learn self-control and that the existing legislation was ineffective since most prostitutes worked clandestinely anyway. Merlin presented her bill in the name of women's rights. She argued that the function of the existing legislation was not to protect public health but the interests of 'men in general, to procure for themselves comfort and safety in their vice, to hold at their discretion every and any woman with the menace of police inquisition, to reaffirm, in spite of public declarations and constitutional principles, masculine privilege and the inequality of the sexes'.[66] The actual bill that was passed was, however, watered down by DC involvement into a more moralising document with less emphasis on helping former prostitutes.

Apart from Merlin, few female voices were heard in this debate. Prostitutes themselves were not consulted although some did write letters of support to Merlin, a selection of which she published to promote her cause. Many men opposed the reform. The arguments they marshalled against it showed that the attitudes of some male Italians had moved on little since the days of Cesare Lombroso. Indeed, even some male 'abolitionists' revealed themselves to be not untainted by such ideas.[67] Many on both sides assumed that prostitutes were inherently corrupt and that the issue was a problem of female, not male, sexuality. Male opposition to Merlin is unsurprising. Italian men in the 1950s were unused to attacks on the privileges of the sexual double standard, privileges officially protected and endorsed by state-approved brothels. As journalist Laura Lilli later noted, 'in brothels, men felt like kings. Lina Merlin wanted to dethrone them.'[68]

Nonetheless, the reform passed easily (385 votes for and 115 against), supported by a cross-party alliance of the Left (who saw prostitution in terms of class oppression) with the DC (who deemed it a moral issue). Parliamentary support was bolstered by medical advances that made venereal diseases less dangerous, and the stand that the United Nations had taken against state-approved prostitution. Italy was the last remaining European country with licensed brothels. Merlin's campaign was, therefore, successful. With regard to her long-term aims, however, it was a complete failure as her law did not bring an end to prostitution.

The same year, 1958, saw another legislative milestone. This gave outworkers (mainly, of course, women) benefits like paid holidays, Christmas bonuses, redundancy pay, social insurance and so on, as well as a right to the piece rates stipulated in collective contracts. This very progressive legislation was, however, extremely ineffective, as an important loophole excluded the self-employed. This was followed by a spate of new laws. In 1959 women were admitted to the police force, albeit only to work on crimes related to 'morality' and in the protection and prosecution of women and children. In 1960 a trade union agreement saw the abolition of female-only categories in collective contracts. However, only in jobs 'normally done by men' did they receive real equal pay. In jobs 'normally done by both sexes', they got only 92.8 per cent of the male wage. Despite its limitations, this agreement did narrow the gender gap and at least a few women now had wage equality. During the 1960s, moreover, various court judgements ruled in favour of equal pay and in 1969 the Court of Cassation declared illegal any collective contract that contradicted Article 37 of the Constitution. In practice, of course, most women remained ghettoised in poorly paid all-female work roles.

In 1963 the marriage bar (which had become increasingly common in the 1950s) was outlawed. The same year saw the removal of all remaining limits to women's access to the professions and public office (apart from in the armed forces, tax inspectorate and police) and to all grades within them. Finally, after a century of campaigning, women could be magistrates. According to Anna Maria Galoppini: 'It was, in the history of women's emancipation, equivalent to the storming of the Bastille.'[69]

In 1963 housewives won pensions. Initially, the new contributory scheme excluded many, but subsequent legislation in 1969 extended rights even to those who had paid no contributions. As well as sparing many from an undignified old age, this reform was important on a symbolic level as it constituted at least some recognition of the social contribution of this large group of women. 1964 saw the abolition of the notorious 'Serpieri Coefficient', a yardstick whereby peasant women's work was deemed worth only a set percentage of a man's, affecting both earnings and inheritance rights. In 1967, new legislation governing child labour was, for the first time, kept separate from the regulation of women's work (albeit itself including gender inequalities: the ban on employing minors in work considered dangerous or particularly dirty set differential age limits for boys (16) and girls (18)).

Overall, by the end of the 1960s, there had been considerable legislative progress on many fronts, particularly in employment law. Despite the polarised politics of the Cold War, women from both sides of the divide had made common cause on some important issues. The early feminist historians clearly overstated the timidity of those who fought for improvements to women's lives in this period. Given the difficulties political women faced and their anomalous position in the public sphere in a time of much rhetoric from both the Church and the Left about the family and women's essential role within it, their achievements were considerable. The political climate of the time, with its divided political system and its faction-ridden and ineffective legislature, which often managed to agree on only unimportant and uncontentious reforms, was unpromising terrain for bold legislative initiatives and even more problematic for any truly autonomous women's politics.

Most of the legislation of the 1950s and 1960s regarded, however, women's role in the public sphere, reflecting the preoccupations and ideas of the major parties of the time. Many laws defending gender inequality remained on the statute books. Reforms to abolish inequalities in the private sphere and matters related to the body (apart from prostitution) had to await the more radical and iconoclastic politics of the following decade. Much had, however, already been achieved. Although the 1970s feminists presented themselves as rebelling against the politics of the previous generation (and indeed, there was much to rebel against, since the political climate in post-war Italy did limit the terms of the gender debate), in many respects it was the dogged perseverance of the 'women's rights constitutionalists', and of UDI and CIF, that paved the way for the more radical politics about to come.

9

'Io Sono Mia': Feminism in the 'Great Cultural Revolution', 1968–80

The 1970s were a watershed period for ideas about gender roles. This decade of political and cultural upheaval saw, as well as a vibrant feminist[1] movement, the rise of the student movement, extra-parliamentary politics, trade union militancy and terrorism of both Left and Right. It was a time of creativity, energy, political passion and utopian dreams but also (eventually) bloody violence and, for most of the movements, defeat. In these years, *détente* destabilised the Cold War stalemate where Communists and Christian Democrats had faced each other in antagonistic symbiosis. Many Western countries saw upheaval in this period but the phenomenon was particularly prolonged in Italy, lasting until the late 1970s. It was also particularly violent: only Germany saw comparable levels of terrorist activity. As elsewhere, it was primarily the young who were involved. Previously, although some Italian teenagers and young adults had been politically active, they had not done so specifically as young persons.

Italian feminists of this decade, like other Western feminists, were often prone to extreme, unrealistic ideas. Unlike the careful strategies of earlier emancipationists, they had a 'no holds barred' approach to politics, iconoclastically attacking 'male power' in all its manifestations, from Marxism to the medical profession. Their political strategy was often poor. Nonetheless, of the various new movements of the 1970s, feminism arguably was the one with the most lasting impact. It reset the agenda for many aspects of gender relations and had a significant impact on the social authority of the Church.

All Western feminisms of this decade (and of earlier periods) struggled with the difference/equality question and most contained a mixture of the two. In Italy, the primary emphasis was on difference. Nonetheless, Italian feminism did share many of the characteristics of other Western feminisms of the time, with its emphasis on change in the private sphere, on sexuality and the body, and on the need for non-hierarchical, autonomous organisation. Despite their rejection of 'mere formal equality', some Italian feminists campaigned for legislative reform.

Up to 1974, feminists worked mainly in small, unco-ordinated groups, often focusing most on debating ideas. During 1974–6, when feminism became more of a mass movement, there was a more public, open phase, including demonstrations and more practical initiatives. During the dark days after 1976, when some of the social movements degenerated into terrorist violence, feminism became confused and complicated. By the 1980s it no longer existed as a movement. It was not, however, dead but gradually mutated into new forms. For many, however, the decline of the movement left them with a profound sense of loss.

The origins of the women's movement

One core factor in the emergence of feminism was the changes wrought by the economic miracle. Urbanisation, improved education and unprecedented material wealth were all important. Many of the previous generation had struggled simply to survive. Young women now wanted more. These changes had been building up over time. As was argued in Chapter 7, by the 1960s some teenagers were increasingly restless about traditional gender roles. The student movement of 1968 acted as a catalyst for this dissatisfaction. Secularisation was also significant, making the feminist challenge to Church authority possible. Feminism, in turn, fuelled secularisation.

Foreign examples were important. Betty Friedan's *The Feminine Mystique* appeared in Italian in 1964. Works by Shulamith Firestone, Kate Millett, Juliet Mitchell and Germaine Greer were translated in the early 1970s, as was *Our Bodies Ourselves* by the Boston Women's Health Collective. The media helped spread news from abroad and some key figures in early Italian feminism, like Carla Lonzi and Serena Castaldi, had spent time in America. The MLD (see below) was set up after a male Radical Party activist collected material on feminism during a trip to America.[2] Many Italian feminists read foreign texts. The Anabasi feminist group founded in 1970, for example, based many of its early meetings on discussions of American feminist readings. French feminism was influential too. An Italian edition of Simone De Beauvoir's *The Second Sex* appeared in 1961 and, especially among certain Milanese feminists, there was much interest in the work of French psychologist Luce Irigaray, who focused, among other things, on the mother–daughter relationship and a critique of Freud.

Italian feminism was not, however, just a carbon copy of foreign movements but had its own national characteristics. Few Italian feminists, for example, shared the aims of the National Organization of Women (NOW), an important part of the US movement. As Yasmine Ergas has commented, 'the closest Italian equivalent of NOW' was UDI, not feminism.[3]

An early sign of what was to come was the foundation in 1966 of Demau (Demistificazione Autoritarismo). This Milanese women's group (although men attended some of its meetings) was the first to call for a new analysis of women's role in society. It was anti-authoritarian and challenged traditional gender roles for both sexes. Its *Manifesto* of 1966 called for, 'opposition to the concept of integrating women into the current society', essentially an attack on UDI-style politics.[4] Demau's ideas were, however, different from those soon to come since, as Aida Ribero argues, they wanted, 'to overcome the idea of "masculine" and "feminine" . . . and build a society where values common to both sexes would prevail'.[5]

Demau, although important evidence that new ideas about gender roles pre-date 1968, was just a small group. Far greater numbers rallied to feminism through the student movement of 1968. Almost a third of the half a million students enrolled at Italian universities in 1968 were female. The student movement was important because of its critique of authoritarian ideas (including the 'authoritarian family'), its call for greater sexual freedoms and its iconoclastic belief that everything should be challenged and questioned.

As in other Western countries many Italian women first became politicised through the sit-ins and mass debates of the student movement, then rebelled against it. They were often sidelined in meetings by more confident men and many male radicals had far from enlightened views about women. In a famous phrase reputedly coined at Trent University, female students were frequently relegated to being *angeli del ciclostile* ('roneo angels').

Women, moreover, found themselves picking up the pieces for the new sexual freedoms. Traditional notions of respectability and honour were swept aside in the student movement. For some this was liberating. For others it was confusing and frightening. Moreover, Fascist anti-contraception laws were still in force. Although some chemists did sell the recently invented Pill (ostensibly as a 'remedy for menstrual disorders'), generally contraception was not freely available. The 'sexual revolution' for many young women ended with a visit to a backstreet abortionist, a sobering event that led them to question the values of their male 'comrades'.

Equality/sameness or difference

Although the ferment of ideas that was Italian feminism was often contradictory, some shared beliefs can be identified.[6] Many Italian feminists rejected the idea of sameness between the sexes and the notion that differences were primarily caused by nurture, not nature. They, instead (like certain intellectual strands of French feminism, in particular the group Psychanalyse et Politique), focused more on the idea of essential differences between the sexes, what they called *differenza sessuale* (sexual difference). They criticised the idea that men were seen as the norm and women as the 'other'. For them, legal, formal equality, although desirable, was not enough. The Italian word *uguaglianza* means both sameness and equality and it was the sameness dimension they rejected. Women, they believed, should not just be added on to the male world, on men's terms, but seek their own identity. The Cerchio Spezzato group of Trent, for example, argued in 1971 that feminists needed to avoid 'the error of mistaking this society for the only one possible, and therefore aiming for equality with men'.[7] The 'Manifesto of Rivolta Femminile' (sometimes described as the founding document of Italian feminism[8]), which was posted in the streets of Rome and published in 1970, expressed this as follows: 'Women must not be defined in relation to men. Consciousness of this underpins both our struggle and our freedom. Man is not the model to be aspired to in women's process of self-discovery. . . . Equality is an ideological attempt to enslave women further.'[9] It ended with, 'we communicate only with women'.

Like other Western feminists, Italian feminists believed that 'the personal is political' and focused on 'private sphere' issues like sexuality, health, gender roles in the family and the transformation of everyday social relations. They wanted greater control of their own bodies, challenging the power of the medical profession and the Church. They advocated contraception and new attitudes to sexuality and opposed violence against women. All these were issues that the traditional Left had sorely neglected. Nonetheless, most, influenced by the strength of class politics in Italy, were anti-capitalist. Some wrote in language with more of a Marxist tinge than in many Western countries, whilst at the same time adopting a denunciatory tone towards the organised Left. Feminist groups varied regionally in this respect: in cities like Turin where the Left was strong, there was most attention to class issues.

One group in particular, Lotta Femminista (founded in Padua in 1971, primarily by former members of the New Left group Potere Operaio and quickly spreading to seven other cities), applied Marxist categories to the role of women. They called for 'wages for housework' and for prostitutes' rights. Most feminists, however, saw economic issues as only one aspect of women's oppression. Liberation had to come in all spheres of life. Most, moreover, rejected the wages for housework idea as one that would trap women in the home.

Organisational questions

Feminists opposed what they considered traditional, hierarchical politics and called for all structures and ways of organising to be rethought. They scorned structures *per se* as male. Rather than attempting to gain the support of male politicians, they lambasted them. They rejected compromise and diplomacy, and the perhaps less radical, but far from ineffective, approach of organisations like UDI. This freed them up considerably whilst at the same time weakening their political impact. They formed no political parties and positioned themselves outside the existing political system.

Instead there was a shifting panorama of hundreds (at times, thousands) of 'collectives' of varying size, often locally orientated. These lacked presidents, constitutions, or any kind of unified national structure (although some, like Rivolta Femminile, had loosely connected member groups in different cities). They varied in size and were often very informal with fluid, shifting memberships. In Turin, for example, 'groups grew, fell apart, reformed, engendered new ways of being, sought homogenisation, fought, clashed and fragmented. This led to schisms, anathemas, heresies, trials and mutual accusations'.[10]

Some groups were bigger, such as the Movimento di Liberazione della Donna (MLD – Movement for the Liberation of Women), which was particularly active in the abortion campaign. Founded in 1970 in Rome, it was affiliated with the Radical Party (and therefore had a greater focus on legislative change than other groups). Unlike other groups it developed a nation-wide network with a national secretariat.

Until 1975, the MLD was mixed, but the other groups were separatist from the start and rejected links with political parties. True autonomy, to enable women to formulate their own demands without male interference, was deemed essential in this period of identity politics, as was the creation and defence of women-only spaces, like women's centres. Autonomy was, of course, a demand of other Western feminisms but in Italy it had particular resonance given the pervasive dominance of political parties in preceding decades. Many women felt more 'at home' in women-only groups. One recalled: 'I wasn't happy in the mixed groups. I definitely wasn't a roneo angel, but neither was I the sort to learn the language, it was as if I was always trying to say the unsayable . . . so I felt really uncomfortable, whereas with women it felt as if all these unsaid things were the starting point for discussion.'[11]

The first collectives emerged in 1969–71. The earliest included Rivolta Femminile (in Milan and Rome, founded by the art historian Carla Lonzi and the first to use consciousness-raising in Italy), Anabasi (Milan), Lotta Femminista (Padua and Rome) and the student group Il Cerchio Spezzato (Trent). Numerous others emerged too, far too many to list here. The better-known ones included the Col di Lana in Milan and the Collettivo Femminista Romano (later called Pompeo Magno). Some were founded by individuals, others by students or former members of New Left parties. They met in private houses or 'women's centres', some of them squats. Although the movement was fragmented, there was much interaction between different groups. In Milan, for example, many groups used the women's centre in Via Cherubini in the early 1970s. Ideas also circulated through magazines and through national meetings like the conference held at Paestum in 1976 (with 1,500 participants).

Many feminists focused only on 'internal aims', dismissing legislative change as peripheral. Such ideological purists, however, were only part of the movement, which always included both those who were only interested in women-only events and exploring women's subjectivity and those who sought to influence the wider world. The 'external' focus tended to grow from the mid-1970s although even then the movement remained diverse. Moreover, as Adler Hellman notes, 'The conflict over external *vs* internal activities – in practice . . . often meant a split between feminists who wished to pursue *both* and those who wanted to focus exclusively on consciousness-raising.'[12]

Some groups concentrated on single issues, like abortion, health self-help or film-making. Feminists also created radio stations, theatre groups and clinics (*consultori*). They produced a good deal of writing, often of an unconventional type, mingling, for example, theoretical ideas with autobiography. A feminist press emerged, notably the magazines *Effè* (whose first editor was Gabriella Parca) and *Quotidiano donna* and the more intellectual *Sottosopra*. There were feminist publishing houses, like Edizioni delle Donne and La Tartaruga, and bookshops, the first opening in Milan in 1975, which, in addition to selling works by female authors, became centres for intellectual activity.

Italian feminism, like other Western feminisms, adopted the practice of consciousness-raising (although the Italian term *autocoscienza* better translates as 'self-awareness'). *Autocoscienza* groups met to discuss how they felt about being women. Here, the political was positioned at the most personal level. The idea was that women, by sharing their innermost thoughts in leaderless, small groups, could discover their own identities and put together a new vision of the world (in order to change it). They sought ideas not in the writings of philosophers or politicians but within themselves. As one woman wrote in 1980, 'consciousness-raising enables a great process of collective identity, extraordinarily synchronised all over Italy. It is quite astonishing how, after spending months in collectives or little groups, when we met in national meetings we found that we'd all understood the same things, we'd gone over similar ground.'[13] For many involved, *autocoscienza* was a life-changing experience. One recalled: 'For me, it was the start of political activity in which, for the first time, I really felt like a protagonist. . . . Each of us said something and whatever we said, large or small, was considered important: I thought it was magnificent! Unique. A unique experience.'[14] Not all experiences, however, were positive. Some women had to see therapists afterwards to deal with unresolved issues that had been raised and some *autocoscienza* groups fell out with each other. Many were fairly short-lived.

Most feminists were young, although a few older women did get involved (Lonzi, for example, was born in 1931), and, according to Passerini, they were predominantly middle class or lower middle class.[15] They did, however, try to reach out to working-class women by, for example, setting up health centres in poor neighbourhoods, and the class and age range of the movement was widened by the involvement of some UDI and trade union women (see below). Because of the movement's anarchic structure, it is difficult to estimate numbers involved. Some indicators exist. *Effe* had a circulation of 50,000[16] and in 1974 there were over a hundred groups in sixty Italian cities.[17] This suggests tens, or at most, hundreds of thousands of activists. Greatest numbers were to be found in large cities, university towns and in the North and Centre. Feminism faced particular challenges in the South (although Naples had a thriving movement). Generally public political space in the South was quite restricted and less than welcoming to women. In Caserta, for example, in the PCI local headquarters: 'If a woman walks through the door, the men look up and wait for her to state her business and leave.'[18] In Caserta feminists were spat at in the streets.[19]

The movement was fluid and constantly changing. Often the same women were involved in various campaigns and groups, or one group was involved in many different campaigns. Because it was so diverse, it could be argued that 1970s feminism was in fact many feminisms. Nonetheless, it did not fracture along ideological lines as occurred in some Western countries. This was partly because abortion, around which large numbers mobilised, helped hold the movement together. It was also because Italy was still a fairly ethnically homogeneous society and the challenge to feminist ideas of 'sisterhood', which came from black women in America, did not surface here until the 1990s.

Some lesbians 'came out' as a result of both feminism and the appearance of Fuori! (Out!), a gay rights organisation. Fuori!, however, was very male dominated and lesbians active in the women's movement often found little acceptance among heterosexual feminists. A handful of previously heterosexual feminists dabbled with lesbianism as a political act, to 'free themselves from male power', but few chose this path and overall, lesbianism was much less visible in the Italian movement than in some other Western feminisms. As Bianca Maria Pomeranzi remembered, when giving a speech at a large feminist conference in 1976: 'I began by saying "I'm a provincial lesbian" and I myself was astonished by the complete silence that followed this statement.'[20] The feminist press, such as *Quotidiano donna* and *Effe*, only began to pay attention to lesbians at the end of the decade and it was then that lesbians themselves began to organise. Nonetheless, the 1970s offered a more favourable climate for Italian lesbians to live their lives freely than previous decades.

Feminism and other political organisations

As the fascinating research by social anthropologist Judith Adler Hellman has shown, the way feminism manifested itself varied regionally depending on the local political situation. In some areas feminist politics took place mainly in autonomous collectives. Elsewhere much activity was expressed through a revitalised, newly 'feminist', UDI.[21]

There were also new trade union groups (this was a decade of union strength after the 'hot autumn' of 1969) which operated in ways similar to feminist collectives. This movement started in Turin with the founding, in 1975, despite the opposition of many male trade unionists, of a 'CGIL–CISL–UIL Women's Intercategory Co-ordinating Group', which bridged the three main union federations. This idea spread, although inter-union and cross-sector co-operation was not achievable everywhere. The early members often included women with experience of feminist collectives outside the unions. Those involved were often from white-collar occupations rather than manual workers.[22] Meetings were run in ways influenced by consciousness-raising. The groups tried to pressurise the unions to prioritise demands which could improve women's position in the workplace ranging from equality in hiring practices to the provision of workplace nurseries. But they also wanted to change the culture of the unions themselves. As 'Alessandra' remembered,

> when I said I wanted to make the union feminist, I really meant that everything needed to be changed, how we did politics, what we campaigned about, the relationships between people, from the largest to the smallest things, from how we elected leaders to how we treated the female clerks employed by the union.[23]

There were even attempts to get unions to champion feminist causes like abortion. This period did see some increased openness to the needs of women in many unions although at the end of the decade they remained male dominated.

Feminist influence spread through the '150 Hours' initiative (originally won by the metalworkers' union, then extended to other categories), which allowed employed persons to take paid time off for study purposes. Among the courses established on this programme were women's studies courses (often focusing on health questions) aimed at raising women workers' consciousness. Such courses, which were particularly numerous in Milan and Turin, became a site of encounter between feminists from the collectives, university lecturers, factory workers, outworkers, white-collar workers and housewives.[24]

Feminists attacked the established parties vigorously for their 'patriarchal' ideology and structures. Most political parties, in turn, initially rejected them.[25] Indeed, as Dau Novelli has noted, 'many of the demands were effectively inconceivable for the world of traditional politics, because they were about private matters, linked to the personal, familial and sexual sphere'.[26] Tina Magnano remembered that, when she gave an impromptu speech at a left-wing meeting in Bologna in 1972, most of those present were shocked: 'I was using a completely different type of language from traditional speakers. I was like a kind of sibyl, but as such I suffered a lot, particularly when I talked about giving birth. The people listening were speechless. It was a painful and exciting experience.'[27]

The small libertarian Radical Party was the only one to fully embrace feminism (rallying to it quickly, with a women's discussion group from 1970), although the Socialists did have some links to the MLD. The DC opposed it. In turn, feminists were highly critical of both the DC and CIF. The relationship with the extra-parliamentary New Left, spawned by the movements of 1968 when they tried to reach out beyond universities to the 'working class', was more complex. Initially a good number of feminists were active in these groups. Practising the uncomfortable choice of 'dual militancy', they sought an alliance, or at least dialogue, between the two movements. Some preferred the activism of these groups to the intense personal approach of consciousness-raising although many who started in the New Left did eventually leave it for feminist politics. By the mid-1970s the New Left had abandoned some of the more creative ideas that had emerged from 1968 in favour of a strictly Marxist–Leninist approach aimed at communist revolution. This was not particularly compatible with feminism. Tension erupted on various occasions, most famously in 1975 at an abortion rally attended by about 20,000 women. There was a clash between the marchers and the marshals of the Lotta Continua group who, incensed by the idea of an all-female demonstration, attacked and beat some of the women. This event helped contribute to the dissolution of Lotta Continua the following year.

Often the feminists' most vitriolic criticisms were directed at the PCI, arguing that the party's campaign for formal rights was useless without change in the private sphere. The Communists, particularly reluctant to challenge Catholic ideas on the family in this period of the 'historic compromise' when they were attempting to go into government with the DC, responded defensively. They dismissed feminism as a bourgeois irrelevance, composed of strident, wrongheaded students and intellectuals. PCI theorist Luciano Gruppi, for example, wrote in 1973 that:

> Far from engaging in practical politics, a typical characteristic of these movements is an existential experience that reaches the doorstep of politics without really penetrating inside. Since it is the personal that prevails . . . the basis of these movements is too individualistic to bring about awareness of the need for a mass movement.[28]

However, because feminism proved strong, even the Communists eventually adopted some feminist ideas and, particularly from the end of the 1970s when the 'historic compromise' dream had faded, PCI conferences increasingly began to discuss issues like contraception and the sexual division of labour in the home. But the PCI's adoption of feminist positions often meant modifying them. They did, for example, support divorce but in the name of strengthening the family (to enable separated persons to remarry). Similarly, abortion was considered a class issue because (they argued) rich women had it already in clinics abroad. Some female members of the PCI and PSI practised their own 'dual militancy', frequenting both feminist collectives and their respective parties. Unlike women in the New Left, PCI women tended not to abandon their party, instead remaining to try to change it.[29]

UDI was fiercely attacked, branded a lackey of the PCI. UDI was by now considerably smaller than in its heyday, although it was still strong in the 'red belt', with, for example, 10,000 members in Reggio Emilia. In the huge cities of Milan and Turin, by contrast, there were only 1,000 and 200 members respectively.[30] The feminists counterposed their ideas ('liberation') with UDI's ('emancipationism'), which they dismissed as dull reformism, aiming only for formal equality and no challenge to power structures in the private sphere. For feminists, the term 'emancipationism' was an insult. Emancipationists, they argued, just wanted to add women to existing institutions and organisations, without changing them, whereas 'liberation' was presented as a positive, revolutionary concept, with the potential both to enhance the position of women and to transform the world. UDI initially rebuffed feminist attacks angrily and with good reason since, although there was some truth in the feminist critique, it most unfairly ignored UDI's considerable achievements.

In some ways this was a generational conflict. As Anna Rossi-Doria has commented, the counterposing of 'liberation' and 'emancipation' was not always as clear-cut as it might seem, for 'we fought against *uguaglianza* not for its own sake but because it had been in particular the banner of the mothers (UDI)'.[31] Similarly, as Rosangela Pesenti has argued, many older UDI members felt threatened by the behaviour of young feminists demanding freedoms that they themselves had been denied.[32] One older *udina* remembered, 'We were shocked when we first saw the feminists, with their crude gestures and their rude language.'[33]

Eventually, however, the hostility waned. Once UDI became active in the abortion campaign (adopting a decidedly more radical stance than the PCI on this issue), this helped bridge the gap with the younger feminists. The change was reciprocal as, in the mid-1970s, some feminists themselves became more interested in legislative reform, UDI's traditional sphere of operations. In 1976, for the first time, UDI and feminists marched together for abortion rights. UDI was gradually rejuvenated by an injection of new ideas and its meetings became less formal. In some areas there was an influx of new, younger members and even some of the older members gradually came to embrace the new politics. By the end of the 1970s, UDI had effectively become a 'feminist' organisation, complementing the work of the radical younger women with its long experience of political lobbying. In some towns feminist collectives even used UDI premises for their meetings.

The 'feministisation' process went one step further when, in 1982 at its XIth Congress, UDI amended its Constitution to dismantle its hierarchical structure. The national leaders all resigned and the mass organisation (200,000 card-carrying members and 30 paid officials[34]) vanished overnight, replaced by local initiatives with little central co-ordination. Not all *udine* embraced the change. Some later believed that it was a mistake. Giovanna Azzini, for example, recently commented that at the time she had been excited by 'this UDI, so ready to change' but now felt that: 'We maybe didn't understand that . . . the structure that held it together didn't enslave us: it was a structure that could be useful, a tool that we abolished quickly.'[35] In areas where UDI had had only a small presence, like strongly Catholic areas and the South, it more or less vanished.

CIF proved less open to change. This was a period of crisis for organised Catholic women with the AC women's sections recently merged into mixed groups and CIF's membership in decline. CIF was not totally out of step with the times, supporting, for example, some of the legal reforms of the decade, but the more radical campaigns were a direct challenge to everything it stood for. Abortion rights were denounced as simply pandering to male sexuality and part of the 'permissive society'. CIF's timid approach to emancipation seemed old-fashioned in the 1970s. Younger Catholics inspired by feminism tended not to join what had become largely a group of Catholic matrons, and sought other ways to reconcile religious faith with the new ideas. In politically 'white' areas like Verona, some women came to feminism via participation in radical Catholic groups.[36] Some, like the theologian Adriana Zarri, combined feminism with a dissident Catholic perspective.[37] But Catholic women were not overall a strong voice in this decade of great challenge to the Church's authority (although, of course, some feminists did retain some kind of personal religious belief, whilst still challenging aspects of Church teachings). It is worth noting, nonetheless, that CIF, like UDI, survived. Both still exist today.

Despite feminist attacks on political parties, women continued to join them. In 1975, women comprised 23.5 per cent of PCI party membership and 37.5 per cent of the DC: little different, therefore, from in previous decades.[38] In terms of voting behaviour, however, some research suggests that female support for the DC was finally waning, and rising for the PCI.[39] Despite the hostility of some feminists to any form of institution, in 1976 feminism gained an official channel for their views with the foundation of the Consulte Femminili (women's consultative committees), whose role was to advise local and central government on women's issues. Some (although not all) proved quite effective.[40]

Legal reform

There was considerable legal reform in this decade. Much was long overdue. Italy's ineffective political system meant that society had changed more than legislation. Feminists were important in setting the agenda and posing the questions that made reform seem important, although they were poor political strategists. They rarely did practical things like draft laws and their suspicion of organised politics made the idea of lobbying problematic. Many marched and demonstrated in support of legal reforms but some scorned the idea of influencing 'male institutions' like parliament. In the case of some of the new legislation, like the maternity law of 1971, it was UDI and trade unions, not feminist groups, who pushed most effectively for change.

Divorce was legalised in 1970. Despite parliamentary delays and Vatican pressure, it passed by a narrow margin (319 votes for and 286 against), opposed only by the DC, the Monarchists and neo-fascists. The actual legislation (originating in a bill presented by Socialist deputy Loris Fortuna in 1965) permitted divorce on grounds of criminal insanity, long prison sentences, crimes of sexual violence, incest and the remarriage abroad of a non-Italian spouse. More significantly, after a five-year separation, any couple could divorce. The DC attempted to abrogate the law by sponsoring a referendum in 1974 but, after much public debate, 59.3 per cent of the electorate voted to keep divorce, thereby demonstrating that public opinion was less influenced by the Vatican than many had thought. This was a sharp dose of reality for the PCI who, believing the 'masses' opposed to it, had provided only luke-warm, ambivalent support to the campaign. The referendum greatly encouraged those who wanted more reform. Now Catholic opposition no longer seemed an insurmountable barrier. The campaign garnered support from some surprising quarters. Even some far from feminist women's magazines like *Grand Hotel* and *Annabella* took a pro-divorce stance.

Numerous other important reforms were passed in this period. In 1971, improvements to the maternity legislation of 1950 were introduced, including extending protection to home workers. The length of maternity leave was increased and mothers could also take unpaid time off if a child under three was ill. 1971 also saw the repeal of the Fascist anti-contraception legislation. The same year, a federally-funded national nursery school system was introduced, something that was much needed given that, at the time, there was only one nursery place per 52,800 residents in Milan and one per 236,000 in Naples.[41] In 1973, legislation regulating outworkers was extended to the self-employed and in 1975 family health clinics, whose role included contraceptive advice, were introduced.

1975 saw the long awaited (UDI had been lobbying for it for ten years) rewriting of the Civil Code, finally abolishing virtually all remaining inequalities. The reform (discussed over three legislatures) was supported by all political parties except the Liberals and neo-fascists. Men and women now became equals in marriage. Men were no longer seen as heads of family. Women no longer had to obtain their husband's permission to obtain a passport, nor did they have to take his name or reside where he decreed. Property was now held in common by both partners (unless they made other arrangements). Dowries were outlawed. Women who married foreigners could retain Italian citizenship. Both parents shared responsibility for taking decisions for their children. Where they disagreed, judicial intervention could be requested. This legislation also gave illegitimate children the same legal rights as children born within marriage. A few inequalities remained. Children still today automatically take their father's name and women add their husband's surname to their own whilst his name remains unchanged.

Another milestone was the 1977 Parity Law (in practice less a product of feminism than of the need to comply with EC Directive 207, of 1976), outlawing sex discrimination in employment and finally ending the long tradition of 'protective legislation'. It covered recruitment, promotions, pensions, training and dismissals. Paternity leave was introduced, including making it possible for a father (instead of the mother) to be the one to take time off if their child was ill. Overall the Parity Law was good on principles but weak on implementation. There was, for example, no real compensation for women who won discrimination cases. They just got their job back, which was not necessarily the ideal solution. Many complainants gave up. Few men in practice took advantage of paternity leave. Nonetheless, this legislation had great symbolic importance, even if it did not always work perfectly. In some cases, moreover, it did open up new jobs for women. In the two years after the law was passed, half of the 17,000 new staff taken on by Fiat in Turin were female.[42]

Abortion

The hardest fought battle was about abortion rights. Abortion posed a deep challenge to Church authority and dramatically brought into the public sphere, through demonstrations and civil disobedience, issues not previously considered political. For many feminists it became a symbol of the political nature of reproduction. Of course abortion was a core issue in other Western feminisms but the call for legalisation had great resonance in Italy because access to contraception was so limited. Even the Ministry of Health estimated the number of illegal terminations at 850,000 per annum. Some argued that it was nearer three million, leading to the death of 20,000 women every year. Many women had a series of terminations over the course of their lives. Unlike many of the other legislative changes, for which UDI had been calling for some time, this campaign was initiated by the feminist movement.

It began in 1971 when the MLD started gathering signatures for a petition to decriminalise abortion, but really took off after the divorce referendum. Feminists had played only a minor role in the divorce campaign, but they were deeply involved in the abortion issue. Their pro-choice campaign sparked an enormous debate, during which many viewpoints were aired. Because of the influence of the Church, all the main political parties opposed legalisation. Even the PCI initially opposed it but then (somewhat reluctantly) rallied to it. The PCI's first abortion bill in 1975 called for abortion free of charge in state facilities, but only for women whose life or health was endangered by the pregnancy, for pregnancies resulting from rape or incest, or where there was serious genetic deformity. Although the PCI did subsequently move closer to feminist ideas, gradually giving in to pressure from female party members, it never truly embraced the idea of a 'woman's right to choose'. The DC was deeply opposed and only the small Radical Party fully championed the pro-choice stance. UDI rallied to the campaign (and this, essentially, was the issue on which UDI at last broke free of the PCI). CIF opposed it.

Feminists (although often divided on questions of approach and tactics, and as individuals sometimes personally troubled about the issue) campaigned vigorously. Some opted for civil disobedience in self-help groups, performing abortions (by the Karman method) or running courier services to clinics

Illustration 9   Abortion demonstration, c. 1975. The placard reads 'Free abortion to avoid dying. Contraceptives to avoid abortions.'
(Reproduced courtesy of Fototeca Storica Nazionale Ando Gilardi.)

abroad. The largest and best organised of these groups were CISA (Centro Italiano per la Sterilizzazione e l'Aborto), linked to the MLD, and CRAC (Comitato Romano per l'Aborto e la Contraccezione). According to Lesley Caldwell, on occasion, CISA betrayed women's trust by tipping off the police so that arrests of women about to abort would help publicise the cause.[43]

Feminists campaigned for free abortion on demand, provided in state medical facilities, with women, not husbands, parents or doctors, taking the decision. They wanted abortion even in quite advanced stages of pregnancy (although this was controversial within the movement itself, as was the age limit for girls seeking abortions). Their campaign was hard-fought but poorly organised, with their interventions often taking little account of the parliamentary timetable. Some feminists simply rejected the campaign, because, as Buttafuoco noted, 'they felt that abortion actually reinforced a concept of genital reproductive sexuality dominated by men, and perpetuated male supremacy'.[44] For them, winning abortion rights was less important than trying to redefine women's sexuality overall.

In 1973, Loris Fortuna presented a moderate bill to legalise abortion for women whose mental or physical health was seriously threatened. There was also a submission made to the Constitutional Court to have the law reinterpreted, and signatures were collected for a referendum. In January 1975 the Constitutional Court legalised therapeutic abortions. After this, various parliamentary parties realised that more reform was possible and presented their own bills. By the end of 1975 a combined bill had been approved by the Senate, but then elections meant that the process had to start afresh. Three years (and nine further bills) later, in June 1978, the law was finally passed. This slow, tortuous progress was often due to delaying tactics by the DC and neo-fascists. The Church spoke out against abortion and there were pro-legalisation demonstrations of about 20,000 women in 1975 and 50,000–100,000 in 1976. About 800,000 people signed a petition calling for a referendum to legalise abortion.

The actual law that was passed (Law 194, 22 May 1978), the result of much bargaining between political parties, fell so far short of feminist demands that the Radicals voted against it. The failure of the PCI to take a radical position and the influence of the DC both help explain its final shape. It permitted state-financed abortions for women in the first 90 days of pregnancy. Private abortions remained illegal. The pregnancy or birth had to be deemed damaging to the woman's physical or mental health, taking into account her economic, social and familial situation and the circumstances in which conception took place (such as rape). Malformation of the foetus was also grounds for termination. In most cases women had to wait for seven days of reflection before going ahead. Only therapeutic abortion was permitted after the 90-day limit. Girls under 18 needed parental consent. The father of the foetus was only consulted if the pregnant woman wished. Medical staff could register as 'conscientious objectors'. So many did so (72 per cent of all doctors by 1979), particularly in the South and Catholic North-east, that backstreet abortion continued (sometimes performed by unscrupulous doctors officially registered as 'conscientious objectors').

The story was not yet over. The law's opponents sought to overturn it by referendum in 1981 but they suffered a crushing defeat: 67.5 per cent of the electorate voted to keep abortion legal. As Catholic historian Paola Gaiotti de Biase has argued, this was evidence of the Church's failure to understand some of the problems of its own faithful. She cites the fact that in some mountain areas inhabited mainly by the elderly and where the DC regularly won 70 per cent of votes at elections, only 50 per cent voted against abortion.[45] Clearly even many DC voters understood the horrors of illegal termination. Most Italians did not, however, want to go further. A simultaneous referendum sponsored by the Radicals for a much more liberal law was rejected by 88.5 per cent.

'Sexual violence'

Rape was a big problem (high levels were reported, probably far more went unreported) and changing social mores offered rapists more opportunities now that women moved around more freely. A feminist campaign, fuelled by a dramatic trial in 1976 of four rapists, one of whose victims, Rosaria Lopez, had died, was launched with demonstrations and *riprendiamoci la notte* ('reclaim the night') marches. Also influential were the publication of *Le violentate* by Maria Adele Teodori and an Italian edition of Susan Brownmiller's *Against Our Will* in 1976.

In this campaign feminists did, at last, intervene in a more organised fashion. In 1977 the MLD set up a short-lived 'rape crisis centre' in Rome. Then a committee of representatives from various women's organisations, including UDI, got together to draft a 'popular initiative bill'. This called for the redefinition of rape as a crime against the person rather than against morality and for the prosecution of marital rape. To be debated in parliament, such bills need 50,000 signatories. The feminist bill, presented in 1980, had 300,000. This potentially effective approach, a new one for the women's movement, was criticised by some feminists as offensive to their purist ideals, which rejected the 'mediations' of laws and the idea of 'delegation' (the notion that a committee could represent other women). They believed that each woman could represent only herself.[46] Some were also unhappy with the idea of allowing the state to prosecute even if the victim herself did not press charges. This, they argued, robbed women of 'self-determination'.

The law on sexual violence took many years to successfully pass through parliament. In one of the reversals, in 1983, when DC opposition prevented its passage, an estimated 50,000 women took to the streets in protest. One related reform, of particular importance to Southern women, was enacted more quickly. From 1981, 'honour' was no longer accepted as a legitimate cause for leniency in sentencing for crimes of violence (including murder), and the barbaric practice of 'reparatory marriage', whereby a rapist could be absolved by marrying his victim, was outlawed. 'Crimes of honour' became rare after this but did not totally vanish. Between 1982 and 1987, for example, one mafioso killed five people, including his own sister-in-law, because he felt dishonoured by their promiscuity.[47]

The decline of feminism as a movement

In the late 1970s, the feminist movement began to decline. To an extent this was simply part of the broader *riflusso* (ebb) of all the new political movements. The broader movement was at least in part destroyed by the meltdown of sections of the New Left into terrorism. Feminists did not flood into terrorism although some research shows that in 'red' terrorist organisations some of the leaders and about a quarter of the members were female. Over half (52 per cent) of these actively took part in armed actions (compared with 62 per cent of male terrorists).[48] Feminists were divided on the question of terrorist women. Although many condemned them, others saw them as women who had broken the mould. Some female terrorists had previously been involved in the women's movement. Others scorned it. Giancarla Ceppi (interviewed 1986), for example, remembered: 'I decided to go to the square to see the women who were "reclaiming the night" and they were dancing and singing songs that were alien to me. I felt a sudden wave of anger: everything I saw was inadequate and inconsistent.'[49] A few acts of violence were carried out in the name of feminism, like an attack on a Turinese gynaecologist who was said to have caused the death of a patient, but such actions were all the work of terrorists, not feminist collectives.

By this time, many feminists were exhausted. It was hard to sustain such a high level of political commitment, particularly with such anarchic forms of organising.[50] The absence of official leaders did not prevent unofficial ones. Without formal structures, meetings could be dominated by a few, a few who were not accountable like elected leaders. Less confident women found it hard to make their voices heard. Many left because they were disillusioned. Groups often fell out among themselves. The assumption that all women somehow had unified aims just because they were women, and that they would all get on, was at best naive and unrealistic, and the failure to develop mechanisms for conflict resolution was highly problematic. As Loretta Montemaggi (born 1930), a Florentine PCI activist, wryly commented, the young feminists had an idealistic view of human nature, for conflict was normal. As she put it: 'they seemed like little nuns'.[51] Feminists failed to acknowledge diversity, in particular, class differences and inequalities of levels of education, preferring instead to paper over the differences between rich and poor, mothers and non-mothers, heterosexuals and lesbians and so on. The very structure of feminism, with many small, often close-knit groups, made it hard to incorporate new members.

The rejection of 'mediations' of women's experiences meant little editing. First-hand-experience accounts were published without comment and this could render accounts of meetings incoherent or unreadably lengthy. This made it easy for a few intellectuals to emerge as spokeswomen, talking personally to the media, and in practice often a few well-educated, confident women wrote the documents supposedly authored collectively. Moreover, as Adler Hellman has aptly noted, although feminists did discuss language and power (seeing men as using language to dominate), they failed to critique Italian traditions of over-intellectual language or fight for the need for clear communication.[52]

Feminist political practice was also time-consuming. Nothing was delegated and everything endlessly discussed. The absence of formal rules (considered 'masculine') or chairs could make meetings directionless. It was difficult to reach a conclusion when all views were equally valid. Some groups collapsed from exhaustion. Success could also render groups obsolete. Feminists called on the state to provide women's clinics but once it did so (albeit as 'family clinics') women's autonomous clinics were sidelined. Similarly, legal abortion took over from self-help initiatives (although some feminists did become active in campaigns to ensure implementation of the law by, for example, denouncing fake 'conscientious objectors' who performed private abortions on the side).

For those involved in this intense period, the experience was a life-changing one. But some just ended up embarking on personal journeys, probing their inner psyches and abandoning attempts to influence formal politics in any way. Some active in trade union groups, for example, rather than continuing to fight to change their union or workplace, left their jobs. Now their horizons were broadened, they sought pastures new.

Feminism: a balance sheet

Utopian rather than practical, the movement of the 1970s greatly advanced thinking about gender roles but there were limitations to its achievements. Although a vast raft of legislation was passed (as in many other countries in this period), some of it was not the best. Both the divorce and abortion laws were moderate, passed to ward off campaigns for more radical legislation. For example, the time limit within which pregnant women had to make up their minds and then find a doctor who was not a conscientious objector was so short that not all who sought them managed to obtain legal abortions. The Parity Law, although good on paper, lacked teeth. Pay inequalities persisted because of the gendered structure of the labour market, and the central questions of childcare and housework were far from resolved. Belittling representations of women persisted in the media (an issue to which Italian feminists paid far too little attention). Even feminist ideology, focusing on 'difference', was not unproblematic. It ran the risk of reinforcing traditional gender roles and it could lead to women simply withdrawing from the general struggle to a safe, reserved space where they discussed 'women's issues' while men continued to rule Italy.

Another problem was that feminists tended to prioritise questions primarily of interest to younger women. As one *udina* from Reggio Emilia commented: 'The younger women . . . understand "sexuality" and "women's health" in terms of their own needs. Issues like rheumatism and menopause are not discussed.'[53] Moreover, feminists seemed more interested in exploring the theme of mothers as symbolic figures, or the difficulties faced by rebellious young feminists in their relationships with their own mothers, than in the problems faced by real mothers themselves. As Passerini has commented, 'the movement of the 1970s was critical of or said little about maternity, and behaved dreadfully towards mothers',[54] certainly a huge change from earlier emancipationists, for whom maternity had been a core issue.

This decade saw some 'firsts' in the world of politics, including the first female cabinet minister, Tina Anselmi (DC), who became Minister of Labour in 1976, and, three years later, the first female president of the Chamber of Deputies, the veteran Communist Nilde Jotti. At the end of the 1970s the number of female deputies in the Chamber of Deputies reached an all-time high. However, this meant only a modest 8.6 per cent and, overall, Italian politics was far from remade in a feminist mould.

By the end of this decade, moreover, many women were still in poor employment. The 1970s did see a reversal of the long downward trend (lasting most of the twentieth century) in female employment. This began to rise in 1971, particularly in the 25 to 35 age group: 1,247,000 of the one and a half million persons newly employed in 1972–80 were women.[55] Feminism was one reason for this: it expanded female horizons and gave women who wanted to work, particularly younger women, the confidence and language to assert their desire to do so. The increase was also due to growth in the tertiary sector, typical of advanced economies, which was increasingly open to women as their educational level rose. Clerical work became increasingly feminised as married women joined the unmarried in the expanding public sector where the timetable was usually fairly compatible with childcare. By 1974, 44 per cent of public-sector white-collar employees were female. They were still mainly clustered in the lower grades but some were beginning to rise up the ranks. The expansion of social services in this decade, such as the new national nursery provisions, also created employment opportunities.

In practice, however, there was often a gulf between the utopian dreams of the feminists and the working lives of many women. As white-collar work became more feminised, for example, it was increasingly 'proletarianised'. Official figures, moreover, give only a partial picture. By 1978, the official participation rate for women in the labour force had reached 24.5 per cent (compared with 54.1 per cent for men). Some research, however, suggests that 10–15 per cent of those officially recorded as 'housewives' in the mid-1970s were in fact employed in the unofficial 'black economy'.[56] This was the period of the rapid growth of the 'Third Italy', the industrial districts of north-eastern and central Italy, dominated by small, mainly family firms and often producing for an international market. Although crucial to economic success and making these areas some of the richest in Italy, such firms frequently offered the many women they employed only precarious, uninsured, low-waged jobs, beyond the reach of trade unions or legislative improvements like the Parity Law. In the same period, many larger firms were beginning to decentralise some of their production (mainly to evade the high cost of labour and extensive regulation of the labour market due to union gains after the 'hot autumn', such as the Statuto dei Lavoratori of 1970), thereby further increasing the growth of small manufacturing units. One estimate put numbers of those in off-the-books manufacturing at 3,745,000 by the end of the 1970s, of whom about 60 per cent were female.[57]

Nonetheless, the 1970s were crucial years for the history of gender relations in Italy. Even if some of the legal reform was not perfect, overall it represented a huge advance for women. On paper at least, they now had equality in both the workplace and the family. They had access to contraception and the abortion legislation drastically reduced deaths from backstreet terminations. Many private-sphere issues had been put on the political agenda for the first time, providing a serious challenge to the Mediterranean honour system and Church authority in this area. The Church, as a result, did not alter its views on sexuality, marriage and so on but it was forced to accept the fact that most Italians, including many practising Catholics, wanted to make up their own minds on these matters.

It is in the sphere of cultural change that the most lasting impact of feminism should be sought. The movement had a huge impact on those involved – for some, amounting to a kind of 'second birth', a moment lived so intensely that their lives seemed to start afresh. Anna Rossi-Doria recently called that time, 'years that in many respects were extraordinary, which shaped the rest of my life, but whose full meaning still eludes me'.[58] Of course, feminists were only a minority of the female population. Amalia Signorelli, however, has argued that this is unimportant since the issues raised, 'were the expression of a widespread state of unease, malaise and unhappiness, which was shared by the majority of Italian women'.[59] Because of extensive media coverage, feminism also affected the attitudes and outlook of many other women (and men) and the results of the divorce and abortion referenda demonstrate that many supported at least part of its agenda.

Feminism gave many women more confidence and greater expectations. Obviously such aspects are difficult to quantify but all commentators agree that some change of this kind did occur. In 1973 an opinion poll carried out by Shell-DOX found that only 6.1 per cent of young women wanted to be like their mothers.[60] Relations between the sexes were very different by the 1980s compared with the 1960s. Now girls and boys mingled freely and sex outside marriage was more or less acceptable. For most women, the desire to work was now seen as legitimate, no longer something to be justified as an extension of maternal duty. Obviously not all of these changes were due to feminism alone, but feminism clearly did help reinforce and accelerate the modernisation of social mores, begun in the period of the economic miracle.

Although the women's movement did not last in an organised sense, its ideological legacy endured. This is because many of its fundamental ideas continued to be relevant in the following years (and indeed, its significance can only really be grasped by taking a longer view). It brought about a sea-change in thinking that went beyond the relatively timid reformulations of gender relations espoused by the associations of the early post-war years. Although, of course, misogynous attitudes remained widespread after this period, they were severely challenged and the legal framework that supported them was swept away. This was to be subsequently built upon as the door had now been opened to further change. Unlike the other movements of the 1970s, feminism resurfaced in new forms in the following decades.

10

The 'Dual Presence': More Work and Fewer Children in the Age of Materialism

The last two decades of the twentieth century saw rapid social, economic, cultural and political change. Italy was now one of the world's richest nations and young women of this period belonged to the first generation without personal experience of the great poverty it had so recently shaken off. Although, to a degree, Italy was becoming more like the rest of Europe, it followed the 'Southern European model' of social development with a very low birth rate, enduring strong family relationships and poor state welfare provisions. On the political front the *partitocrazia* (party-rule, as the Italian political system of this period has been dubbed) survived in the 1980s but, in the early 1990s, imploded in a maelstrom of corruption trials, finally bringing to an end half a century of DC rule. In these years, Italy became increasingly ethnically diverse with migrant workers, including many women, arriving from all over the world.

Secularisation slowed. While the percentage of Italians regularly attending Mass had fallen steadily from 1956 to 1981, thereafter it stabilised at around 40 per cent (rallying a little in the 1980s, then declining slightly again).[1] However, by this time, Italy's practising Catholics were mainly of the 'pick-and-mix' variety, selecting the aspects they liked without actually following the precepts of Catholicism on matters like sexuality and birth control. Church welfare organisations continued to make up for some of the deficiencies of state provisions.

For women, this was a period of great strides forward in both education and employment, although less so in the world of politics. At the same time, the rapidly proliferating private television channels, mainly owned by media mogul Silvio Berlusconi, offered very different representations of Italian women, broadcasting a nightly parade of scantily-clad 'hostesses' and showgirls. The more progress, it seemed, women made in other spheres, the greater the appetite for such belittling images.

Feminism: the 'long wave'

Italian feminism as a movement waned although it far from vanished. As Donatella Della Porta has noted, 'the mobilization of the 1970s set the basis for what can be called the long wave of the women's movement that continued well into the 1990s'.[2] In this period, feminism became what has been called 'diffuse feminism', a term used to denote the spread of feminist ideas into general cultural values and into institutional and political spheres. The question of 'liberation' versus 'emancipation' was no longer an issue. Key terms, instead, were the compatible aims of parity and diversity, the latter embracing both women's difference from men as well as diversity among women themselves. Feminists continued to organise albeit in a new manner. In Florence, for example, a whole range of different groups were active, many of them founded after the 1970s, often by women who had been active in that decade, and built around networks formed at that time.[3]

Feminist groups of this period were often small, locally-based and focused on specific, defined aims (like peace, artistic activities, historical research and so on). Many were more pragmatic in their approach than the 1970s collectives and more interested in influencing institutions and locations of power. Some became more professionalised and less afraid of 'delegation' to other women and indeed of structures (although informal, alternative methods of organising persisted). Particularly in areas where the Left was in power, they worked with local authorities and looked to them for funding for specific projects. Some younger women became involved, although they were not always prepared to just adopt 1970s ideas wholesale. Anna, a young woman involved in the women's section of the mixed organisation ARCI (Associazione Ricreativa Culturale Italiana) in the mid-1980s, for example, described the idea of totally separatist groups as, 'a depressing, self-punishing spectre, giving up trying to succeed in the world, searching for an island'.[4]

Some groups offered services or training for women but cultural and intellectual activities were particularly important. By 1986, when they held their first nationwide conference in Siena, there were already about 100 women's cultural centres.[5] Such intellectual activity remained largely outside institutional contexts, in contrast to, for example, the UK, where women's studies was increasingly finding a place in mainstream education. Italian universities remained fairly impervious to such ideas (although by the turn of the century this was beginning to change) and so women's studies emerged mainly outside the academy, in bookshops, publications and seminars. Postgraduate training in women's history, for example, was pioneered by a residential summer school run annually from 1990 by the Società delle Storiche (Female Historians' Association – founded in 1989).

This was the period when lesbian groups finally emerged, like the Collegamento tra Lesbiche Italiane (Rome) and Phoenix (Milan), carving out a distinct identity for themselves between the gay organisation Fuori! and the women's movement. From 1981 a series of national lesbian meetings were held.[6]

UDI continued to function. After the dramatic 1982 conference in which the national directorate resigned, some older *udine* who felt uncomfortable with this new situation left to return to more familiar party work, like membership drives, in the PCI or PSI. Nonetheless, UDI did continue as a loose association and its national magazine *Noi donne* stayed in print. At the beginning of the twenty-first century, UDI once again began to rebuild its organisational structure and rebaptised itself Unione Donne in Italia (Union of Women in Italy), to be more open to migrant women.

Political parties and parliament

In the 1980s, the PCI began to take feminist ideas seriously, finally acknowledging that sexual oppression was not just a subsection of class oppression. In 1984 the VII Congress of Communist Women embraced the idea of autonomy, and 1986 saw the publication of the Charter of Women Communists (subtitled 'Women's Strength Comes from Women'), a document which applied the concept of sexual difference to a range of political questions. This conversion to feminism of one of Italy's main political parties was highly significant. The PCI also co-opted Livia Turco to its highest executive body to represent women's issues and launched a new policy of quotas (subsequently continued by the PDS – the Democratic Party of the Left – the successor to the PCI) for women on its representative and executive bodies. This boosted numbers selected as PCI candidates, and many women appeared high up on PCI electoral lists. The policy bore fruit immediately: in the 1987 election, numbers of female Communist parliamentarians doubled. Consequently, numbers of female senators and deputies hit an all-time high. Such policies may help explain why, in this period of declining membership, fewer women deserted the party than men. Women were 24 per cent of PCI membership in 1976, 26.9 per cent in 1989 and (in the PDS) 28 per cent in 1992.[7]

The PSI adopted a similar approach of reserving seats for women on its executive bodies, with some success. Women continued to be far less represented at the high levels of the DC. Despite this, female DC membership peaked in the 1980s with, in 1986, 37.5 per cent of overall membership and, in the South, over 40 per cent. However, given the importance of clientelism in recruitment, this does not necessarily imply high levels of female politicisation.[8]

In the 1990s, Italy's political system went into meltdown with the disappearance of the DC and the transformation of the PCI into the social-democratic PDS. The end of the DC did not mean an end to many of the values it promoted. Some of the new political forces spawned by the redrafting of the Italian political scene, such as Silvio Berlusconi's Forza Italia, similarly stressed family values. The 1994 elections, won by Berlusconi and his Centre–Right alliance, brought some new right-wing women to prominence, like Irene Pivetti (Lega Nord) and Tiziana Parenti (Forza Italia), who were highly critical of feminism. Cristina Matranga (Forza Italia), for example, called it, 'an ideology that aimed to annihilate men and destroy femininity'.[9] New electoral systems were tried, some favouring, some hindering, women's chances of election. Intriguingly, women politicians appear to have had virtually no involvement at all in the systemic corruption uncovered by the spectacular trials of the early 1990s (affecting mainly, but far from exclusively, the DC and the PSI). Even prominent DC politicians like Tina Anselmi seem to have had 'clean hands'. Historian Emma Fattorini has argued that this was because women were more ethical in politics.[10] Whether or not she is right, it does suggest that even women who had risen to leading positions had been excluded from the real corridors of party power.

TABLE 2 Women in Parliament, 1983–2006

	1983	**1987**	**1992**	**1994**	**1996**	**2001**	**2006**
% of women in the Chamber of Deputies	7.9	12.9	8.0	14.7	10.6	11.5	17.1
% of women in the Senate	4.9	6.5	9.5	9.2	8.2	8.1	14.0

Sources:
1983–92: M. Guadagnini, 'A "Partitocrazia" without Women: the Case of the Italian Party System', in J. Lowenduski and P. Norris (eds), *Gender and Party Politics* (London: Sage, 1993), p. 189.
1994–2006: 'Donne elette al Parlamento italiano, per legislatura e camera di appartenenza', at www.istat.it/salastampa/comunicati/non_calendario/20070307_00/17_parlamento.pdf

Despite all the political upheaval, cross-party solidarity between female deputies was still possible. In February 1996 the lengthy feminist campaign to reform rape legislation finally bore fruit. Sponsored by 67 female deputies from various different parties (including even the neo-fascist Alessandra Mussolini, granddaughter of the Duce), the new legislation finally inscribed into law the feminist demand that rape be seen as a crime against the person rather than against public morality. It raised the minimum sentence from three to five years (with a maximum of ten) and to six–twelve years for rapes committed with specific aggravating circumstances (such as if the victim was under fourteen). It also introduced automatic state prosecution. Sex with a minor incurred prosecution for statutory rape but, controversially, consensual sex between minors aged thirteen to sixteen was permitted.[11]

As Table 2 shows, numbers of female parliamentarians remained low. A host of factors contributed to this situation including specific features of the electoral system. It was also a product of low numbers in areas of professional and political life which could serve as springboards to a national political career like office-holding in local government or a role in the higher echelons of business. This was particularly problematic in less centralised parties like the DC, where patronage networks were essential to selection. But such structural factors were compounded by enduring good old-fashioned male prejudice, the male-dominated atmosphere of parliament and women's domestic responsibilities. One (unidentified) female deputy explained, in 1996, that few women got involved in politics, 'because this is male politics, its rhythms, processes and language are all male. For a woman, getting involved in this kind of politics means a lot of hard work, a lot of physiological and physical effort . . .'[12]

A radical attempt to boost numbers came in 1993 when, partly due to the political skills of veteran parliamentarian Tina Anselmi, a gender clause was included in the new electoral law (Law 277 – part of the attempt to redraw Italy's political map). The clause introduced a controversial quota system whereby parties had to list candidates on electoral lists for the Chamber of Deputies in alternate order by sex (in a context where 25 per cent of deputies were elected from lists, the rest in single member constituencies). As a result, many more women were elected in the 1994 general election, but the quotas provoked heated debates. Their main supporters were women in the Centre–Left coalition. Others (including some feminists) opposed them. Emma Bonino (Radical Party), for example, argued that: 'Relationships between women and politics cannot be laid down by law. This protection, graciously bestowed upon women, diminishes their role and is no more than a frame of mimosas around an unpresentable picture.'[13] Quotas were also tried in local government where, historically, few women were elected (only 8.5 per cent in 1991). Law 81 of 1993 stipulated that in electoral lists neither sex could have over two-thirds of candidates in larger municipalities or more than three-quarters in smaller ones. In 1995, this was implemented in regional elections.

In July 1995, however, the Constitutional Court declared all the quotas illegal. Electoral legislation, it stated, should be rigorously egalitarian. Consequently, at the historic elections of 1996, which saw the first ever parliamentary victory of the Left, far fewer women stood and far fewer were elected. Eventually, however, in 2003, a new constitutional amendment (inspired by a similar French law and by a growing awareness of how Italy lagged behind much of the EU in this respect) permitted 'special measures' to promote equal opportunities for both sexes in access to public offices and elective posts. This amendment was supported even by female parliamentarians from right-wing parties.[14]

During the 1980s and 1990s there were a number of female government ministers although they still tended to be given 'female' portfolios, like equal opportunities (a new ministry founded in 1996, first headed by Anna Finocchiaro) or education. There were some exceptions, like Nilde Jotti and Irene Pivetti (leaders of the Chamber of Deputies in 1979–92 and 1994–6 respectively), Susanna Agnelli (Foreign Minister in 1995–6) and Rosa Russo Jervolino (Interior Minister in 1998–9), but, to date, Italy has had neither a female Prime Minister nor President of the Republic.

Education

This period saw a dramatic turn of events in education. Confounding centuries of prejudice about female intellectual inferiority, girls overtook boys. As in other Western nations, they forged ahead in enrolments and achievement. Already in the early 1980s girls had caught up with boys in secondary education. By 1983–4, two-thirds of the pupils in the prestigious *liceo classico* were female as were 44.1 per cent of those graduating from university.[15] Between 1982 and 1995, although numbers of girls and boys in secondary education remained roughly equal, more girls successfully completed school and fewer had to repeat a failed year.

In 1992, for the first time ever, more than 50 per cent of Italian university enrolments were women. They also overtook in numbers graduating (53.1 per cent in 1995) and among those successfully completing secondary education.[16] Their forward momentum continued after this and by the end of the century boys had fallen even further behind. The expansion in female education was particularly marked in the South given how far behind it had been only a few decades earlier. By the 1990s, the differences between North and South were negligible.[17]

Illustration 10   Forging ahead in education: girls sitting school-leaving examinations, 26 June 1989.
(Reproduced courtesy of Fototeca Panizzi, Reggio Emilia.)

Although girls were ahead in terms of raw achievement, the sexes still tended to prefer different subjects with boys predominating in professional and technical training and girls in 'general' schools. By the 1990s, however, although this was still true, the picture became slightly less clear-cut as some girls moved into previously predominantly 'male' institutions like scientific grammar schools. At university too, women were increasingly present in faculties with potentially good career prospects like Medicine, Law, Engineering and Architecture.[18]

All this suggests that the women of twenty-first-century Italy, having already outperformed boys at school, may well be poised to advance into areas of employment where they were previously poorly represented. However, because only about half the age cohort of either sex actually completed secondary school and small numbers (by European standards) attended university, these changes primarily affected the middle class. Education, moreover, is only one, albeit an important one, of a range of factors that determine levels of employment.

Employment

By this time, the idea that women's 'normal' role was to be a housewife and mother was finally dead. This norm was replaced by the concept of the 'dual presence', in which both work and family commitments were seen as part of women's core identity. Most Italian women now expected, or at least hoped, to combine both roles. Maternity was no longer seen as inherently incompatible with employment.

Official statistics showed a continuation of the rise, begun in the 1970s, in female employment. Numbers rose both of women seeking work and of those actually employed. In 1971, official statistics put 25.1 per cent of women as 'economically active', rising to 26.7 in 1981, 30.1 in 1991, and 37.6 in 2001.[19] In parts of the North and Centre rates were much higher. Nationally, real levels were doubtless higher than official statistics, due to the informal economy. Earnings differentials, however, persisted. Although the gap narrowed, in the mid-1990s women only received, on average, 75 per cent of male earnings in manual work and 56 per cent among managers.[20]

Levels of employment varied according to region, marital status and level of education. According to one study, at the beginning of the 1990s,

> there is a 96 per cent probability that a forty-year-old woman from the Centre–North will find employment at least once if she is an unmarried graduate, but the figure will be only 75 per cent if she is, or has been, married and only reached the fifth year of primary school. In the South the difference between these two categories is even greater: 96 per cent compared with 40.6 per cent.[21]

Nonetheless, increasing numbers of wives did work. The old pattern of women working until marriage and then leaving the workforce was gone. Surveys carried out during the 1990s show a high proportion of women with very young children still in employment.[22] Women's new educational achievements proved useful. In 1987, 35 per cent of working women, compared with 25 per cent of employed men, had secondary or higher education qualifications.[23]

In this period, new equal opportunities legislation was added, much of it (like the Parity Law) inspired by EC/EU norms. Trade union feminists were also important advocates of the idea of equal opportunities. In 1983, under Italy's first socialist prime minister (Bettino Craxi), a national equal opportunities committee was created in the Employment Ministry, mainly to do research and draft legislative proposals. The following year this was joined by a, somewhat overlapping, equal opportunities commission attached to the prime minister's office. Its remit was to promote equal opportunities broadly, including in politics; to advise the government on equal opportunity matters; to do research and to act as a kind of ombudsman for equality issues; 1984 also saw the creation of a new figure, the Equal Opportunities Officer, who operated in regional committees regulating the labour market. Some (mainly northern) local authorities also set up equal opportunities commissions. Overall, such bodies have not had a huge impact on policy-makers although they have done useful research and helped inform women about their rights.

In 1991, positive discrimination legislation was introduced which aimed to tackle both direct and indirect discrimination at work and encouraged a reorganisation of working practices to accommodate those with family responsibilities. Large firms had to submit a gender analysis of their workforce every two years. Despite its clearly advanced aims, this legislation proved fairly ineffective. Positive action was only made compulsory in the public sector. For private firms, it was voluntary.[24]

Legislative advances are doubtless not the main reason for the increase in women's employment. Far more significant are cultural changes (women's new desire for the 'emancipation' of work), the expansion of the tertiary sector and the growth of the nursery school system. In 1988, 88 per cent of Italian children aged 3–5 attended public or private nursery school. Although little was available for those younger than three, many women could turn to female kin, particularly grandmothers, for help. As Franca Bimbi has argued, this 'active solidarity of women of different generations' made the Italian situation 'a mix of rapid modernization and traditional family relationships'.[25]

As elsewhere in Europe, gender segregation of the labour market persisted. Women did advance into new areas of work. The 1980s saw, for example, the first female mountain guides, croupiers and airline pilots. However, examples like these suggested greater change than was actually happening: most women remained in 'female occupations'. Numbers continued to decline in agriculture, and, after a slight rise in the 1970s, also in industry.

In public administration and commerce, the upward trend continued and almost all the overall increase in female employment in this period was due to expansion in this sector;[26] 47 per cent of all employed women in 1972, and 67 per cent in 1989, were in the tertiary sector.[27] The public sector was a large component of this, employing, by 1999, 1,709,592 women. In 2000, for the first time, they slightly outnumbered men.[28] This is of enormous significance given the perceived desirability of such positions. Many Italians aspired to public-sector employment since, despite low pay and often frustrating working conditions, it provided real job security and good pensions.

Teaching became even more feminised. Women were 89 per cent of Italian primary teachers (the highest percentage in Europe) in 1989, but only 60 per cent of middle school and secondary teachers and even less at university level. The pyramid-like gender structure of the profession lingered on and men mainly still held the reins of power: 65 per cent of head-teachers in middle schools and 82 per cent in secondary schools were male in 1990.[29]

A hallmark of the Italian economy was the large number of self-employed persons and small businesses. In 1994, 24.1 per cent of the labour force was self-employed (compared with 11.2 per cent in the UK).[30] This form of employment could be appealing to women, with its potential for flexible working hours, and numbers of self-employed women rose. By 2004, 23.5 per cent of Italian businesses, many of them in the commercial or agricultural sectors, were classified as 'female businesses' – enterprises where all or most of the managers or investors were female. Numbers were boosted by Law 215 of 1992, which fostered female entrepreneurship in various ways, including providing start-up loans. Many businesses were extremely small, often just one woman working alone. Some were flourishing concerns. Others were not really self-employed at all but 'contracted labour', an exploitative ruse that enabled employers to circumvent labour legislation.[31]

In the 'Third Italy', women had a central role as both workers and entrepreneurs. Rates of female employment here were higher than the national average. This was partly because many of the small firms had developed out of sharecropping households where, of course, women had always worked, but it was also because the continuing strength of kin networks meant many babysitters for working mothers.[32]

Women advanced greatly in the professions. Numbers of doctors, magistrates, journalists and so on, rose. There were still some legal hurdles to overcome. Although women gained entry to the new state police force on equal terms with men (thereby abolishing the separate women-only force) in 1981, they were not admitted to the armed forces until 2000 and only if unmarried (although this was later declared unconstitutional). After this the only profession which formally excluded them was the priesthood of the Catholic Church.

However, the 'glass ceiling' was firmly in place in many professions and other high-status forms of employment. At the end of the century most top jobs were still held by men, with women disproportionately clustered in the lower ranks. The reasons for this were complex but clearly included both male prejudice and women's difficulties in juggling the demands of jobs with high levels of responsibility and domestic commitments.

In overall numbers, moreover, Italy lagged behind much of the EU. The 36.1 per cent of Italian women officially recorded as in employment in 1996 was considerably below the EU average of 50.2 per cent.[33] One reason for this was structural unemployment, particularly in the South where, unlike in other areas, there were still many young housewives. Many here just could not find work. This was also true of Southern men (indeed, Italian rates of male employment were also below the EU average – 65.3 per cent in 1996, compared with an EU average of 69.7) but unemployment was persistently higher among women. In

1996 the national rate was 9.7 per cent for men and 16.6 per cent for women.[34] Continuing male prejudice was also a factor. Some employers found ways around the Parity Law. The State Railways, for example, kept numbers of female ticket inspectors to a minimum by testing candidates' ability in heavy tasks like manually unhooking carriages, which, in practice, were now performed electronically.[35]

Female employment was also held back by a shortage of part-time work (although the timetable for many public employees – 8 am to 2 pm, six days a week – could make full-time work suitable for mothers). In 1989, only 10.9 per cent of employed Italian women worked part-time (the EU average was 29 per cent). By 1994, the figure had risen only to 12.4 per cent.[36] Unions did little to promote flexible working hours. Indeed, they generally opposed part-time working as likely to divide the working class. There were few incentives in Italian labour legislation for employers to adopt it. They could, for example, achieve workforce flexibility through a subsidised lay-off system. New legislation introduced in the 1990s did introduce slightly more flexibility in the labour market, which potentially could, in the long run, increase part-time opportunities, but, by the turn of the century, this had so far had little impact.[37] Women who sought more flexible hours were often pushed to the margins of the labour market into the informal economy, undefended by legislation or trade unions. Some deliberately opted for the unofficial economy, despite often exploitative pay and conditions, for this specific reason (and not just to avoid taxes as is often suggested). Surveys done in the early 1990s showed that the real number of women working part-time (including unofficial employment) was distinctly higher than official figures suggested. Estimates range from 13.9 to 26.3 per cent.[38]

Women also turned to the unofficial economy if they could not find legal work. Far from untypical was Assunta, a forty-year-old mother of two who, when interviewed in the mid-1990s, had been registered as unemployed for ten years, after being made redundant from a Turinese factory. Although the much longed for, decently-paid, legal job had not emerged: 'I haven't sat around doing nothing. I've worked all over the place, but always off the books. I did cleaning . . . I did night-care for the elderly.'[39] Large numbers of women continued to do outwork at home or in sweatshops. One survey estimated that about 2 million women did such, often very poorly paid, work in 1997, making goods like clothes and shoes at home.[40]

Female employment was also, somewhat perversely, held back by trade union success in reducing wage differentials (in the official economy), which were smaller (particularly for lower-qualified work) than in many EU countries. Although clearly a gain for those already working, this could decrease the incentive to recruit women, as could the relative generosity of Italian maternity pay. Until the mid-1990s, women's participation was further reduced by a mandatory retirement age for women of 55 in the private sector, which discouraged a return to employment after childbearing.

The limitations of the Italian welfare state were also a factor. Welfare spending increased in post-war Italy in a comparable manner to other European countries, but the use of the system for clientelist ends made provisions regionally uneven and often poor. Admittedly, Italy did set up a national health service in 1978 on universalist principles but generally welfare policy tended to favour transfer payments (usually tied to employment) rather than service provisions. Pensions, for example, were generous (absorbing 52.2 per cent of welfare spending in 1996)[41] whereas provisions like residential care for the elderly were scarce. Generally speaking the state tended to devolve responsibility for family problems to families themselves, rather than helping them. The limited welfare sector reduced employment opportunities (since the welfare state was a major female employer in many countries) and placed the burden of care for the sick or the elderly (a pressing issue given increasing longevity) on daughters, giving them what Chiara Valentini has called a 'triple presence'.[42] Even for those with 'only' a 'dual presence', women's often conflicting obligations at home and work could be problematic. Some Italian women squared this particular circle by employing other, often migrant, women.

By the end of the twentieth century, Italy had large numbers of domestic servants, a work role that many had thought technology and 'modernisation' would make redundant. This resurgence in paid domestic labour was, of course, apparent in other Western countries too, similarly linked to rising levels of female employment, but some argue that migrant domestics were particularly prevalent in Italy.[43] Moreover, a particular feature in Italy was the revival of the 'premodern' form of domestic service: live-in servants.

By 1981 domestic service employed only 0.9 per cent of the 'active population' (compared with 1.9 per cent in 1961) and co-resident servants had virtually disappeared. From the mid-1980s, however, numbers rose again, accelerating in the late 1990s. One statistical reconstruction put their numbers at 314,700 in 1980, 801,100 in 1990, and 1,058,600 in 2000 (although these figures also include those working in institutions like orphanages, and a few men). By 2000, 8.1 per cent of Italian families (about 1.8 million families) employed domestics. In 1980, mostly only well-off families had done so. By 2000, although this was still true for daily helps, some more modest families employed co-resident servants.[44] By the end of the century, although the majority of daily domestics were Italians, they were no longer prepared to do live-in work. Admittedly, co-resident servants were a minority (according to one survey, in 2003, 0.4 per cent of Italian families had live-in help),[45] but all were migrants, largely employed to care for the elderly or disabled.

Migrant women

In the final quarter of the twentieth century, Italy, with its long tradition of emigration and internal migration, became a migrant destination. Some migrants, like Somalis, came as a result of colonial ties or (particularly Filipinos and Cape Verdeans) because Italy is a Catholic country. Many more, from a range of East European and Third World countries, were drawn by Italy's wealth, the opportunities for undocumented workers in the informal economy and because it was one of the last European nations to impose immigration controls. Even after controls were introduced, Italy's borders remained remarkably leaky.

Italy has had marked gender-specific immigration, with men predominating among migrants from Moslem and certain African countries and women among those from Catholic countries and former colonies in the Horn of Africa. About 50 per cent of migrants between 1965 and 1985 were female. After this, the proportion of men increased.[46] Significant numbers of lone female migrants have come to Italy, mainly to work as domestic servants or (to a lesser extent) prostitutes. Sometimes women were recruited directly. In Cape Verde, for example, Capuchin friars acted as intermediaries, placing women in Italian families. Other migrant women, including many from North Africa, came to join their husbands, their arrival facilitated by a law of 1986 enabling family reunification. Many of these wives, too, became servants.

Life for migrants was often tough due to racism, violence and a shortage of housing and welfare facilities (because of a lack of planning for their arrival). Particularly vulnerable were undocumented migrants. Many had to turn to charities, like the Catholic charity Caritas, which provides extensive services for migrants. Housing problems trapped many in otherwise unappealing, live-in work. Many migrant women suffered great poverty, remitting most of their earnings home. Social isolation was common. One study of Somali and Filipina migrants in Rome found that most had no Italian friends or even friends from other national groups.[47]

Early migrants were often the most exploited. As migrant communities matured, however, they saw increasing levels of family reunification and some employment diversification. By the turn of the century, some migrant women were beginning to set up their own organisations, and in some areas, like Emilia-Romagna, projects, funded by the EU or local authorities, were founded to help them. One sign of change was the election, in 1999, of the Nicaraguan Lidia Obando, as head of ACLI-COLF, the national Catholic organisation for domestic servants.

Whilst male migrants did a range of different jobs (sometimes including domestic service), domestic service was overwhelmingly the main employer of migrant women. As Antonia, a Cape Verdean migrant, put it: 'You have to resign yourself to domestic work, they are not going to give you a job in a factory or even to do cleaning in hospitals or nursing. Domestic work is, however, clean and honest work. Italian women do not want to do it so they cannot say that we're stealing their work from them. You've got absolutely no chance of getting office work.'[48] This was true even for educated migrants (one survey in the late 1990s found that one in ten migrant domestic workers had attended university).[49] Ardah from Somalia said: 'The work in Italy is really horrible . . . but in Rome, even if you have a degree, if you are a foreigner, all you will find is domestic work.'[50]

Migrant women's own 'dual presence' was often particularly difficult. For some live-in domestics it meant forgoing maternity altogether. Others left their children in their country of origin (sometimes with a paid carer) or placed them in residential care institutions (mainly Church-run) in Italy. Rosemarie Samaniego, a maid in Rome, said: 'When the girl that I take care of calls her mother "Mamma" my heart jumps . . . I begin thinking . . . I should be taking care of my very own children and not someone else's. . . . Some days, I just start crying while I am sweeping the floor because I am thinking about my children in the Philippines.'[51] The life of the co-resident domestic was difficult in many other ways too, with long hours (often on call round the clock and with only two half-days off per week) and little privacy.

For some middle-class families, servants were a status symbol. Most, however, were employed to enable Italian women to reconcile work and family obligations in a society which clung to deeply-held cultural beliefs about proper family life such as the need for daily shopping, high standards of cleaning and home-cooked food, and where men did little at home. As Andall argues, the demand for live-ins was partly 'symptomatic of an inability to conceptualise an alternative model to the pre-existing one. In effect, live-in domestic work replicates in structure the traditional role of the wife and mother'.[52]

Although some migrant domestics did acquire new authority in their community and family of origin through remittances, for many, life in Italy could hardly be seen as emancipating. It is difficult to escape the conclusion that some Italian women 'emancipated' themselves on the backs of migrants. Italian feminists proved somewhat reluctant to grasp this particular nettle, which jars with the notion of 'sexual difference' and the implied commonality of all women. For example, in 1992, at a round table in Rome on migration, when a Tunisian speaker denounced the fact that migrants had to work '24 hours like a slave', the (Italian) feminist Elvira Panotti commented somewhat dismissively that: 'Salua Dridi's protest should be extended to the lives of all women because a 24-hour day is a normal day for all women and all housewives. So, we can say that what is being proposed for domestic workers is relevant for all women.'[53] Other feminists have been more perceptive. Anna Rossi-Doria, for example, wrote in 1991 that, 'There is no other European country where . . . there is a comparable demand for live-in domestic workers. This is a sign of Italian women's high level of emancipation (which is riven with contradiction and which perhaps partly explains our current silences regarding female migrants).'[54]

Another numerous (and very visible, given the openness of street trade and the illegality of brothels) group of migrants were sex-workers. Lina Merlin's hopes that her law would end prostitution proved totally wrong: it very much continued to be a feature of Italian life. By the end of the century, Italian-born prostitutes were increasingly rare, replaced by vulnerable young foreigners. Some migrated alone and then worked independently, sometimes as call-girls or 'hostesses' but also on the streets. There was also a tide of human misery consisting of women who were tricked into coming to Italy (or occasionally directly kidnapped) and coerced by various means into working. The latter group (mainly Nigerians and Albanians) usually worked the streets, living lives characterised by brutality, violence and exploitation.[55] Numbers of migrant prostitutes are very uncertain. Research done in 1996 estimated about 19,000–25,000 of them, with high concentrations in Milan and Rome.[56] Women were not just victims, however. Disturbingly, some involved in trafficking and organising the work of prostitutes were themselves female, such as the 'madams' involved in recruiting Nigerian girls.

Family and demography

The salient features of the Italian family in the final decades of the twentieth century were its diminishing size, the failure of adult children to leave the parental nest, and growing longevity. Confounding the predictions of those who opposed it, divorce (made easier in 1987, with the minimum separation time reduced from five to three years) did not lead to a disintegration of the family. On the contrary, the family remained extremely strong right up to the end of the century and beyond, as a central point of identification for most Italians. This was partly for cultural reasons but also because, in a society without the cushion of an efficient welfare state and where much employment was provided by family businesses to its members, there were many reasons for families to stick together. Dynamics within the family, however, changed. The old idea of the authoritarian *pater familias*, with great power over his wife and children, was now virtually gone. Indeed, the role of fathers became somewhat unclear and ambivalent.[57] Instead Italian families, if anything, became more centred around the figure of the mother, the new 'supermother' who, juggling the many balls of family responsibilities and employment, was determined to prove that she could cope.[58]

Although attitudes to sexuality changed greatly and female virginity at marriage was no longer seen as significant, virtually all children were born in wedlock. In 1993, only 7.3 per cent of Italian births were outside marriage compared with an EU average of 21.7.[59] Marriage as an institution remained strong and by the end of the twentieth century Italy still granted no legal rights to cohabiting couples (whether heterosexual or gay). In a survey of 1996, only 12 per cent of women aged 20–24 agreed with the idea that marriage was 'an out-of-date institution'.[60] In 1992, at 26 years old, the mean age at marriage was almost exactly the EU average of 26.1. The divorce rate of 0.4 per 1,000 of population in 1993, in contrast, was well below the EU figure of 1.7.[61] Cohabiting, unwed couples were mainly either divorced or separated persons awaiting a divorce to remarry, or single people, living together temporarily on the road to marriage. Few saw it as an alternative to marriage.[62]

There were, however, some signs of change. Numbers of single-parent families rose slightly (from 5.5 per cent of families with children under 18 in 1983 to 7.2 per cent in 1993–4) and they were increasingly headed by divorced or single mothers (mainly middle-class, employed women), rather than mainly widows or widowers, as previously.[63] By the turn of the century, moreover, although divorce, one-parent families and so on were still low, they were increasing. There was also a much greater propensity to put off marriage. In 1981, only 13 per cent of men aged 35 and 14 per cent of women aged 30 were unmarried. By 2001, the figures were 32 per cent and 38 per cent respectively.[64]

In 2001, 7.5 million Italians were aged over 75 (compared with 5 million in 1981).[65] This increasing longevity meant that many children had grandparents in their lives, usually not living in the same house but often close by. Because of outliving men, increasing numbers of elderly women lived alone, although they were usually not isolated because of the close proximity of family members and because many helped care for grandchildren. The institutionalisation of the elderly was very low, only about 2–3 per cent in the early 1990s,[66] and most of the frail elderly were looked after by daughters in their fifties and sixties.

Although the vast majority of Italians lived in nuclear families (with slightly more extended families in the 'Third Italy' regions), kinship ties remained extremely strong with many adults living close to their parents and seeing them frequently. One large survey in 1993 found that 69 per cent of adults aged over 25 resided in the same municipality as their parents (albeit usually in a separate home).[67] Most adult 'children' only left home to marry. Indeed, in the 1990s, young persons left home later than in the 1970s and 1980s. In the early 1990s, 91.3 per cent of Italians aged 45–54, and 57.7 per cent of those aged 55–64, had co-resident 'children'.[68] This situation was undoubtedly evidence of Italians' continuing emotional attachment to their families but it also had obvious financial advantages (particularly in a country with high levels of youth unemployment). Moreover, because paternal authority had weakened (particularly in the North), many no longer felt the need to leave home to achieve a degree of personal freedom. Given that most mothers continued to cook and clean for adult 'children', particularly sons, this increased women's workload.

Maternity was still important in most women's lives and, actual birth statistics notwithstanding, a cultural emphasis on women's maternal role persisted. Various surveys have shown that young women at the end of the century still saw maternity as an essential part of their future lives (albeit combined with employment).[69] At the end of the century, 80 per cent of Italian women had had at least one child by the age of 40. However, many stopped there, particularly in the Centre–North (two was more common in the South). This added up to dramatic fertility decline and gave Italy one of the lowest birth rates in the world, rivalled only by other Mediterranean countries like Spain and Greece. Births per 1,000 persons plummeted from 14.0 in 1975, to 11.3 in 1980, 10.1 in 1985, and only 9.1 in 1995. The fertility rate in 1975, at 2.0, was already below the 'substitution rate' of 2.1. By 1980 it was 1.49, falling to 1.36 in 1990, and 1.18 in 1995.[70] After this it rallied slightly, although not hugely.

The explanations for this trend are complex and controversial. As will be clear from previous chapters, it was not new but the continuation of a long decline. What was surprising was how extreme it became by the end of the century. It is important to note that it was not just women who chose to have fewer children: research done in 1996 found that the preferred contraception of 30 per cent of Italian couples was *coitus interruptus* and, for 23 per cent, condoms.[71] However, all commentators concur that women's rising education, their 'dual presence' and their new desire for 'emancipation', are important. Also relevant are rising expectations of what parents should provide for children, the availability of effective birth control and the fact that many increasingly put off the responsibilities of parenthood.

All these factors are similar to other advanced economies and fail to explain why birth rates fell more in Italy than northern European countries with higher rates of female employment. Factors particular to Italy include the timetable in most schools (8 am to 1 pm, six days a week), which made it hard for mothers to work (particularly given the shortage of part-time employment) unless they themselves were in public employment with a similar timetable or could rely on other help. The instability of the job market, the shortage of affordable rented accommodation, and high youth unemployment, were also disincentives to starting a family. All these led many to put off starting a family and, once the decision was taken, for some it was already too late.

The 'long family' may have been a deterrent for some. Adult children still at home were often very comfortable. Parents usually wanted them to stay and often demanded no contribution to household finances or to domestic chores. This could discourage some from setting up their own household. Although the mean age of women having their first child in Italy was not particularly high (in 1996 it was 27.8 years, similar to the UK and France), the numbers of those who never had children were rising. According to Gianpiero Dalla Zuanna, this may be partly due to a reluctance to leave the safety of 'the golden cage of Italian youth', leaving it so late that they ended up single.[72] He also argues that this prolonged period of cushioned life made young people risk-averse, and risk-taking is needed to have children.

Italy, somewhat perversely, was still a society where children were highly valued and loved. This led, however, not to having more children but to lavishing clothes, toys and expectations on only one or two. This idea was reinforced by the fact that Italy in the post-miracle years was a *nouveau riche* society where conspicuous consumption, encouraged by deluges of television advertising, was prevalent. Italian parents spent more per child than elsewhere in Europe and this led some to believe that they could not afford many. Prioritising what they saw as quality over quantity, they aimed for one or, at most, two perfectly reared children, who, they hoped, would do well in life. Cultural norms about home life were also relevant. Italian high standards of housework rendered unacceptable the slightly grubby, untidy homes of many new parents in countries like Britain.

One survey in 2003 (interviewing 50,000 women who had had their first child 18–21 months previously)[73] found that many did in theory want to have more children. One major impediment they cited was the difficulty of reconciling work and maternity and the shortage of public childcare. In this survey, 60 per cent of babies were cared for by grandparents. Only 20 per cent went to crèches. The role of fathers was striking. Only 7 per cent in the sample had made use of their legal right to paternity leave as the idea was stigmatised. The survey also demonstrated how few new fathers helped with housework: 73 per cent of mothers stated that nobody helped them. Among those who did get help, 38 per cent were assisted by a domestic help, 28 per cent by their partner and 21 per cent by their own parents.

Apart from in a minority of middle-class couples, housework was still seen as women's work. Dino Giovannini's study of fathers in Emilia Romagna found that: 'there is no equal sharing either of childcare or of family work. The father is a support, a prop, but does not share. Usually he perceives and admits the inequality of sharing the workload by showing understanding and admiration for what his partner does.'[74] In the early 1990s a survey of 20,000 families found that 28.3 per cent of fathers did housework on the day they were surveyed and 99 per cent of mothers. The fathers spent only 48 minutes on such activities compared with 5.5 hours for mothers. This survey even found that single mothers did less than married mothers as they only had children to look after, not a husband as well. Daughters, too, did far more than sons. Even unemployed young males living at home and still awaiting their first job were indulged and pampered in this respect and expected to do virtually nothing, whereas young women in the same situation were loaded with chores.[75] Men, in these surveys, devoted far more time to leisure activities than women.

Patterns were, therefore, already firmly established before marriage. Given how few Italian bachelors lived alone, but, instead, went straight from the 'golden cage' of their mother's care to the marital home, they never learned how to fend for themselves. Many Italian women did seem to accept this situation as normal and perhaps inevitable. As Chiara Valentini wrote in 1997, 'in many couples . . . women are tacitly accepting an age-old custom which, on the eve of the year 2000, is making their lives absurdly complicated'.[76] A subsequent study in 2003 found some change. By then, women's share of housework and caring activities in the home had declined by 7 per cent but this still left them with 77.7 per cent of the burden in the average household.[77]

The relationship between all these factors and fertility decline is, however, complex and sometimes regionally specific. Emilia Romagna, for example, had one of the lowest regional birth rates, despite having some of the best crèche provisions in Italy. In the South, where birth rates were higher, men were even less likely to contribute to housework than their Northern counterparts.

Government policy on the family was ambiguous, consisting in an often contradictory set of policies which had emerged over time.[78] Addressing fertility decline itself was something of a taboo subject, since, until the 1970s, pronatalism was so strongly associated with Mussolini as to render even academic debate on the issue problematic. Once the subject was opened up, there were frequent alarmist headlines in the press about the plummeting birth rate but it remained difficult for politicians to address the question. In the 1980s, nothing was done. Assistance to families amounted to little more than the (admittedly good) nursery system and miserly family allowances. Tax allowances, for example, were considerably higher for a dependent spouse than for dependent children. Instituted by the Fascists in the 1930s, family allowances (tax exempt and means tested) were based on the male-breadwinner model, paid to workers for their spouse and children, not directly to mothers. Unemployed parents got nothing. The low priority given to this is evidenced by the fact that considerably more was collected in contributions to the scheme than was paid out, the balance being diverted to areas like pensions. Although until the 1970s Italy spent nearly 3 per cent of GDP on family support subsidies, from the 1980s this fell to under 1 per cent, a very poor level compared with other EU countries.[79] This made families themselves the primary source of assistance to their members, with the state coming decidedly second. The truly needy often had to turn to local sources of assistance, which meant great variations regionally.

However, in the 1990s, fertility decline began to be discussed across the political spectrum. The Church too intervened. Cardinal Ruini, in 1994, called the demographic issue 'a really urgent matter for Italy'.[80] It was only when the Left won the 1996 election that a government felt able to officially adopt a pro-natalist stance. It was easier for Left politicians as they were less likely to be branded latter-day Fascists. A package of reforms was proposed, ranging from fiscal benefits for people with children, to increased family allowances, to priority in housing for young couples. Livia Turco, Minister for Social Solidarity (a feminist and practising Catholic), presented them as a form of welfare assistance in the name of women's (and couples') right to choose to have more children. She stated in an interview:

> I was involved in feminism, but I am not ashamed to say that children are worth it. I grew up with the idea that both things could be reconciled. I became a mother so late. I have a five-year-old son and I'm sorry he doesn't have a brother or sister. I mean, the experience of maternity is absolutely incomparable: it's not like any other experience in life.[81]

Modernity and tradition

Some of the apparent contradictions of late twentieth-century Italian gender relations stemmed from the fact that Italian society still combined a fascinating mixture of 'modernity' and tradition. Arguably, the modernisation of society and the economy was so rapid in Italy that many elements of the past, both good and bad, remained. In this context, Italians invented their own version of modernity, one that did not involve too abrupt a change with 'tradition'. This included a strong family.

At the end of the twentieth century, Italian families stuck together, they sat down together to eat proper meals of fresh, home-cooked food in clean homes and they lavished attention and care on their one or two children. Single parenthood was relatively rare and there was a widespread belief that the elderly should be able to remain at home. Many would argue that there is much to be applauded in this approach to modernity in one of the world's wealthiest nations. Sometimes this created opportunities, such as the fact that many young mothers could rely on childcare help from older female kin. However, it also meant enormous challenges for Italian women, besieged with conflicting responsibilities at home and at work. They coped by having fewer children and by employing outside help. Perhaps the core reason for fertility decline was not exactly women's emancipation but more, as Paul Ginsborg has put it, their 'partial emancipation'.[82] Given that Italian men were unwilling at the end of the century to do more than a token amount of housework, and given that the state offered little support, this reproductive 'go-slow' made perfect sense.

Conclusion

Many different female figures appear in the pages of this book, from toiling peasants and outworkers to the urban housewife astonished by her first indoor bathroom, from Catholic, Communist or Fascist organisers to feminists of many hues. There are women prepared to carry bombs to liberate their country, commit murder to save a daughter's honour, risk their lives in backstreet abortion or even willing to die for Mussolini. There are women blazing the trail in employment, education or politics and many welfare activists, some doing 'God's work' and others for whom welfare was imbued with deeply political, sometimes feminist or even national meanings. There are browbeaten daughters-in-law in sharecropping households, white widows, schoolgirls, migrant live-in carers, cabinet ministers and Fascist gymnasts.

These examples give just a flavour of the huge diversity of Italian women's lives in this century of change. In 1900 women had a subordinate position in family law, needed a 'marital authorisation' for many legal transactions and could not vote or stand for political office. Cultural norms reinforced legal subordination and, despite widespread female employment, it was as wives and mothers that women were primarily valued. There were many restrictions on what they could do and where they could go. Millions were peasants, with a surfeit of work but little 'emancipation'. Morality on many issues, despite the rise of socialism and the new social science, was largely defined by Church precepts (although these were far from always followed to the letter, as is clear from the prevalence of abortion).

By 2000, Italy was a wealthy, largely urban nation with one of the lowest birth rates in the world. Women were in many respects much freer than their great-grandmothers. Indeed their lives would have been barely recognisable to those great-grandmothers. A sea-change in female identity had occurred. Women's expectations were far higher, as were the opportunities open to them. They had advanced into many professions and educational levels had been revolutionised from a situation where anything above very basic or domestic education for girls was regarded with suspicion to one where women outperformed men. All legal impediments to equality had been swept aside. The power of the Church, although still present, was much diminished. Attitudes to sex were transformed. The woman afraid to undress before her husband, quoted in Chapter 4, forms a stark contrast to the sexually free behaviour of many by the end of the century. Some of the female figures who appeared in the media were quite new (indeed would have been shockingly unthinkable a hundred years earlier), like assertive young lesbians ready to debate with Church and state alike for the right to live their lives as they chose. Only a small number, however, had succeeded in the world of politics.

For many the norm (or at least the aspiration) was no longer full-time moth-erhood but a 'dual presence' combining work and family. The model of the *pater familias* had been replaced by a new, less hierarchical ideal of far greater equality between husband and wife and, as male authority declined, wom-en's role became more central in the family. The family itself was both smaller (as fertility dropped and the nuclear family became virtually universal) and longer, with life expectancy stretching out into previously unthinkable dec-ades. Although by the end of the century they were having very few children, women were still valued, and valued themselves, as mothers.

The causes of all this change are, of course, complex. One is clearly the pat-tern, timing and pace of economic growth, which have all had a huge impact on society and gender roles, as has secularisation, although Catholicism itself proved remarkably resilient. Catholicism should not, of course, be seen as simply a source of women's oppression. Catholicism also produced pioneers like Armida Barelli and Tina Anselmi, both positive, modern role models. The series of different political systems experimented (or endured) by Italy over the course of the century brought different problems and benefits for gender rela-tions. Even Fascism, its emphasis on women's domestic destiny notwithstand-ing, carved out new female spaces and, despite all the suffering they brought, both world wars did push women more into the public sphere, whether as war workers, rioters, partisans or black marketeers. Some change came from abroad. Foreign thinkers from Bebel to Brownmiller inspired Italian feminists of various kinds, foreign examples helped Italian women get the vote, and the EU was a driving force in equal opportunities legislation.

A huge agent of change has been, of course, women themselves. Greater gender equality did not simply arrive, the automatic product of 'modernity'. Instead, many fought long and hard for it. It is a striking feature of my nar-rative that, in every decade of the twentieth century (even the dark years of Fascist dictatorship), albeit in their own ways and shaped by the values and possibilities of their time, there were women willing to challenge at least aspects of the patriarchal order. They ranged from puritanical, earnest early feminists endeavouring to prove women's worth by good works, to 1970s iconoclasts demanding sexual freedom, from Catholic evangelisers to UDI stal-warts. Success, however, came slowly. It took the combined persistence, over nearly a century, of successive generations of emancipationists and feminists, to successfully unpick the iniquities of the Pisanelli Code.

Although, perhaps inevitably, this has been very much a tale of progress, it is not a simple or linear story. Patterns of employment are an excellent illustration of this. Employment has been a persistent theme of this book and we have encountered many working women including midwives, rice-weeders, servants, garment-makers, factory hands, teachers, lawyers, civil servants and prostitutes. By the end of the century many legal and cultural barriers to female employ-ment had fallen and women had gained entry to careers previously closed to them. However, this is far from a simple 'forward march' narrative. Although there were changes in what women actually did (rice-weeders were replaced by chemical weedkillers, 'handywomen' by trained midwives, and so on), occupa-tional sex-typing remained an enduring feature of the labour market throughout the century. Moreover, as far as can be told from census statistics (and a repeated theme of this book has been the unreliability of such figures), women's employment actually declined steadily over most of the century, only rallying in the 1970s. The figures reveal the perhaps startling fact that in 2001 the percentage of women recorded by official statistics as working was only a little higher than in 1901 and slightly lower than in 1881.

What did change was not how many worked but the meaning of work and who worked. The idea that employment was essentially only an adjunct to women's primary mission as mothers was gone and the early twentieth-century pattern, whereby only peasant and working-class women worked and middle-class women did not, vanished. By the end of the century the reverse was increasingly true. Those most likely to work were middle-class and educated. The pattern of Northern women being more likely to work than those from the South did, however, persist.

Employment was facilitated for some by migrant labour. At the end of the twentieth century, just as at the beginning, poor vulnerable women mainly from rural areas worked as live-in servants for Italian families and serviced men as sex workers. What had changed was the globalisation of the system as Italy was transformed from a sender of emigrants to a migrant destination. Some of the new female migrants' lives were as difficult and unfree as those of Italian peasants who migrated into cities at the beginning of the century. Remarkably, in 2000, Italy had more, not fewer, domestic workers than a hundred years before.

There are other elements of continuity in women's situation over the course of the century. One is the great resilience of the family with, even after divorce was introduced, a low rate of marital breakdown. Another is family limitation: during the whole century there were Italian women who at least attempted to control their fertility. Their ability to do so was, however, much improved over time by sex education and access to legal and relatively safe contraception.

At the end of the century, however, many inequalities persisted. Although the old hierarchical, patriarchal family had gone, the domestic division of gender roles had not. Italian men had changed but somewhat less than their northern European counterparts and patronising and discriminatory behaviour towards women had far from disappeared. Luisa Passerini summed this up well in 1996, when she wrote that:

> Women have become more visible in a range of places and situations and more visible to one another. For all that, Italy remains a country in which gender relations are still often formed in the mould of an underlying masculinism – old-fashioned or newfangled, covert or manifest – and this masculinism both sustains old traditions and invents new ones.[1]

In the year 2000, most Italian men still saw housework as women's work and few, particularly in comparison with northern Europe, had begun to take on a share of this burden. A UN survey presented at the 1995 international women's conference in Beijing showed that in other industrialised nations women worked on average 13 per cent more than men but Italian women (taking an embarrassing first place in this particular league table) did 28 per cent more.[2] This situation should not, however, be entirely blamed on men. Research in the 1990s does suggest that the stereotypical image of Italian sons indulged and pampered by their mothers is not without foundation.

In other areas too, inequalities persisted. Although women did make great strides forward in politics, by 2000 they had neither managed to carve out a prominent place for themselves in parliament nor changed the political culture itself. Representations of women in the media were radically transformed but whether the scantily dressed dancers and elegant, stiletto-heeled hostesses of many end-of-century television programmes are a more emancipated vision than the virginal, stern Red Cross nurses of the First World War is debatable. The fundamental issue of how to reconcile employment with maternity was still largely unresolved.

Nonetheless, Italian women have made astonishing progress over the course of the last century. By any yardstick, Italy in 2000 had far greater gender equality than it did a hundred years before and it was largely women themselves who achieved this. The result, however, was riven with contradictions. Italy at the end of the millennium was a nation that loved children but produced few, where many practised both Catholicism and birth control, a place where most working women continued to do all the housework and, indeed, where that housework continued to be done to a very high standard. It was a land of formal legal equality but persistent inequalities, a land where most families were nuclear yet kin networks remained vitally important, where grandmothers, not the nurseries feminists had fought for, were the main source of childcare for mothers. In short, Italian gender relations at the end of the twentieth century were a fascinating mix of modernity and tradition. This book has sought to explore some of the ways in which Italy arrived at this contradictory outcome at the end of what was, in virtually all respects, a century of advance and achievement for Italian women.

Notes

Introduction

1. On Italian women's and gender history, see M. De Giorgio, 'Women's History in Italy (Nineteenth and Twentieth Centuries)', *Journal of Modern Italian Studies*, 1 (1996): 413–43; M. Palazzi, 'Storia delle donne e storia di genere in Italia', in S. Bellassai and M. Malatesta (eds), *Genere e mascolinità. Uno sguardo storico* (Rome: Bulzoni, 2000); P. Willson, '*In Memoriam* Memoria', *Gender and History*, 5 (1993): 416–20; A. Rossi-Doria (ed.), *A che punto è la storia delle donne in Italia* (Rome: Viella, 2003); M. Palazzi and I. Porciani (eds), *Storiche di ieri e di oggi. Dalle autrici dell'Ottocento alle riviste di storia delle donne* (Rome: Viella, 2004); R. De Longis, 'La storia delle donne', in P. Di Cori (ed.), *Gli studi delle donne in Italia. Una guida critica* (Rome: Carocci, 2001).
2. See, for example, the various volumes of Laterza's *Storia delle donne in Italia*, published from 1994 onwards, and A. Bravo et al., *Storia sociale delle donne nell'Italia contemporanea* (Rome-Bari: Laterza, 2001).
3. S. Soldani, 'L'incerto profilo degli studi di storia contemporanea', in Rossi-Doria (ed.), *A che punto*, p. 72.

1   Italian Women at the Dawn of the Twentieth Century

1. Cited in M. Raicich, 'Liceo, università, professioni. Un percorso difficile', in S. Soldani (ed.), *L'educazione delle donne. Scuole e modelli di vita femminile nell'Italia dell'Ottocento* (Milan: Angeli, 1989), p. 173. Raicich describes Ravà as a 'diligent ministerial civil servant' (p. 174n).
2. Mortality fell from 30.3 per thousand in 1862–71 to 21.3 per thousand in 1902–11.
3. M. Livi-Bacci, *A History of Italian Fertility during the Last Two Centuries* (Princeton: Princeton University Press, 1977), p. 52.
4. M. Pelaia, 'Il cambiamento dei comportamenti sessuali', in A. Bravo et al., *Storia sociale delle donne nell'Italia contemporanea* (Rome-Bari: Laterza, 2001), p. 187.
5. www.vatican.va/holy_father
6. M. D'Amelia, *La mamma* (Bologna: Il Mulino, 2005), chap. 4.
7. See M. Seymour, *Debating Divorce in Italy: Marriage and the Making of Modern Italians, 1860–1974* (Basingstoke: Palgrave Macmillan, 2006).
8. Cited in G. Landucci, 'I positivisti e la "servitù" della donna', in Soldani (ed.), *L'educazione delle donne*, p. 483.

9. See P. Ungari, *Storia del diritto di famiglia in Italia (1796–1942)* (Bologna: Il Mulino, 1974); C. Saraceno, 'Women, Family, and the Law', *Journal of Family History*, 15 (1990): 427–42.

10. Before unification most Italian states had legal systems which privileged first-born males and gave unequal rights for males and females. All had *patria potestas* (the subjection of all household members to the authority of the, normally male, head of household). But certain parts of pre-unification Italy had divorce and (restricted) female suffrage.

11. On widows, see M. Palazzi, *Donne sole. Storia dell'altra faccia dell'Italia tra antico regime e società contemporanea* (Milan: Bruno Mondadori, 1997), pp. 88–93.

12. On family structure, see the classic M. Barbagli, *Sotto lo stesso tetto. Mutamenti della famiglia in Italia dal XV al XX secolo* (Bologna: Il Mulino, 1984).

13. G. Montroni, 'La famiglia borghese', in P. Melograni (ed.), *La famiglia italiana dall'Ottocento a oggi* (Rome-Bari: Laterza, 1988), p. 132.

14. *Capoccia* and *reggitrice* are local terms. These figures had different names in different regions but their roles were more or less the same.

15. L. Scaraffia, 'Essere uomo, essere donna', in Bravo et al., *Storia sociale delle donne*, p. 17.

16. On the rules of behaviour for middle-class adolescent girls, see M. De Giorgio, *Le italiane dall'Unità a oggi. Modelli culturali e comportamenti sociali* (Rome-Bari: Laterza, 1992), chap. 2. On courtship, see Barbagli, *Sotto lo stesso tetto*, chap. 8.

17. Livi-Bacci, *A History of Italian Fertility*, p. 75.

18. Pelaia, 'Il cambiamento dei comportamenti sessuali'.

19. Cited in De Giorgio, *Le italiane*, p. 292.

20. On power relations within peasant families see, for example, F. Zanolla, 'Suocere, nuore e cognate nel primo '900 a P. nel Friuli', *Quaderni Storici*, 44 (1980): 429–50.

21. Barbagli, *Sotto lo stesso tetto*, p. 401.

22. Palazzi, *Donne sole*, pp. 408–9.

23. Ibid., p. 259.

24. Barbagli, *Sotto lo stesso tetto*, p. 498.

25. On white widows, see P. Corti, 'Donne che vanno, donne che restano. Emigrazione e comportamenti femminili', *Annali Cervi*, 12 (1990): 213–35.

26. Palazzi, *Donne sole*, p. 371.

27. G. Obici and G. Marchesini, *Le 'amicizie' di collegio. Ricerche sulle prime manifestazioni dell'amore sessuale* (Rome: D. Alighieri, 1898).

28. M. Gibson, 'Labelling Women Deviant: Heterosexual Women, Prostitutes and Lesbians in Early Criminological Discourse', in P. Willson (ed.), *Gender, Family and Sexuality: The Private Sphere in Italy, 1860–1945* (Basingstoke: Palgrave Macmillan, 2004), p. 97.

29. A. Bravo, 'Madri fra oppressione ed emancipazione', in Bravo et al., *Storia sociale delle donne*, p. 78.
30. D'Amelia, *La mamma*.
31. Cited in ibid., p. 96.
32. Scaraffia, 'Essere uomo, essere donna', p. 12.
33. Barbagli, *Sotto lo stesso tetto*, p. 425.
34. Cited in A. Hallamore Caesar, 'About Town: the City and the Female Reader, 1860–1900', *Modern Italy*, 7 (2002): 129–41, p. 140n.
35. A. Hallamore Caesar, 'Women and the Public/Private Divide: the Salotto, Home and Theatre in Late Nineteenth-Century Italy', in Willson, *Gender, Family and Sexuality*.
36. Cited in De Giorgio, *Le italiane*, p. 92.
37. G. Bonetta, 'Igiene e ginnastica femminile nell'Italia liberale', in Soldani, *L'educazione delle donne*.
38. S. Pivato and A. Tonelli, *Italia vagabonda. Il tempo libero degli italiani dal melodramma alla pay-tv* (Rome: Carocci, 2001), p. 64.
39. M. Barbagli, *Educating for Unemployment: Politics, Labor Markets and the School System. Italy, 1859–1973* (New York: Columbia University Press, 1982).
40. Cited in D. Dolza, *Essere figlie di Lombroso* (Milan: Angeli, 1990), p. 49.
41. C. Covato, *Un'identità divisa. Diventare maestra in Italia fra Otto e Novecento* (Rome: Archivio Guido Izzi, 1996), pp. 53–4.
42. Cited in ibid., pp. 57–8.
43. S. Franchini, 'L'istruzione femminile in Italia dopo l'Unità: Percorsi di una ricerca sugli educandati pubblici di elite', *Passato e presente*, 10 (1986): 53–94, p. 82.
44. She was not, however, the first female graduate in Italy. Maria Pellegrina Amoretti, for example, had graduated in law at Pavia in 1777.
45. O. Vitali, *Aspetti dello sviluppo economico italiano alla luce della ricostruzione della popolazione attiva* (Rome: Istituto di demografia, 1970); S. Patriarca, 'Gender Trouble: Women and the Making of Italy's "Active Population" 1861–1936', *Journal of Modern Italian Studies*, 3 (1998): 144–63.
46. See R. Sarti, 'Work and Toil: the Breadwinner Ideology and Women's Work in 19th and 20th Century Italy', conference paper (Salzburg, 1999), published at www.uniurb.it/scipol/drs_work_and_toil.pdf
47. A. Pescarolo, 'Il lavoro e le risorse delle donne', in Bravo et al., *Storia sociale delle donne*, p. 156.
48. A. Kelikian, 'Convitti operai cattolici e forza lavoro femminile', in A. Gigli Marchetti and N. Torcellan (eds), *Donna lombarda* (Milan: Angeli, 1992).
49. Cited in F. Reggiani, 'Un problema tecnico e un problema morale: la crisi delle domestiche a Milano (1890–1914)', in ibid., p. 149.
50. M. Gibson, *Prostitution and the State in Italy, 1860–1915* (New Brunswick: Rutgers University Press, 1986), p. 31.
51. Cited in R. Macrelli, *L'indegna schiavitù. Anna Maria Mozzoni e la lotta contro la prostituzione di Stato* (Rome: Riuniti, 1981), p. 65.
52. J. Morris, *The Political Economy of Shopkeeping in Milan, 1886–1922* (Cambridge: Cambridge University Press, 1993), pp. 41–3.

53. M. P. Bigaran, 'Progetti e dibattiti parlamentari sul suffragio femminile: da Peruzzi a Giolitti', in *Rivista di storia contemporanea*, 14, 1 (1985): 50–82, p. 79.

54. See M. De Giorgio, 'Donne e professioni', in M. Malatesta (ed.), *Storia d'Italia. Annali 10. I professionisti* (Turin: Einaudi, 1996); B. Montesi, 'Donne, professioni, cittadinanza', *Storia e problemi contemporanei*, 31 (2002): 147–66.

55. S. Follacchio, ' "L'ingegno aveva acuto e la mente aperta". Teresa Labriola. Appunti per una biografia', *Storia e problemi contemporanei*, 17 (1996): 65–89, p. 68.

56. See F. Tacchi, 'Donne e avvocatura. Dall'età liberale a oggi', *Rassegna forense*, 35 (2002): 461–99; F. Tacchi, 'Il lungo cammino delle laureate in giurisprudenza', in *Società e storia*, 103 (2004): 97–125.

57. S. Soldani, 'Lo Stato e il lavoro delle donne nell'Italia liberale', *Passato e presente*, 24 (1990): 23–71, pp. 62–4.

58. S. Patriarca, 'Journalists and Essay-writers, 1850–1915', in L. Panizza and S. Wood (eds), *A History of Women's Writing in Italy* (Cambridge: Cambridge University Press, 2000). See also S. Wood, *Italian Women's Writing, 1860–1994* (London: Athlone, 1995).

59. See Hallamore Caesar, 'About town'.

60. Cited in A. Buttafuoco, *Cronache femminili. Temi e momenti della stampa emancipazionista in Italia dall'Unità al fascismo* (Siena: Università degli Studi, 1988), p. 24n.

61. C. Gasparini, 'Ricordi di una maestra', *Scuola italiana moderna* (1987), pp. 23–6, p. 24.

62. Elena Gianini Belotti has recently published a novel about Donati. See *Prima della quiete: storia di Itala Donati* (Milan: Rizzoli, 2003).

2 The 'Tower of Babel': First-Wave Feminism

1. I have used the term 'feminism' here for simplicity. Some of the persons discussed here did use this word themselves but others preferred 'emancipationism' or 'the woman question'. See M. De Giorgio, *Le italiane dall'Unità a oggi* (Rome-Bari: Laterza, 1992), pp. 494–507.

2. A. Buttafuoco, *Questioni di cittadinanza: donne e diritti sociali nell'Italia liberale* (Siena: Protagon, 1997), p. 47. On Buttafuoco's influential work, see A. Rossi-Doria (ed.), *Annarita Buttafuoco. Ritratto di una storica* (Rome: Jouvence, 2001); P. Gabrielli, *Questioni di femminismo e di cittadinanza. Leggere Annarita Buttafuoco* (Siena: Università degli Studi, 2001); P. Gabrielli, 'Protagonists and Politics in the Italian Women's Movement: a Reflection on the Work of Annarita Buttafuoco', *Journal of Modern Italian Studies*, 7 (2002): 74–87.

3. See A. Buttafuoco, *Cronache femminili. Temi e momenti della stampa emancipazionista in Italia dall'Unità al fascismo* (Siena: Università degli Studi, 1988).

4. Cited in A. Buttafuoco, 'Vite esemplari. Donne del primo Novecento', in A. Buttafuoco and M. Zancan (eds), *Svelamento. Sibilla Aleramo: una biografia intellettuale* (Milan: Feltrinelli, 1988), p. 151.

5. On the many ways in which the idea of the 'new woman' was used in this period, see M. De Giorgio, 'Dalla "donna nuova" alla donna della "nuova" Italia', in D. Leoni and C. Zadra (eds), *La Grande Guerra. Esperienze, memoria, immagine* (Bologna: Il Mulino, 1986).

6. Cited in Buttafuoco, *Cronache femminili*, p. 89.

7. De Giorgio, *Le italiane*, p. 500.

8. See M. D'Amelia, *La mamma* (Bologna: Il Mulino, 2005), chap. 3 on how certain mothers of patriots, including Mazzini's own mother Maria Drago, were venerated as heroic figures.

9. On these early feminists, see J. Jeffrey Howard, 'Patriot Mothers in the Post-Risorgimento: Women after the Italian Revolution', in C. R. Berkin and C. M. Lovett (eds), *Women, War and Revolution* (New York: Holmes & Meier, 1980); F. Pieroni Bortolotti, *Alle origini del movimento femminile in Italia, 1848–1892* (Turin: Einaudi, 1963); Buttafuoco, *Cronache femminili*, chap. 1.

10. See G. Biadene, 'Solidareità e amicizia: il gruppo de "La donna" (1870–1880)', *Nuova DWF*, 10–11 (1979): 48–79.

11. On Mozzoni, see, for example, the critical edition of a selection of her writings, A. M. Mozzoni, *La liberazione della donna*, ed. F. Pieroni Bortolotti (Milan: Mazzotta, 1975).

12. Buttafuoco, *Questioni di cittadinanza*, pp. 54–6.

13. M. Tesoro, 'Presenza delle donne nei partiti politici, 1890–1914', *Storia e problemi contemporanei*, 4 (1989): 59–60.

14. M. Casalini, '"Sebben che siamo donne . . .". Il movimento operaio e la questione delle lavoratrici', *Passato e presente*, 45 (1998): 113–34, p. 133.

15. Ibid., p. 114.

16. Ibid., pp. 115–16.

17. On Malnati, see E. Scaramuzza, 'La maestra italiana tra Ottocento e Novecento. Una figura esemplare di educatrice socialista: Linda Malnati', in L. Rossi (ed.), *Cultura, istruzione e socialismo nell'età giolittiana* (Milan: Angeli, 1991).

18. M. Casalini, 'Femminismo e socialismo in Anna Kuliscioff, 1890–1907', *Italia contemporanea*, 143 (1981), p. 26. See also C. La Vigna, 'The Marxist Ambivalence Towards Women: Between Socialism and Feminism in the Italian Socialist Party', in M. J. Boxer and J. Quartaert (eds), *Socialist Women* (New York: Elsevier, 1978).

19. 'Feminism and Socialism in Anna Kuliscioff's writings', in R. Pickering-Iazzi (ed.), *Mothers of Invention* (Minneapolis: Minnesota University Press, 1995), p. 2.

20. On the 1902 and 1910 legislation see C. Ficola, 'Legislazione sociale e tutela della maternità nell'età giolittiana', in M. L. Betri and A. Gigli Marchetti (eds), *Salute e classi lavoratrici in Italia dell'Unità al fascismo* (Milan: Angeli, 1982).

21. On Ersilia Majno, see the entries in F. Andreucci and T. Detti (eds), *Il movimento operaio italiano. Dizionario biografico (1853–1943)*, vol. 3 (Rome: Riuniti, 1977), and R. Farina (ed.), *Dizionario biografico delle donne lombarde, 568–1968* (Milan: Baldini & Castoldi, 1995).

22. On the educational role of feminist organisations, see A. Buttafuoco, 'La filantropia come politica. Esperienze dell'emancipazionismo italiano nel Novecento', in L. Ferrante et al. (eds), *Ragnatele di rapporti. Patronage e reti di relazione nella storia delle donne* (Turin: Rosenberg & Sellier, 1988).

23. On the Uffici, see A. Buttafuoco, 'Tra cittadinanza politica e cittadinanza sociale. Progetti ed esperienze del movimento politico delle donne nell'Italia liberale', in G. Bonacchi and A. Groppi (eds), *Il dilemma della cittadinanza. Diritti e doveri delle donne* (Bari-Rome: Laterza, 1993).

24. M. P. Bigaran, 'Progetti e dibattiti parlamentari sul suffragio femminile: da Peruzzi a Giolitti', *Rivista di storia contemporanea*, 14, 1 (1985): 50–82, p. 74.

25. On these initiatives see Buttafuoco, *Questioni di cittadinanza*, chap. 3.

26. UFN, *Relazione 1906* (Milan, Ramberti, no date [1907]), p. 5, cited in ibid., p. 175.

27. F. Pieroni Bortolotti, *Socialismo e questione femminile in Italia, 1892–1922* (Milan: Mazzotta, 1974), p. 25.

28. D. Meyer, *Sex and Power: The Rise of Women in America, Russia, Sweden and Italy* (Middletown: Wesleyan University Press, 1987), p. 131.

29. Buttafuoco, *Questioni di cittadinanza*, pp. 22–3. See also Buttafuoco, '*La trama di una tradizione'. Leggere Franca Pieroni Bortolotti* (Siena: Università degli Studi, 2001).

30. See A. Buttafuoco, 'Motherhood as a Political Strategy: the Role of the Italian Women's Movement in the Creation of the Cassa Nazionale di Maternità', in G. Bock and P. Thane (eds), *Maternity and Gender Politics: Women and the Rise of the European Welfare States, 1880s–1950s* (London: Routledge, 1991).

31. Buttafuoco, *Cronache femminili*, p. 109.

32. On early 'Catholic feminism' see P. Gaiotti de Biase, *Le origini del movimento cattolico femminile* (Brescia: Morcelliana, 2002 [Ist edn 1963]); Gaiotti de Biase, 'Da una cittadinanza all'altra. Il duplice protagonismo delle donne cattoliche', in Bonacchi and Groppi (eds), *Il dilemma della cittadinanza*; Buttafuoco, *Cronache femminili*, pp. 71–88.

33. On the CNDI, see C. Gori, *Crisalidi. Emancipazioniste liberali in età giolittiana* (Milan: Angeli, 2003); F. Taricone, *L'associazionismo femminile in Italia dall'Unità al Fascismo* (Milan: Unicoplo, 1996).

34. See De Giorgio, *Le italiane*, p. 502.

35. See Gori, *Crisalidi*, chap. 3.

36. Cited in Gaiotti de Biase, *Le origini del movimento*, p. 166.

37. C. Dau Novelli, 'L'associazionismo femminile cattolico (1908–1960)', *Bollettino dell'archivio per la storia del movimento sociale cattolico in Italia*, 33 (1998): p. 113.

38. Ibid., p. 117.

39. Cited in Gaiotti de Biase, *Le origini del movimento*, p. 100.

40. On anti-suffrage arguments, see Bigaran, 'Progetti e dibattiti parlamentari'.

41. Buttafuoco, *Cronache femminili*, p. 14.

42. Ibid., p. 233.

43. On feminists as role models for other women and on the Majno–Aleramo controversy, see Buttafuoco, 'Vite esemplari'.

44. A. Buttafuoco, *Le Mariuccine: Storia di un'istituzione laica. L'Asilo Mariuccia* (Milan: Angeli, 1985).

45. On feminist campaigns to combat prostitution see M. Gibson, *Prostitution and the State in Italy, 1860–1915* (New Brunswick: Rutgers University Press, 1986); R. Macrelli, *L'indegna schiavitù. Anna Maria Mozzoni e la lotta contro la prostituzione di stato* (Rome: Riuniti, 1981).

46. Cited in Buttafuoco, 'Vite esemplari', p. 146.

3   On the 'Home Front': World War One and its Aftermath, 1915–20

1. M. Randolph Higonnet and P. L.-R. Higonnet, 'The Double Helix', in M. R. Higonnet et al. (eds), *Behind the Lines: Gender and the Two World Wars* (New Haven, CT: Yale University Press, 1987), p. 39.

2. On Italy's experience of the war, see, for example, A. Gibelli, *La Grande Guerra degli italiani, 1915–1918* (Milan: Sansoni, 1998), which includes a useful bibliography of some of the vast historiography on this topic.

3. See ibid., pp. 291–302.

4. A. Fava, 'Assistenza e propaganda nel regime di guerra (1915–18)', in *Storia e politica* (1981): 513–48, 700–18, p. 517.

5. On masculinity, see, for example, A. Arru (ed.), *La costruzione dell'identità maschile nell'età moderna e contemporanea* (Rome: Biblink, 2001); A. Arru (ed.), *Pater familias* (Rome: Biblink, 2002); S. Bellassai and M. Malatesta (eds), *Genere e mascolinità. Uno sguardo storico* (Rome: Bulzoni, 2000); *Mascolinità*, themed issue of *Genesis*, II/2 (2003); *Italian Masculinities*, special issue of *Journal of Modern Italian Studies*, 10, 3 (2005).

6. On widows, see F. Lagorio, 'Italian Widows of the First World War', in F. Coetzee and M. Shevin Coetzee (eds), *Authority, Identity and the Social History of the Great War* (Providence and Oxford: Berghahn, 1995); F. Lagorio, 'Appunti per una storia sulle vedove di guerra italiane nei conflitti mondiali', *Rivista di storia contemporanea*, 23–4 (1994–5): 170–93.

7. Cited in Gibelli, *La Grande Guerra degli italiani*, p. 199.

8. S. Soldani, 'La Grande Guerra lontano dal fronte', in *Storia d'Italia. Le regioni dall'Unità ad oggi*, vol. IV: *La Toscana*, ed. G. Mori (Turin: Einaudi, 1986), p. 402.

9. On these committees, see ibid.; Fava, 'Assistenza e propaganda'.

10. Fava, 'Assistenza e propaganda'.

11. See M. C. Dentoni, ' "L'arte di viver bene mangiando poco." Signore e contadine di fronte ai problemi alimentari', *Annali Cervi*, 13 (1991): 133–47.

12. P. Di Cori, 'Storia, sentimenti, solidarietà nelle organizzazioni femminili cattoliche dall'età giolittiana al fascismo', *Nuova DWF*, 10–11 (1979): 80–124, p. 115.

13. B. Pisa, 'La mobilitazione civile e politica delle italiane nella Grande Guerra', in *Giornale di storia contemporanea*, 4, 2 (2001): 79–103, pp. 82–3.

14. On feminist interventionists, see E. Schiavon, 'L'interventismo femminista', *Passato e presente*, 54 (2001): 59–72.

15. On Labriola in this period, see S. Follacchio, ' "L'ingegno aveva acuto e la mente aperta". Teresa Labriola. Appunti per una biografia', *Storia e problemi contemporanei*, 17 (1996).

16. M. Casalini, 'I socialisti e le donne. Dalla "mobilitazione pacifista" alla smobilitazione postbellica', *Italia contemporanea*, 222 (2001): 5–42, pp. 10–14.

17. Cited in Pisa, 'La mobilitazione civile', p. 86.

18. Ibid., pp. 89–90.

19. On feminists in war welfare work, see ibid.; S. Bartoloni, 'L'associazionismo femminile nella prima guerra mondiale e la mobilitazione per l'assistenza civile e la propaganda', in A. Gigli Marchetti and N. Torcellan (eds), *Donna lombarda* (Milan: Angeli, 1992).

20. On the FNCA, see E. Schiavon, 'Interventismo al femminile nella Grande Guerra. Assistenza e propaganda a Milano e in Italia', *Italia contemporanea*, 234 (2004): 89–104.

21. Bartoloni, 'L'associazionismo femminile', p. 85.

22. Pisa, 'La mobilitazione civile', p. 90.

23. A. Buttafuoco, *Cronache femminili. Temi e momenti della stampa emancipazionista in Italia dall'Unità al fascismo* (Siena: Università degli Studi, 1988), chap. 5.

24. See Bartoloni, 'L'associazionismo femminile', pp. 82–3.

25. Fava, 'Assistenza e propaganda', p. 711.

26. See Bartoloni, 'L'associazionismo femminile', p. 79.

27. S. Bartoloni, 'Al capezzale del malato. Le scuole per la formazione delle infermiere', in S. Bartoloni (ed.), *Per le strade del mondo* (Bologna: Il Mulino, 2007).

28. On Red Cross nurses, see the excellent S. Bartoloni, *Italiane alla guerra. L'assistenza ai feriti, 1915–1918* (Venice: Marsilio, 2003).

29. Ibid., p. 72.

30. Cited in ibid., p. 126.

31. Because of the diffuse nature of production, figures are approximate. See B. Pisa, 'Una azienda di Stato a domicilio: la confezione di indumenti militari durante la Grande Guerra', *Storia contemporanea*, 20 (1989): 953–1006, pp. 969–70.

32. On the organisation of this work, see ibid.; B. Pisa, 'La questione del vestiario militare fra mobilitazione civile e strategie logistiche', in A. Staderini, L. Zani, and F. Magni (eds), *La Grande Guerra e il fronte interno. Studi in onore di George Mosse* (Camerino: Università degli studi, 1998).

33. Soldani, 'La Grande Guerra', p. 421.

34. Pisa, 'La questione del vestiario', pp. 203–4.

35. B. Curli, *Italiane al lavoro, 1914–1920* (Venice: Marsilio, 1998).

36. Ibid., pp. 166–8.

37. Ibid., chaps 5–6.

38. A. Bravo, 'Donne contadine e prima guerra mondiale', *Società e storia*, 10 (1980), p. 847.

39. Cited in Gibelli, *La Grande Guerra degli italiani*, p. 194.
40. S. Soldani, 'Donne senza pace: esperienze di lavoro e di lotta, di vita tra guerra e dopoguerra (1915–1920)', *Annali Cervi*, 13 (1991): 13–55, p. 24.
41. A. Bull and P. Corner, *From Peasant to Entrepreneur: The Survival of the Family Economy in Italy* (Oxford: Berg, 1993), pp. 61–3.
42. E. Franzina, 'Il tempo libero della guerra. Case del soldato e postriboli militari', in D. Leoni and C. Zadra (eds), *La Grande Guerra. Esperienze, memoria, immagine* (Bologna: Il Mulino, 1986), pp. 215–16.
43. On social protest see G. Procacci, 'Popular Protest and Labour Conflict in Italy, 1915–18', *Social History*, 14 (1989): 31–58.
44. Ibid., p. 46.
45. See G. Procacci, 'La protesta delle donne delle campagne in tempo di guerra', *Annali Cervi*, 13 (1991).
46. Ibid., p. 63.
47. Procacci, 'Popular Protest and Labour Conflict', p. 42.
48. Soldani, 'La Grande Guerra', p. 444.
49. Soldani, 'Donne senza pace', p. 30.
50. On public opinion after Caporetto, see G. Procacci, 'Aspetti della mentalità collettiva durante la guerra. L'Italia dopo Caporetto', in Leoni and Zadra (eds), *La Grande Guerra*, pp. 261–90.
51. On the suffrage issue during the war and in 1919, see M. Bigaran, 'Il voto alle donne in Italia dal 1912 al fascismo', *Rivista di storia contemporanea*, 16 (1987): 240–65.
52. S. Soldani, 'Lo Stato e il lavoro delle donne nell'Italia liberale', *Passato e presente*, 24 (1990): 23–71, p. 69.
53. Soldani, 'Donne senza pace', p. 31.
54. L. Tomassini, 'Mercato del lavoro e lotte sindacali nel biennio rosso', *Annali Cervi*, 13 (1991): 87–117, p. 89.
55. M. Palazzi, *Donne sole. Storia dell'altra faccia dell'Italia tra antico regime e società contemporanea* (Milan: B. Mondadori, 1997), p. 421.
56. See F. Thébaud, 'The Great War and the Triumph of Sexual Division', in G. Duby and M. Perrot (eds), *A History of Women in the West*, vol. V: *Towards a Cultural Identity in the Twentieth Century* (Cambridge, MA: Belknap, 1994), pp. 30–1.
57. Cited in Curli, *Italiane al lavoro*, p. 286.
58. Casalini, 'I socialisti e le donne', p. 22.
59. See P. Di Cori, 'The Double Gaze: Visibility of Sexual Difference in Photographic Representation (1908–1918)', in M. Cicioni and N. Prunster (eds), *Visions and Revisions* (Oxford: Berg, 1993).
60. M. De Giorgio, 'Dalla "donna nuova" alla donna della "nuova" Italia', in Leoni and Zadra (eds), *La Grande Guerra*, p. 323.
61. S. Bartoloni, *Donne al fronte. Le infermiere volontarie nella Grande Guerra* (Rome: Jouvence, 1998).
62. See M. D'Amelia, *La mamma* (Bologna: Il Mulino, 2005), chap. 5.
63. On women and rural strikes in 1919–20, see Tomassini, 'Mercato del lavoro', p. 89.

4 'Exemplary Wives and Mothers': Under Fascist Dictatorship

1. P. Meldini, *Sposa e madre esemplare. Ideologia e politica della donna e della famiglia durante il fascismo* (Rimini-Florence: Guaraldi, 1975).
2. See, for example, I. Vaccari (ed.), *La donna nel ventennio fascista, 1919–1943* (Milan: Vangelista, 1978).
3. V. De Grazia, *How Fascism Ruled Women: Italy, 1922–1945* (Berkeley: California University Press, 1992).
4. Cited in S. Bellassai, *La mascolinità contemporanea* (Rome: Carocci, 2004), p. 84. See also B. Spackman, *Fascist Virilities* (Minnesota University Press: Minneapolis, 1996).
5. Cited in T. Koon, *Believe, Obey, Fight: Political Socialization of Youth in Fascist Italy* (Chapel Hill: University of North Carolina Press, 1985), p. 25.
6. For the text of the Ascension Day speech, see http://cronologia.leonardo. it/storia/a1927v.htm
7. On the loans, see M. Salvante, 'I prestiti matrimoniali: una misura pro-natalista nella Germania nazista e nell'Italia fascista', *Passato e presente*, 60 (2003): 39–58.
8. On sexuality in this period, see, for example, Bruno P. F. Wanrooij, *Storia del pudore. La questione sessuale in Italia, 1860–1940* (Venice: Marsilio, 1990).
9. N. Revelli, *L'anello forte. La donna: storie di vita contadina* (Turin: Einaudi, 1985), pp. 58–60.
10. D. Detriagache, 'L'Italie fasciste et la repression de l'avortement', *Mélanges de l'École Française de Rome*, 92 (1980): 691–735.
11. Testimony of an unidentified midwife in L. Lanzardo, *Il mestiere prezioso. Le ostetriche raccontano* (Turin: Forma, 1985), p. 26.
12. A. Gissi, *Le segrete manovre delle donne* (Rome: Biblink, 2006), p. 87. On midwives, see also A. Gissi, 'Between Tradition and Profession: Italian Midwives during the Fascist Period', in P. Willson (ed.), *Gender, Family and Sexuality: The Private Sphere in Italy, 1860–1945* (Basingstoke: Palgrave Macmillan, 2004); N. Triolo, 'Fascist Unionization and the Professionalization of Midwives in Italy: a Sicilian Case Study', *Medical Anthropology Quarterly*, 8 (1994): 259–81.
13. Police report cited in Gissi, *Le segrete manovre*, p. 82.
14. See P. Willson, 'Flowers for the Doctor: Pro-natalism and Abortion in Fascist Milan', *Modern Italy*, 1 (1996): 44–62.
15. On gay men under Fascism there is a growing literature. See, for example, M. Ebner, 'The Persecution of Homosexual Men under Fascism', in Willson, *Gender, Family and Sexuality*; L. Benadusi, *L'omosessualità nell'esperimento totalitario fascista* (Milan: Feltrinelli, 2005).
16. Luigi Vercellotti, cited in L. Passerini, *Torino operaia e fascismo. Una storia orale* (Rome-Bari: Laterza, 1984), p. 182.
17. C. Saraceno, 'Constructing Families, Shaping Women's Lives: the Making of Italian Families between Market Economy and State Interventions', in

J. Gillis et al. (eds), *The European Experience of Declining Fertility, 1850–1970* (Oxford: Blackwell, 1992), p. 260.

18. On ONMI, see, for example, A. Bresci, 'L'Opera Nazionale maternità e infanzia nel ventennio fascista', *Italia contemporanea*, 192 (1993): 421–42; P. Willson, 'Opera nazionale per la maternità e l'infanzia (Onmi)', in S. Luzzatto and V. De Grazia (eds), *Dizionario del fascismo*, vol. II (Turin: Einaudi, 2003); C. Ipsen, *Dictating Demography: The Problem of Population in Fascist Italy* (Cambridge: Cambridge University Press, 1996).

19. On infant abandonment, see, for example, D. Kertzer, *Sacrificed for Honour: Italian Infant Abandonment and the Politics of Reproductive Control* (Boston, MA: Beacon, 1993); M. S. Quine, *Italy's Social Revolution: Charity and Welfare from Liberalism to Fascism* (Basingstoke: Palgrave Macmillan, 2002); G. Pomata, 'Madri illegittime tra Ottocento e Novecento: Storie cliniche e storie di vita', *Quaderni storici*, 44 (1980): 497–542.

20. Passerini, *Torino operaia e fascista*, p. 187.

21. De Grazia, *How Fascism Ruled Women*, p. 154.

22. J. Charnitzky, *Fascismo e scuola. La politica scolastica del regime (1922–1943)* (Florence: La Nuova Italia, 1994), p. 499.

23. On Fascist propaganda in primary schools, see Koon, *Believe, Obey, Fight*, chap. 3.

24. De Grazia, *How Fascism Ruled Women*, p. 154.

25. Koon, *Believe, Obey, Fight*, p. 49.

26. A. M. Galoppini, *Il lungo viaggio verso la parità* (Pisa: Tacchi, 1992), pp. 131–2.

27. On gender and the Charter, see Charnitzky, *Fascismo e scuola*, pp. 447–9.

28. De Grazia, *How Fascism Ruled Women*, p. 154.

29. Cited in S. Ulivieri, 'Alfabetizzazione, processi di scolarizzazione femminile e percorsi professionali tra tradizione e mutamento', in S. Ulivieri (ed.), *Educazione e ruolo femminile. La condizione delle donne in Italia dal dopoguerra a oggi* (Florence: La Nuova Italia, 1992), p. 187.

30. A. De Grand, 'Women under Italian Fascism', *Historical Journal*, 19 (1976): 947–68, p. 966.

31. Charnitzky, *Fascismo e scuola*, p. 513.

32. Ibid., p. 431.

33. M. Castellani, *Donne italiane di ieri e di oggi* (Florence: Bemporad, 1936–7), p. 82.

34. B. Mussolini, 'Macchina e donna', *Il popolo d'Italia*, 206 (31 August 1934).

35. Castellani, *Donne italiane di ieri*, p. 109.

36. De Grand, 'Women under Italian Fascism', p. 967.

37. M. Barbagli, *Disoccupazione intellettuale e sistema scolastico in Italia* (Bologna: Il Mulino, 1974), p. 245.

38. Castellani, *Donne italiane di ieri*, p. 113.

39. On these colleges, see Anon., 'Le tre Scuole Superiori Femminili del Partito si riapriranno nella prima decade di ottobre', *Giornale della donna*, 15 Sept. 1933, pp. 1–2.

40. P. Ferrara, 'Le donne negli uffici (1863–2002)', in G. Melis (ed.), *Impiegati* (Turin: Roscnberg & Sellier, 2004), p. 141.

41. Castellani, *Donne italiane di ieri*, p. 114.

42. Ferrara, 'Le donne negli uffici', p. 145.

43. Cited in Ipsen, *Dictating Demography*, p. 163.

44. De Grand, 'Women under Italian Fascism', p. 956.

45. M. Salvati, *Il regime e gli impiegati* (Rome-Bari: Laterza, 1992), p. 203.

46. Figures from O. Vitali, *Aspetti dello sviluppo economico italiano alla luce della ricostruzione della popolazione attiva* (Rome: Università di Roma, 1970), pp. 366–9.

47. S. Soldani, 'Lo stato e il lavoro delle donne', *Passato e presente*, 24 (1990): 23–71, p. 62n.

48. See P. Sabbatucci Severini and A. Trento, 'Alcuni cenni sul mercato di lavoro durante il fascismo', *Quaderni storici*, 10 (1975): 550–78.

49. See E. Noether, 'Italian Women and Fascism: a Re-evaluation', *Italian Quarterly*, 23, 90 (1982): 69–80, p. 72.

50. See O. Vitali, *La popolazione attiva in agricoltura attraverso i censimenti (1881–1961)* (Rome: Failli, 1968); O. Vitali, 'I censimenti e la composizione sociale dell'agricoltura italiana', in P. Bevilacqua (ed.), *Storia dell'agricoltura italiana*, vol. II: *Uomini e classi* (Venice: Marsilio, 1990).

51. S. Salvatici, *Contadine nell'Italia fascista. Presenze, ruoli, immagini* (Turin: Rosenberg & Sellier, 1999). See also P. Willson, *Peasant Women and Politics in Fascist Italy: The Massaie Rurali* (London: Routledge, 2002), chap. 1.

52. See B. Bianchi, 'I tessili: lavoro, salute, conflitti', *Annali Feltrinelli*, 20 (1979–80): 973–1070.

53. See, P. Willson, *The Clockwork Factory: Women and Work in Fascist Italy* (Oxford: Oxford University Press, 1993).

54. R. Sarti, 'La domesticité en Italie durant la période du fascisme (1922–1943)', *Sextant*, 15–16 (2001): 174–5.

55. See A. Dadà, 'Partire per un figlio altrui', in D. Corsi (ed.), *Altrove. Viaggi di donne dall'antichità al Novecento* (Rome: Viella, 1999).

56. Sarti, 'La domesticité en Italie', p. 190.

57. S. Bellassai, *La legge del desiderio. Il progetto Merlin e l'Italia degli anni cinquanta* (Rome: Carocci, 2006), pp. 25–7.

58. 'Maria G.' in Willson, *The Clockwork Factory*, p. 204.

59. On fashion in this period, see N. Aspesi, *Il lusso e l'autarchia. Storia dell'eleganza italiana, 1930–1944* (Milan: Rizzoli, 1982).

60. See S. Salvatici, 'Il rotocalco femminile: una presenza nuova negli anni del fascismo', in S. Franchini and S. Soldani (eds), *Donne e giornalismo. Percorsi e presenze di una storia di genere* (Milan: Angeli, 2004).

61. De Grazia, *How Fascism Ruled Women*, pp. 119–20.

5 Doing their Duty for Nation (or Church): Mass Mobilisation during the Fascist *Ventennio*

1. Cited in F. Taricone, *L'associazionismo femminile in Italia dall'Unità al fascismo* (Milan: Unicopli, 1996), p. 83.

2. I. Vaccari, *La donna nel ventennio fascista (1919–1943)* (Bologna: Vangelista, 1977), p. 114.

3. On anti-fascist women, see, for example, P. Gabrielli, *Fenicotteri in volo. Donne comuniste nel ventennio fascista* (Rome: Carocci, 1999); G. De Luna, *Donne in oggetto. L'antifascismo nella società italiana (1922–1939)* (Turin: Bollati Boringhieri, 1996); M. Gibson, 'Women and the Left in the Shadow of Fascism in Interwar Italy', in H. Gruber and P. Graves (eds), *Women and Socialism: Socialism and Women* (New York and Oxford: Berghahn, 1998).

4. On Catholic women's organisations under Fascism, see C. Dau Novelli, *Famiglia e modernizzazione in Italia tra le due guerre* (Rome: Studium, 1994), chap. 5; M. De Giorgio, 'Metodi e tempi di un'educazione sentimentale. La Gioventù Femminile Cattolica Italiana negli anni venti', *Nuova DWF*, 10–11 (1979): 126–45; P. di Cori, 'Rosso e bianco. La devozione al Sacro Cuore di Gesù nel primo dopoguerra', *Memoria*, 5 (1982): 82–107; P. di Cori, 'Storia, sentimenti, solidareità nelle organizzazioni femminili cattoliche dall'età giolittiana al fascismo', *Nuova DWF*, 10–11 (1979): 80–124.

5. M. De Giorgio, *Le italiane dall'Unità a oggi* (Rome-Bari: Laterza, 1992), p. 48.

6. Di Cori, 'Storia, sentimenti, solidareità', p. 121.

7. S. Salvatici and A. Scattigno, *In una stagione diversa. Le donne in Palazzo Vecchio, 1946/1970* (Florence: Edizioni Comune Aperto, 1998), p. 169.

8. R. Sarti, 'La domesticité en Italie durant la période du fascisme (1922–1943)', *Sextant*, 15–16 (2001): 165–202, pp. 193–8.

9. On early Fascist women, see D. Detriagache, 'Il fascismo femminile da San Sepolcro all'affare Matteotti (1919–1925)', *Storia contemporanea*, 14 (1983): 211–51; S. Bartoloni, 'Dalla crisi del movimento delle donne alle origini del fascismo. L'"Almanacco della donna italiana" e la "Rassegna femminile italiana"', in A. Crispino (ed.), *Esperienza storica femminile nell'età moderna e contemporanea* (Rome: UDI, 1988).

10. See I. Rinaldi, 'Ines Donati. Realtà e mito di un'"eroina" fascista', *Quaderni di Resistenza Marche*, 13 (1987): 48–89.

11. On the FF, see P. Willson, 'Italy', in K. Passmore (ed.), *Women, Gender and Fascism in Europe, 1919–1945* (Manchester: Manchester University Press, 2003); V. De Grazia, *How Fascism Ruled Women: Italy, 1922–1945* (Berkeley: California University Press, 1992), chap. 8; H. Dittrich-Johansen, *Le 'militi dell'idee'. Storia delle organizzazioni femminili del Partito Nazionale Fascista* (Florence: Olschki, 2002).

12. Little research has been done on the lives of prominent female Fascists. A few biographical works exist. See, for example, H. Dittrich-Johansen, 'Strategie femminili nel ventennio fascista: la carriera politica di Piera Gatteschi Fondelli nello "Stato degli uomini" (1919–1943)', *Storia e problemi contemporanei*, 21 (1998): 65–86; D. Detriagache, 'Du socialisme au fascisme naissant: formation et itinéraire de Regina Terruzzi', in R. Thalmann (ed.), *Femmes et fascismes* (Paris: Tierce, 1986); P. Willson, '"The Fairy Tale Witch": Laura Marani Argnani and the Women's Fasci of Reggio Emilia, 1929–1940', *Contemporary European History*, 15 (2006): 23–42.

13. On the class composition of the early leaders, see H. Dittrich-Johansen, 'Le professioniste del Pnf', *Studi storici*, 42 (2001): 181–201, pp. 190–4.

14. Cited in G. Gaballo, *Ero, sono e sarò fascista. Un percorso attraverso il fondo archivistico di Angela Maria Guerra* (Genoa: Le Mani, 2001), p. 18.

15. Cited in L. Motti, 'Le "Orvietine" e l'Accademia: un'esperienza di confine tra appartenenza e senso di sé', in M. Rossi Caponeri and L. Motti (eds), *Accademiste di Orvieto. Donne ed educazione fisica nell'Italia fascista, 1932–1943* (Perugia: Quattroemme, 1996), p. 106.

16. Bartoloni, 'Dalla crisi del movimento', p. 130.

17. Cited in A. M. Galoppini, *Il lungo viaggio verso la parità* (Pisa: Tacchi, 1992), p. 103.

18. On suffrage, see M. Bigaran, 'Il voto alle donne in Italia dal 1912 al fascismo', *Rivista di storia contemporanea*, 16 (1987): 240–65.

19. Although supposedly the FF official organ, this newspaper was entirely personally financed by Majer Rizzioli herself. See S. Bartoloni, 'Il fascismo femminile e la sua stampa: la "Rassegna femminile italiana" (1925–1930)', *Nuova DWF*, 21 (1982): 143–69.

20. Cited in Willson, 'Italy', p. 16.

21. Although Labriola often wrote in the Fascist women's press, she was never really involved in the FF. Indeed she alienated many Fascist women by her intellectual and arrogant tone. (See S. Follacchio, '"L'ingegno aveva acuto e la mente aperta". Teresa Labriola. Appunti per una biografia', *Storia e problemi contemporanei*, 17 (1996): 65–89, pp. 84–5.)

22. V. De Grazia, *How Fascism Ruled Women*, p. 238.

23. P. Willson, 'Empire, Gender and the "Home Front" in Fascist Italy', *Women's History Review*, 16 (2007): 487–500.

24. See P. Willson, *Peasant Women and Politics in Fascist Italy: the Massaie Rurali* (London: Routledge, 2002).

25. Ibid., p. 78.

26. See P. Willson, 'Sezione operaie e lavoranti a domicilio', in V. De Grazia and S. Luzzatto (eds), *Dizionario critico del fascismo*, vol. 2 (Turin: Einaudi, 2003).

27. Cited in Willson, *Peasant Women and Politics*, p. 190.

28. Testimony of 'Clorinda C' in M. Mietto and M. G. Ruggerini, '"Faber est suae quisque fortunae." Gli studenti del Liceo Classico e dell'Istituto Magistrale a Reggio Emilia', *Contributi*, 21–2 (1987): 232–391, p. 359.

29. Gaballo, *Ero, sono e sarò fascista*.

30. H. Dittrich-Johansen, 'Per la Patria e per il Duce. Storie di Fedeltà Femminili nell'Italia fascista', *Genesis*, I/1 (2002): 125–56.

31. Willson, *Peasant Women and Politics*, p. 97n.

32. On the Sant'Alessio College, see ibid., chap. 7.

33. On the youth groups, see T. Koon, *Believe, Obey, Fight: Political Socialization of Youth in Fascist Italy, 1922–1943* (Chapel Hill: North Carolina University Press, 1985).

34. Cited in P. Ferrara, 'Corpo e politica: storia di un'Accademia al femminile (1919–45)', in Rossi Caponeri and Motti (eds), *Accademiste di Orvieto*, p. 54.

35. Motti, 'Le "Orvietine"', p. 118.

36. Anna Maria Zanardo Fanello (interviewed 1995), cited in ibid., p. 132.

37. Cited in M. D'Amelia, *La mamma* (Bologna: Il Mulino, 2005), p. 211.

38. Koon, *Believe, Obey, Fight*, pp. 173, 175.

6 War Comes to Women, 1940–45

1. Much has been written about the military history of this war. For a concise account, see B. Holden Reid, 'Italian campaign', in I. C. B. Dear (ed.), *The Oxford Companion to World War II* (Oxford: Oxford University Press, 1995), pp. 451–6.

2. For a thoughtful reflection on recent trends in this historiography, see D. Gagliani, 'Resistenza alla guerra, diritti universali, diritti delle donne', in D. Gagliani (ed.), *Guerra, resistenza, politica. Storie di donne* (Reggio Emilia: Aliberti, 2006).

3. A. Lepre, *Le illusioni, la paura, la rabbia. Il fronte interno italiano, 1940–1943* (Naples: Edizioni Scientifiche Italiane, 1989), p. 20.

4. Cited in F. Koch, 'Lo sfollamento nella memoria femminile. Proposta di lettura di alcuni testi dell'Archivio diaristico nazionale', *L'impegno*, 13 (1993): 32–40.

5. On the mobilisation of civilians, see P. Ferrazza, 'La mobilitazione civile in Italia 1940–1943', *Italia contemporanea*, 214 (1999): 21–42.

6. M. Mafai, *Pane nero: donne e vita quotidiana nella Seconda Guerra Mondiale* (Milan: Mondadori, 1987), pp. 57–8.

7. L. Baldissara, ' "Senza onore e senza pane". Industrie di guerra, classe operaia e condizioni di vita a Bologna', *Annali della Fondazione Micheletti*, 5 (1990–91): 463–89, p. 488.

8. Ferrazza, 'La mobilitazione civile', p. 31.

9. Ibid., p. 40.

10. In March 1942, female factory workers were allowed to aspire to the (hitherto male) grade of *operaio qualificato* (skilled worker) (ibid., p. 37).

11. On air-raid protection, see Lepre, *Le illusioni, la paura*, pp. 57–60.

12. On rationing, see ibid., pp. 83–91.

13. Mafai, *Pane nero*, p. 144.

14. Cited in P. Cavallo, *Italiani in guerra. Sentimenti e immagini dal 1940 al 1943* (Bologna: Il Mulino, 1997), p. 272.

15. G. De Luna, 'Torino in guerra: la ricerca di un'esistenza collettiva', *Annali della Fondazione Micheletti*, 5 (1990–91): 885–902.

16. For an overview of this copious historiography, see P. Willson, 'Saints and Heroines: Re-writing the History of Italian Women in the Resistance', in T. Kirk and A. McElligot (eds), *Opposing Fascism* (Cambridge: Cambridge University Press, 1999). A useful text in English is J. Slaughter, *Women and the Italian Resistance, 1943–1945* (Denver, CO: Arden, 1997).

17. Testimony of Tersilla Fenoglio Oppedisano, in A. M. Bruzzone and R. Farina, *La resistenza taciuta. Dodici vite di partigiane piemontesi* (Turin: Bollati Boringhieri, 2003 [Ist edn 1976]), p. 173.

18. See, for example, V. Serafini, 'Lina Merlin: dalle donne in politica alla politica delle donne', in Gagliani, *Guerra, resistenza, politica*.

19. L. Passerini, *Torino, operaio e fascista. Una storia orale* (Rome-Bari: Laterza, 1984), p. 19.
20. Slaughter, *Women and the Italian Resistance*, p. 58.
21. See A. Bravo, 'Simboli del materno', in A. Bravo (ed.), *Donne e uomini nelle gverre mondiali* (Rome-Bari: Laterza, 1991), p. 110.
22. Cited in M. Addis Saba, *Partigiane. Tutte le donne della Resistenza* (Milan: Mursia, 1998), p. 99.
23. See, for example, G. Sciola, 'Società rurale e Resistenza nelle vallate bresciane', in R. Anni et al. (eds), *I gesti ed i sentimenti: le donne nella Resistenza bresciana* (Brescia: Comune di Brescia, 1990), pp. 50–4.
24. On 'civilian Resistance', see A. Bravo, 'Armed and Unarmed: Struggles without Weapons in Europe and in Italy', *Journal of Modern Italian Studies*, 10 (2005): 468–84; J. Semelin, *Unarmed Against Hitler: Civilian Resistance in Europe, 1939–1943* (Westport, CT: Praeger, 1993).
25. Bravo, 'Simboli del materno'.
26. R. Overy, 'Strategic Air Offensives', in *The Oxford Companion to World War II*, p. 837.
27. On how peasant women remembered such events (often blaming the partisans for provoking massacres), see, for example, G. Contini, 'Ricordare le stragi naziste: le contadine toscane', *Genesis*, I/1 (2002): 242–50.
28. L. Picciotto Fargion, *Il libro della memoria. Gli ebrei deportati dall'Italia (1943–1945)* (Milan: Mursia, 1991), p. 342.
29. On rapes in the German occupied area, see C. Venturoli, 'La violenza taciuta. Percorsi di ricerca sugli abusi sessuali fra il passaggio e l'arrestarsi del fronte', in D. Gagliani et al. (eds), *Donne, guerra, politica* (Bologna: CLUEB, 2000).
30. Testimony of Rosanna Rolando in Bruzzone and Farina, *La Resistenza taciuta*, p. 25.
31. On the Allied governance of the South, see D. W. Ellwood, *Italy 1943–45* (London: Leicester University Press, 1985).
32. Ibid., p. 127.
33. G. Gribaudi, *Guerra totale. Tra bombe alleate e violenze naziste. Napoli e il fronte meridionale 1940–44* (Turin: Bollati Boringhieri, 2005), p. 528.
34. P. Masino, 'Di qui è passato il lupo', *Noi Donne*, 21 Oct. 1951, cited in V. Chiurlotto, 'Donne come noi: Marocchinate 1944 – Bosniache 1993', *DWF*, 17 (1993): 42–67, pp. 57–8.
35. Gribaudi, *Guerra totale*, p. 532.
36. Masino, 'Di qui è passato il lupo', pp. 45–9.
37. J. C. Notin, *La Campagne d'Italie. Les victoires oubliées de la France, 1943–1945* (Paris: Perrin, 2002); Gribaudi, *Guerra totale*, chap. 10.
38. See M. Fraddosio, 'The Fallen Hero: the Myth of Mussolini and Fascist Women in the Italian Social Republic', *Journal of Contemporary History*, 31 (1996): 99–124.
39. On the SAF, see, for example, F. Alberico, 'Ausiliarie di Salò. Videointerviste come fonti di studio della Rsi', *Storia e memoria*, 15 (2006): 199–225; D. Gagliani, 'Donne e armi. Il caso della Repubblica Sociale Italiana', in

D. Gagliani and M. Salvati (eds), *Donne e spazio nel processo di moderizzazi-one* (Bologna: CLUEB, 1996).

40. M. Fraddosio, 'La donna e la guerra. Aspetti delle militanza femminile nel fascismo: dalla mobilitazione civile alle origini del Saf nella Repubblica Sociale Italiana', *Storia contemporanea*, 10 (1989): 1105–81.

41. Cited in M. Fraddosio, 'La mobilitazione femminile: i Gruppi fascisti repubblicani femminili e il Saf', *Annali della Fondazione Luigi Micheletti*, 2 (1986): 257–74, pp. 265–6.

42. Cited in Alberico, 'Ausiliarie di Salò', p. 212.

43. S. D'Alessandro, 'Le ausiliarie nella repubblica sociale italiana', *Studi e ricerche di storia contemporanea*, 46 (1996): 5–26, pp. 10, 20.

44. The theme of such collaboration is a relatively new one for Italian histo-riography. For some early findings, see M. Firmani, 'Oltre il SAF: storie di collaborazioniste della RSI', S. Lunadei, 'Donne processate a Roma per collaborazionismo', both in Gagliani (ed.), *Guerra, resistenza, politica*. See also, S. D'Alessandro, 'Ausiliarie e partigiane. Due mondi diversi', *Studi e ricerche di storia contemporanea*, 47 (1997): 47–70.

45. See Bravo, 'Simboli del materno', pp. 122–4.

46. F. Lagorio, 'Appunti per una storia sulle vedove di guerra italiane nei conflitti mondiali', in *Rivista di storia contemporanea*, 23–4 (1994–5): 170–93, p. 184.

47. This view is put strongly in A. Bravo, 'Guerre e mutamenti nelle strutture di genere', *Italia contemporanea*, 195 (1994): 367–74.

7 Moving into Town: New Social and Economic Roles, 1945–67

1. C. Dau Novelli, *Sorelle d'Italia. Casalinghe, impiegate e militanti nel Nove-cento* (Rome: AVE, 1996), pp. 107–8.

2. G. Crainz, *Storia del miracolo italiano. Culture, identità, trasformazioni fra anni cinquanta e sessanta* (Rome: Donzelli, 2005), p. vii.

3. Oral testimony cited in G. Bonansea, 'Tra immaginario contadino e realtà operaia. Donne a Torino negli anni Cinquanta', *Annali Cervi*, 13 (1991): 329–43, p. 337.

4. Cited in A. Bravo, 'Madri fra oppressione ed emancipazione', in A. Bravo et al., *Storia sociale delle donne nell'Italia contemporanea* (Rome-Bari: Laterza, 2001), p. 106.

5. S. Bellassai, *La legge del desiderio. Il progretto Merlin e l'Italia degli anni Cinquanta* (Rome: Carocci, 2006).

6. See S. Gundle, 'Feminine Beauty, National Identity and Political Conflict in Postwar Italy, 1945–1954', *Contemporary European History*, 8 (1999): 359–78.

7. S. Bellassai, *La mascolinità contemporanea* (Rome: Carocci, 2004), chap. 5.

8. E. Capussotti, 'Modelli femminili e giovani spettrici. Donne e cinema negli anni Cinquanta', in N. M. Filippini et al. (eds), *Corpi e storia. Donne e uomini dal mondo antico all'età contemporanea* (Rome: Viella, 2002).

9. Cited in M. C. Liguori, 'Donne e consumi nell'Italia degli anni cinquanta', *Italia contemporanea*, 205 (1996): 665–89, p. 675.

10. S. Piccone Stella, *La prima generazione. Ragazze e ragazzi nel miracolo economico italiano* (Milan: Angeli, 1993).

11. Ibid., p. 106.

12. Cited in ibid., p. 60.

13. I. Bakker, 'Women's Employment in Comparative Perspective', in J. Jenson et al. (eds), *Feminization of the Labour Force: Paradoxes and Promises* (Cambridge: Polity, 1988), p. 19.

14. O. Vitali, *Aspetti dello sviluppo economico italiano alla luce della ricostruzione della popolazione attiva* (Rome: Università di Roma, 1970), pp. 325–7.

15. A. Signorelli, 'La condizione femminile nel tramonto della società rurale tradizionale (1945–1960)', *Annali Cervi*, 13 (1991): 249–75.

16. D. Del Boca, 'Women in a Changing Workplace: the Case of Italy', in Jenson et al., *Feminization of the Labour Force*, p. 122.

17. F. Pristinger, 'Il lavoro delle donne: passato e presente', in S. Ulivieri (ed.), *Educazione e ruolo femminile. La condizione delle donne in Italia dal dopoguerra a oggi* (Florence: La Nuova Italia, 1992), p. 149.

18. G. Vicarelli, 'Il medico al femminile. Le donne nello sviluppo della professione medica in Italia', *Polis*, 3 (1989): 225–48, p. 229.

19. S. Ulivieri, 'Donne e insegnamento dal dopoguerra a oggi. La femminilizzazione del corpo insegnante', in S. Ulivieri, *Essere donne insegnanti. Storia, professionalità e cultura di genere* (Turin: Rosenberg & Sellier, 1996), p. 75.

20. Cited in ibid., p. 62.

21. R. Sarti, 'La domesticité en Italie durant la période du fascisme (1922–1943)', *Sextant*, 15–16 (2001): 165–202, p. 171.

22. Cited in Crainz, *Storia del miracolo*, p. 120.

23. Piccone Stella, *La prima generazione*, p. 98.

24. L. Passerini, 'The Ambivalent Image of Women in Mass Culture', in F. Thébaud (ed.), *A History of Women in the West*. vol. V: *Toward a Cultural Identity in the Twentieth Century* (Cambridge, MA: Belknap, 1994), p. 339.

25. For details of this survey, see F. Taricone, *Il Centro Italiano Femminile: dalle origini agli anni settanta* (Milan: Angeli, 2001), pp. 99–117.

26. Dau Novelli, *Sorelle d'Italia*, p. 120.

27. Cited in Piccone Stella, *La prima generazione*, p. 104.

28. Passerini, 'The Ambivalent Image of Women', p. 335.

29. Cited in Bonansea, 'Tra immaginario contadino', p. 334.

30. Cited in Liguori, 'Donne e consumi', p. 677.

31. See E. Asquer, 'Per una storia sociale della lavatrice in Italia. Donne, elettrodomestici e consumi negli anni cinquanta e sessanta', *Italia contemporanea*, 241 (2005): 449–70.

32. See, for example, C. Hardyment, *From Mangle to Microwave: The Mechanization of Household Work* (Cambridge: Polity, 1988).

33. Asquer, 'Per una storia sociale', p. 461.

34. See M. D'Amelia, *La mamma* (Bologna: Il Mulino, 2005), chap. 1.

35. M. De Giorgio, *Le italiane dall'Unità a oggi* (Rome-Bari: Laterza, 1992), p. 309.

36. On such court judgements, see R. Canosa, *Il giudice e la donna. Cento anni di sentenze sulla condizione femminile in Italia* (Milan: Mazzotta, 1978).

37. Bellassai, *La mascolinità contemporanea*, pp. 103–4.

38. G. Parca, *Italian Women Confess* (London: Allen & Unwin, 1963), p. 92.

39. L. Caldwell, 'The Family in the Fifties: a Notion in Conflict with Reality', in C. Duggan and C. Wagstaff (eds), *Italy in the Cold War: Politics, Culture and Society, 1948–58* (Oxford: Berg, 1995), pp. 154–5.

40. C. Saraceno, 'The Italian Family from the 1960s to the Present', *Modern Italy*, 9 (2004): 47–57, p. 48.

41. L. Caldwell, 'Church, State and Family: the Women's Movement in Italy', in A. Kuhn and A. M. Wolpe (eds), *Feminism and Materialism* (London: Routledge, 1978), p. 84.

42. On these debates, see A. Treves, *Le nascite e la politica nell'Italia del Novecento* (Milan: LED, 2001), chap. 12.

43. M. Cacioppo, 'Condizione di vita familiare negli anni cinquanta', *Memoria*, 6 (1982): 83–90, p. 84.

44. All figures are from A. Nobile, 'Popolazione femminile e trasformazioni demografiche delle campagne (1951–1971)', *Annali Cervi*, 13 (1991): 303–28.

45. A. Boschi, *Nuove questioni matrimoniali* (Turin: Marietti, 1952 [Ist edn 1949]), pp. 30–1. Cited in S. Bernini, 'Natural Mothers: Teaching Morals and Parent-craft in Italy, 1945–60', *Modern Italy*, 9 (2004): 21–33, p. 27.

46. Cited in Treves, *Le nascite e la politica*, p. 425.

47. See Bernini, 'Natural Mothers', pp. 21–33.

48. On Parca, see P. Morris, 'The Harem Exposed: Gabriella Parca's *Le italiane si confessano*', in P. Morris (ed.), *Women in Italy, 1945–1960: An Interdisciplinary Study* (New York: Palgrave Macmillan, 2006).

49. On advice columns, see P. Morris, 'A Window on the Private Sphere: Advice Columns, Marriage, and the Evolving Family in 1950s Italy', *The Italianist*, 27 (2007): 304–32.

50. Introduction to G. Parca, *Le italiane si confessano* (Milan: Feltrinelli, 1977 [Ist edn 1959]), p. 2.

51. Piccone Stella, *La prima generazione*, p. 86.

52. Parca, *Italian Women Confess*, p. 19.

53. Piccone Stella, *La prima generazione*, p. 87.

54. L. Harrison, *The Wantons* (London: Ortolan, 1966), pp. 45–6.

55. Ibid., p. 53.

56. Ibid., p. 124.

57. M. Pelaia, 'Il cambiamento dei comportamenti sessuali', in Bravo et al., *Storia sociale delle donne*, p. 201.

58. On this comparison, see S. Piccone Stella, ' "Donne all'Americana?": Immagini convenzionali e realtà di fatto', in P. P. D'Attore (ed.), *Nemici per la pelle: sogno americano e mito sovietico nell'Italia contemporanea* (Milan: Angeli, 1991).

59. L. Passerini, *Storie di donne e femministe* (Turin: Rosenberg & Sellier, 1987), p. 143.

8 Women's Politics in the Shadow of the Cold War, 1945–67

1. CIF, *Memorie di donne a cinquant'anni dalla Costituente* (Pisa-Rome: Istituti editoriali e poligrafici internazionali, 1997), p. 87.

2. See B. Pisa, 'Angela Guidi Cingolani: politica e modelli femminili fra fede e modernizzazione', *Giornale di storia contemporanea*, 9 (2006): 95–136.

3. Cited in G. Ascoli, 'L'UDI tra emancipazione e liberazione (1943–64)', in G. Ascoli et al., *La questione femminile in Italia* (Milan: Angeli, 1977), p. 119.

4. S. Portaccio, 'Buona e bella. I periodici femminili cattolici negli anni '50', *Memoria*, 4 (1982): 140–4, p. 142.

5. Cited in Ascoli, 'L'UDI tra emancipazione', p. 143.

6. S. Bellassai, *La morale comunista. Pubblico e privato nella rappresentazione del PCI (1947–1956)* (Rome: Carocci, 2000).

7. S. Salvatici and A. Scattigno, *In una stagione diversa. Le donne in Palazzo Vecchio, 1946/1970* (Florence: Edizioni Comune Aperto, 1998), p. 43.

8. Bellassai, *La morale comunista*, p. 228.

9. See M. Casalini, *Le donne della sinistra (1944–48)* (Rome: Carocci, 2005), chap. 7.

10. Essential reading on this topic is the work of A. Rossi-Doria, in particular her *Diventare cittadine. Il voto alle donne in Italia* (Florence: Giunti, 1996).

11. A. M. Galoppini, *Il lungo viaggio verso la parità* (Pisa: Tacchi, 1992), p. 179.

12. A. Rossi-Doria, 'Una celebrazione inusuale', in L. Derossi (ed.), *1945. Il voto alle donne* (Milan: Angeli, 1998), p. 44.

13. CIF, *Memorie di donne*, p. 90.

14. Rossi-Doria makes this point in many of her writings. See, for example, 'Le donne sulla scena politica', in *Storia dell'Italia repubblicana*, vol. 1: *La costruzione della democrazia. Dalla caduta del fascismo agli anni cinquanta* (Turin: Einaudi, 1994), p. 792.

15. Maria Casalini, however, in an innovative recent book, pays some long due attention to the influence of the legacies of the past on post-war women's politics. See her *Le donne della sinistra*.

16. G. Galeotti, *Storia del voto alle donne in Italia* (Rome: Biblink, 2006), pp. 232, 270.

17. C. Dau Novelli, *Sorelle d'Italia: casalinghe, impiegate e militanti nel Novecento* (Rome: AVE, 1996), p. 175n.

18. Cited in Galoppini, *Il lungo viaggio*, p. 188.

19. Cited in C. Dau Novelli, 'Il CIF e la società italiana (1944–1981)', in C. Dau Novelli (ed.), *Donne del nostro tempo. Il Centro Italiano Femminile (1945–1995)* (Rome: Studium, 1995), p. 5.

20. See M. D'Amelia (ed.), *Donne alle urne. La conquista del voto. Documenti 1864–1946* (Rome: Biblink, 2006), p. 141.

21. Cited in Galeotti, *Storia del voto*, p. 261.

22. Cited in A. Rossi-Doria, 'Italian Women Enter Politics', in C. Duchen and I. Bandhauer Schoffman (eds), *When the War was Over: Women, War and Peace in Europe, 1940–56* (London: Leicester University Press, 2000), p. 97.

23. Cited in Salvatici and Scattigno, *In una stagione diversa*, p. 43.

24. P. Gaiotti de Biase, 'Il CIF e la conquista della cittadinanza', in Dau Novelli (ed.), *Donne del nostro tempo*, p. 102.

25. For biographical details of these pioneers, see Galeotti, *Storia del voto*, pp. 271–9.

26. Cited in Galoppini, *Il lungo viaggio*, p. 187.

27. A. Buttafuoco, 'Cittadine italiane al voto', *Passato e presente*, 40 (1997): 5–11, p. 10.

28. C. Saraceno, 'Le donne dalla battaglia per il voto alla "tutela fascista"', in Derossi (ed.), *1945. Il voto alle donne*, p. 38.

29. Cited in R. Canosa, *Il giudice e la donna. Cento anni di sentenze sulla condizione femminile in Italia* (Milan: Mazzotta, 1978), p. 133.

30. Cited in P. Zappaterra, 'Autobiografia e tensione alla politica nelle comuniste bolognesi, 1945–1955', *Storia e problemi contemporanei*, 20 (1997): 49–62, p. 56.

31. P. Ginsborg, *A History of Contemporary Italy* (Harmondsworth: Penguin, 1990), p. 127. On the southern rural unrest, see F. Faeta, 'Contadini, donne, conflittualità di classe in un paese meridionale del secondo dopoguerra', *Annali Cervi*, 13 (1991): 277–92.

32. See P. Willson, *Peasant Women and Politics in Fascist Italy* (London: Routledge, 2002), epilogue.

33. On the GF in this period, see Dau Novelli, *Sorelle d'Italia*, chap. 3.

34. F. Taricone, *Il Centro Italiano Femminile: dalle origini agli anni Settanta* (Milan: Angeli, 2001), pp. 154–6.

35. Salvatici and Scattigno, *In una stagione diversa*, pp. 38–9.

36. G. Poggi et al., *L'organizzazione partitica del PCI e della DC* (Bologna: Il Mulino, 1968), pp. 417–24.

37. Ibid., chap. 3.

38. On UDI, see, for example, M. Michetti et al., *UDI. Laboratorio di politica delle donne* (Rome: Libera Stampa, 1984); M. Rodano, 'In quanto donna. L'Udi dal 1952 al 1964', in A. Crispino (ed.), *Esperienza storica femminile nell'età moderna e contemporanea* (Rome: UDI, 1988).

39. Ascoli, 'L'UDI tra emancipazione', p. 111.

40. G. Galli and A. Prandi, *Patterns of Political Participation in Italy* (New Haven, CT: Yale University Press, 1970), p. 199.

41. S. Casmirri, *L'Unione Donne Italiane (1944–1948)* (Rome: Quaderni del Fiap, 1978), p. 89n.

42. Casalini, *Le donne della sinistra*, pp. 134–5.

43. A. Ribero, *Una questione di libertà. Il femminismo degli anni Settanta* (Turin: Rosenberg & Sellier, 1999), p. 67.

44. M. Gavioli and P. Zappaterra, '"Viaggiare su di un filo": militanti comuniste al crocevia tra storia personale e impegno politico nel "partito nuovo"', *Storia e problemi contemporanei*, 25 (2000): 79–101, p. 91.

45. C. Liotti et al., *'Volevamo cambiare il mondo'. Memorie e storie delle donne dell'UDI in Emilia Romagna* (Rome: Carocci, 2002), p. 124.

46. See M. Casalini, 'Il dilemma delle comuniste. Politiche di genere della sinistra nel secondo dopoguerra', in N. Filippini and A. Scattigno (eds), *Una democrazia incompiuta. Donne e politica in Italia dall'Ottocento ai nostri giorni* (Milan: Angeli, 2007), p. 148.

47. M. Seymour, *Debating Divorce in Italy: Marriage and the Making of Modern Italians, 1860–1974* (Basingstoke: Palgrave Macmillan, 2006), chap. 7.

48. On the relationship between the various Catholic organisations, see M. C. Giuntella, 'Il rapporto con gli altri movimenti cattolici in Italia', in Dau Novelli (ed.), *Donne del nostro tempo.*

49. Galli and Prandi, *Patterns of Political Participation*, p. 192.

50. C. Dau Novelli, ' "Daremo sei milioni di voti". Il movimento delle donne cattoliche nei primi anni della Repubblica', *Memoria*, 21 (1987): 45–55, p. 52.

51. Taricone, *Il Centro Italiano Femminile*, pp. 78–99.

52. P. Gabrielli, *'Il club delle virtuose'. Udi e Cif nelle Marche dall'antifascismo alla guerra fredda* (Ancona: Il lavoro editoriale, 2000), p. 112.

53. D. Gagliani, 'Welfare State come umanesimo e antipatronage. Un'esperienza delle donne nel secondo dopoguerra', in D. Gagliani and M. Salvati (eds), *La sfera pubblica femminile. Percorsi di storia delle donne in età contemporanea* (Bologna: Clueb, 1992).

54. Taricone, *Il Centro Italiano Femminile*, p. 51.

55. L. Caldwell, *Italian Family Matters* (Basingstoke: Macmillan, 1991), p. 48.

56. On the CIF and UDI rituals and festivals, see Gabrielli, *'Il club delle virtuose'*, pp. 211–45.

57. However, for a highly critical view of UDI and CIF's approach to emancipation, see N. Rothenberg, 'The Catholic and the Communist Women's Press in Post-War Italy: an Analysis of *Cronache* and *Noi Donne*', *Modern Italy*, 11 (2006): 285–304.

58. S. Piccone Stella, *La prima generazione* (Milan: Angeli, 1993), pp. 127–8.

59. Salvatici and Scattigno, *In una stagione diversa*, p. 108.

60. Testimony in M. Addis Saba et al. (eds), *Donne e Costituente* (Rome: Presidenza del Consiglio dei Ministri, 1996), p. 13.

61. Guadagnini, 'Le donne nel Parlamento', p. 145.

62. A. Verzelli, 'Politica e altre fatiche. Le donne in consiglio comunale a Bologna 1945–1985', in Gagliani and Salvati (eds), *La sfera pubblica.*

63. A. Garofalo, *L'italiana in Italia* (Bari: Laterza, 1956), p. 105.

64. M. Tambor, 'Prostitutes and Politicians: the Women's Rights Movement in the Legge Merlin Debates', in P. Morris (ed.), *Women in Italy, 1945–1960* (London: Palgrave Macmillan, 2007), p. 132.

65. Cited in S. Bellassai, *La legge del desiderio. Il progetto Merlin e l'Italia degli anni Cinquanta* (Rome: Carocci, 2006), p. 107.

66. Cited in Tambor, 'Prostitutes and Politicians', p. 137.

67. On male attitudes to the Merlin law, see S. Bellassai, 'Un mondo senza Wanda. Opinione maschile e legge Merlin (1948–1958)', *Genesis*, II/2 (2003), 67–98.

68. Cited in Galoppini, *Il lungo viaggio*, p. 236.

69. Ibid., p. 283.

9 'Io Sono Mia': Feminism in the 'Great Cultural Revolution', 1968–80

1. Some Italians call the women's movement of the 1970s 'neo-feminism' (to distinguish it from what in English would be called first-wave feminism). I have used 'feminism' as more readily comprehensible to English-language readers.
2. Interview with MLD activist Liliana Ingargiola, in *Memoria*, 19–20 (1987): 49–65, p. 51.
3. Y. Ergas, 'Feminisms of the 1970s', in F. Thébaud (ed.), *A History of Women in the West*, vol. V: *Toward a Cultural Identity in the Twentieth Century* (Cambridge, MA: Belknap Harvard, 1994), p. 533.
4. Cited in F. Lussana, 'Le donne e la modernizzazione: il neofemminismo degli anni settanta', in *Storia dell'Italia repubblicana*, vol. 3: *L'Italia nella crisi mondiale. L'ultimo ventennio* (Turin: Einaudi, 1997), p. 524.
5. A. Ribero, *Una questione di libertà. Il femminismo degli anni Settanta* (Turin: Rosenberg & Sellier, 1999), p. 106.
6. Two useful guides to Italian feminist thinking are P. Bono and S. Kemp (eds), *Italian Feminist Thought: A Reader* (Oxford: Blackwell, 1991); S. Kemp and P. Bono (eds), *The Lonely Mirror: Italian Perspectives on Feminist Theory* (London: Routledge, 1993).
7. Cited in A. Rossi-Doria, 'Ipotesi per una storia che verrà', in T. Bertilotti and A. Scattigno (eds), *Il femminismo degli anni Settanta* (Rome: Viella, 2005), p. 5.
8. L. Passerini, 'Gender Relations', in D. Forgacs and R. Lumley (eds), *Italian Cultural Studies: An Introduction* (Oxford: Oxford University Press, 1996), p. 150.
9. Cited in R. Lumley, *States of Emergency: Cultures of Revolt in Italy from 1968 to 1978*, (London: Verso, 1990), p. 317.
10. Ribero, *Una questione di libertà*, p. 139.
11. Cited in E. Guerra, 'Una nuova soggettività: femminismo e femminismi nel passaggio degli anni Settanta', in Bertilotti and Scattigno, *Il femminismo degli anni Settanta*, p. 42.
12. J. Adler Hellman, *Journeys Among Women: Feminism in Five Italian Cities* (New York: Oxford University Press, 1987), p. 68.
13. A. Crispino, cited in Rossi-Doria, 'Ipotesi per una storia che verrà', p. 7.
14. Cited in Guerra, 'Una nuova soggettività', p. 42.
15. L. Passerini, *Storie di donne e femministe* (Turin: Rosenberg & Sellier, 1987), p. 168.
16. D. Colombo, 'The Italian Feminist Movement', *Women's Studies International Quarterly*, 4 (1981): 461–9, p. 465.
17. L. Passerini, 'The Women's Movement in Italy and the Events of 1968', in M. Cicioni and N. Prunster (eds), *Visions and Revisions: Women in Italian Culture* (Providence: Berg, 1993), p. 178n.
18. Adler Hellman, *Journeys Among Women*, pp. 169, 172.
19. Ibid., p. 169.
20. Testimony of Bianca Maria Pomeranzi, *Memoria*, 19–20 (1987): 207–10, p. 209.

21. See Adler Hellman, *Journeys Among Women*.
22. L. Ellena, 'Spazi e culture politiche nel femminismo torinese. Un percorso tra memoria e ricerca storica dagli anni Novanta ad oggi', in Bertilotti and Scattigno, *Il femminismo degli anni Settanta*, pp. 231–2.
23. Cited in Passerini, *Storie di donne e femministe*, p. 120.
24. See L. Caldwell, 'Courses for Women: the Example of the 150 Hours in Italy', *Feminist Review*, 14 (1983): 71–83.
25. See Y. Ergas, '1968–79. Feminism and the Italian Party System: Women's Politics in a Decade of Turmoil', *Comparative Politics*, 14 (1981–2): 253–79.
26. C. Dau Novelli, 'Il CIF e la società italiana (1944–1981)', in C. Dau Novelli (ed.), *Donne del nostro tempo. Il Centro Italiano Femminile (1945–1995)* (Rome: Studium, 1995), p. 27.
27. Testimony of Tina Magnano, in *Memoria*, 19–20 (1987): 215–18, p. 217.
28. Cited in A. Buttafuoco, 'Italy: the Feminist Challenge', in C. Bloggs and D. Plotke (eds), *The Politics of Eurocommunism: Socialism in Transition* (Boston: South End Press, 1980), pp. 198–9.
29. See G. Zuffa, 'Le doppie militanze. Donna comunista, donna femminista', *Memoria*, 19–20 (1987): 38–47.
30. Adler Hellman, *Journeys Among Women*, pp. 102, 118.
31. Rossi-Doria, 'Ipotesi per una storia che verrà', p. 6.
32. R. Pesenti, 'Fuori scena', in C. Liotti et al., *'Volevamo cambiare il mondo'. Memorie e storie delle donne dell'UDI in Emilia Romagna* (Rome: Carocci, 2002), p. 78.
33. Adler Hellman, *Journeys Among Women*, p. 121.
34. Ibid., p. 217.
35. Cited in Liotti et al., *'Volevamo cambiare il mondo'*, p. 92.
36. Adler Hellman, *Journeys Among Women*, pp. 144–5.
37. See L. Chiavola Birnbaum, *Liberazione della donna: Feminism in Italy* (Middletown: Wesleyan University Press, 1986), chap. 9.
38. M. Weber, 'Italy', in J. Lowenduski and J. Hills (eds), *The Politics of the Second Electorate* (London: Routledge & Kegan Paul, 1981), p. 193.
39. Ibid., p. 203.
40. Ribero, *Una questione di libertà*, p. 151.
41. L. Caldwell, 'Church, State and Family: the Women's Movement in Italy', in A. Kuhn and A. M. Wolpe (eds), *Feminism and Materialism* (London: Routledge & Kegan Paul, 1978), p. 84.
42. J. Barkan, *Visions of Emancipation: The Italian Workers' Movement since 1945* (New York: Praeger, 1984), p. 140.
43. L. Caldwell, 'Abortion in Italy', *Feminist Review*, 7 (1981): 49–63, p. 61.
44. Buttafuoco, 'Italy: the Feminist Challenge', p. 202.
45. P. Gaiotti de Biase, 'Cattoliche e cattolici di fronte all'aborto e il mutamento degli equilibri della Repubblica', *Genesis*, III/I (2004): 57–86, p. 67.
46. See T. Pitch, 'Tra diritti sociali e cittadinanza. Il movimento delle donne e la legge sulla violenza sessuale', *Problemi del socialismo*, 27/28 (1983): 192–214.
47. V. Pizzini Gambetta, 'Becoming Visible: Did the Emancipation of Women Reach the Sicilian Mafia?', in A. Cento Bull and A. Giorgio (eds), *Speaking Out and Silencing: Culture, Society and Politics in Italy in the 1970s* (Oxford: Legenda, 2006), p. 207.

48. D. Della Porta, 'Specificità delle donne e violenza politica', *Rivista di storia contemporanea*, 18 (1989): 116–26.

49. Cited in Passerini, *Storie di donne e femministe*, p. 69.

50. On the causes of the decline of the movement, two good analyses are Adler Hellman, *Journeys Among Women*, chap. 8; Rossi-Doria, 'Ipotesi per una storia che verrà'.

51. S. Salvatici and A. Scattigno, *In una stagione diversa. Le donne in Palazzo Vecchio 1946/1970* (Florence: Edizioni Comune Aperto, 1998), p. 74.

52. Adler Hellman, *Journeys Among Women*, pp. 199–200.

53. Cited in ibid., p. 121.

54. L. Passerini, 'Quale memoria storica per il movimento delle donne in Italia?' in M. Palazzi and A. Scattigno, *Discutendo di storia, soggettività, ricerca, biografia* (Turin: Rosenberg & Sellier, 1990), p. 46.

55. D. Del Boca, 'Women in a Changing Workplace: the Case of Italy', in J. Jenson, E. Hagan and C. Reddy (eds), *Feminization of the Labour Force: Paradoxes and Promises* (Cambridge: Polity Press, 1988), p. 123.

56. Weber, 'Italy', p. 192.

57. Del Boca, 'Women in a Changing Workplace', p. 124.

58. Rossi-Doria, 'Ipotesi per una storia che verrà', p. 1.

59. A. Signorelli, 'Women in Italy in the 1970s', in Cento Bull and Giorgio, *Speaking Out and Silencing*, p. 42.

60. M. De Giorgio, ' "Donne e società". Dieci anni della rivista del movimento femminile DC', *Memoria*, 2 (1981): 128–32, p. 131.

10 The 'Dual Presence': More Work and Fewer Children in the Age of Materialism

1. M. Pisati, 'La domenica andando alla messa', *Polis*, 14 (2000): 115–36.

2. D. Della Porta, 'The Women's Movement, the Left, and the State: Continuities and Changes in the Italian Case', in L. A. Banaszak et al. (eds), *Women's Movements Facing the Reconfigured State* (Cambridge: Cambridge University Press, 2003), p. 49.

3. Ibid.

4. F. Chiaromonte, 'Autonomia in uno spazio misto. L'Arci donna', *Memoria*, 13 (1986): 63–71, p. 67.

5. P. Bono and S. Kemp (eds), *Italian Feminist Thought: A Reader* (Oxford: Blackwell, 1991), p. 139.

6. B. M. Pomeranzi, 'Differenza lesbica e lesbofemminismo', *Memoria*, 13 (1986): 72–8.

7. M. Guadagnini, 'A "Partitocrazia" without Women: the Case of the Italian Party System', in J. Lowenduski and P. Norris (eds), *Gender and Party Politics* (London: Sage, 1993), p. 178.

8. F. Anderlini, 'La DC: iscritti e modello di partito', *Polis*, 3 (1989): 277–304, pp. 295–7.

9. Cited in C. Valentini, *Le donne fanno paura* (Milan: Il Saggiatore, 1997), p. 178.

10. E. Fattorini, 'L'impegno politico delle donne cattoliche', in *Una memoria mancata. Donne cattoliche nel '900 italiano* (Milan: Vita e Pensiero, 1998), p. 161.

11. See A. J. Everhart, 'Predicting the Effect of Italy's Long-awaited Rape Law Reform on the "Land of Machismo"', *Vanderbilt Journal of Transnational Law*, 31 (1998): 671–718.

12. Cited in A. Babbini, 'La rappresentanza femminile alla Camera dei Deputati nella XII Legislatura', in M. Addis Saba et al. (eds), *Alle origini della Repubblica. Donne e Costituente* (Rome: Commissione nazionale per la parità e le pari opportunità tra uomo e donna, 1996), p. 187.

13. Cited in M. Guadagnini, 'The Debate on Women's Quotas in Italian Electoral Legislation', *Swiss Review of Political Science*, 4 (1998): 97–102, p. 98.

14. See M. Guadagnini, 'Gendering the Debate on Political Representation in Italy: a Difficult Challenge', in J. Lovenduski (ed.), *State Feminism and Political Representation* (Cambridge: Cambridge University Press, 2005).

15. S. Ulivieri, 'Alfabetizzazione, processi di scolarizzazione femminile e percorsi professionali tra tradizione e mutamento', in S. Ulivieri (ed.), *Educazione e ruolo femminile. La condizione delle donne in Italia dal dopoguerra a oggi* (Florence: La Nuova Italia, 1992), pp. 193, 209.

16. M. Dei, 'Donne e istruzione: verso una parità apparente? Recenti tendenze della componente femminile dell'istruzione in Italia', *Polis*, 12 (1998): 459–79, p. 460.

17. Valentini, *Le donne fanno paura*, p. 87.

18. Dei, 'Donne e istruzione'.

19. A. Colombo, 'Il mito del lavoro domestico: struttura e cambiamenti in Italia (1970–2003)', *Polis*, 14 (2005): 435–64, p. 443.

20. A. Del Re, 'The Paradoxes of Italian Law and Practice', in L. Hantrais (ed.), *Gendered Policies in Europe* (London: Macmillan, 2000), p. 112.

21. I. Bison, M. Pisati and A. Schizzerotto, 'Disuguaglianze di genere e storie lavorative', in S. Piccone Stella and C. Saraceno (eds), *Genere. La costruzione sociale del femminile e del maschile* (Bologna: Il Mulino, 1996), p. 277.

22. C. Saraceno, 'The Italian Family from the 1960s to the Present', *Modern Italy*, 9 (2004): 47–57, p. 50.

23. M. C. Meini, 'Lavoro e professioni femminili in Italia: dirlo con i numeri', *Polis*, 3 (1989): 249–73, p. 256.

24. Del Re, 'The Paradoxes of Italian Law', pp. 116–18.

25. F. Bimbi, 'Gender, "Gift Relationship" and Welfare State Cultures in Italy', in J. Lewis (ed.), *Women and Social Policies in Europe* (Aldershot: Edward Elgar, 1993), p. 146.

26. Meini, 'Lavoro e professioni femminili', pp. 252–3.

27. Bimbi, 'Gender, "Gift Relationship"', p. 145.

28. P. Ferrara, 'Le donne negli uffici (1863–2002)', in G. Melis (ed.), *Impiegati* (Turin: Rosenberg & Sellier, 2004), p. 149.

29. S. Ulivieri, 'Donne e insegnamento dal dopoguerra a oggi. La femminilizzazione del corpo insegnante', in *Essere donne insegnanti. Storia, professionalità e cultura di genere* (Turin: Rosenberg & Sellier, 1996), p. 79.

30. D. Del Boca, 'Labour Policies, Economic Flexibility and Women's Work: the Italian Experience', in E. Drew et al. (eds), *Women, Work and the Family in Europe* (London: Routledge, 1998), p. 126.

31. R. Tarro, 'La donna e l'impresa', in R. Longo (ed.), *Donne e lavoro* (Rome: Bonanno, 2006), pp. 163–4.

32. M. Blim, 'Italian Women after Development: Employment, Entrepreneurship and Domestic Work in the Third Italy', *History of the Family*, 6 (2001): 257–70.

33. J. Rubery (ed.), *Women's Employment in Europe: Trends and Prospects* (London: Routledge, 1999), p. 55.

34. Ibid., p. 56.

35. Valentini, *Le donne fanno paura*, p. 99.

36. Rubery, *Women's Employment in Europe*, p. 255.

37. Del Boca, 'Labour Policies, Economic Flexibility', pp. 129–30.

38. R. Trifiletti, 'La famiglia e il lavoro delle donne', in M. Barbagli and C. Saraceno (eds), *Lo stato delle famiglie in Italia* (Bologna: Il Mulino, 1997), p. 210.

39. Cited in Valentini, *Le donne fanno paura*, p. 136.

40. Ibid., p. 148.

41. P. Ginsborg, *Italy and its Discontents, 1980–2001* (London: Penguin, 2001), p. 313.

42. Valentini, *Le donne fanno paura*, p. 80.

43. J. Henshall Momsen, 'Maids on the Move: Victim or Victor', in J. Momsen (ed.), *Gender, Migration and Domestic Service* (London: Routledge, 1999), p. 7.

44. Colombo, 'Il mito del lavoro domestico'.

45. Ibid., p. 446.

46. M. Orsini-Jones and F. Gattullo, 'Migrant Women in Italy: National Trends and Local Perspectives', in F. Anthias and G. Lazaridis (eds), *Gender and Migration in Southern Europe: Women on the Move* (Oxford: Berg, 2000), p. 127.

47. V. Chell-Robinson, 'Female Migrants in Italy: Coping in a Country of New Immigration', in ibid., p. 115.

48. Cited in J. Andall, *Gender, Migration and Domestic Service: The Politics of Black Women in Italy* (Aldershot: Ashgate, 2000), p. 159.

49. J. Andall, 'Hierarchy and Interdependence: the Emergence of a Service Caste in Europe', in J. Andall (ed.), *Gender and Ethnicity in Contemporary Europe* (Oxford: Berg, 2003), p. 49.

50. Cited in Andall, *Gender, Migration*, p. 170.

51. Cited in R. Salazar Parreñas, *Servants of Globalisation: Women, Migration and Domestic Work* (Stanford, CA: Stanford University Press, 2001), p. 119.

52. Andall, *Gender, Migration*, p. 34.

53. Cited in ibid., p. 265.

54. Cited in ibid., p. 286.

55. A. Roversi, 'La prostituzione da strada delle donne immigrate a Modena', *Polis*, 15 (2001): 35–54.

56. G. Campani, 'Migrant Women in Southern Europe: Social Exclusion, Domestic Work and Prostitution in Italy', in R. King et al. (eds), *Eldorado or Fortress: Migration to Southern Europe* (London: Macmillan, 2000), p. 155.

57. Ginsborg, *Italy and its Discontents*, p. 77.

58. Valentini, *Le donne fanno paura*, p. 65.

59. Rubery, *Women's Employment in Europe*, p. 96.

60. M. Barbagli et al., *Fare famiglia in Italia. Un secolo di cambiamenti* (Bologna: Il Mulino, 2003), p. 122.

61. Rubery, *Women's Employment in Europe*, p. 95.

62. L. L. Sabbadini, 'Le convivenze "more-uxorio"', in Barbagli and Saraceno (eds), *Lo stato delle famiglie*.

63. A. L. Zanatta, 'Le famiglie con un solo genitore', in Barbagli and Saraceno (eds), *Lo stato delle famiglie*.

64. Barbagli et al., *Fare famiglia in Italia*, p. 75.

65. Ibid., p. 204.

66. C. Facchini, 'Gli anziani e la solidarietà tra generazioni', in Barbagli and Saraceno (eds), *Lo stato delle famiglie*, p. 288.

67. M. Barbagli, 'Family and Kinship in Italy', in M. Gullestad and M. Segalen (eds), *Family and Kinship in Europe* (London: Pinter, 1997), p. 34.

68. L. L. Sabbadini and R. Palomba, *Tempi diversi. L'uso del tempo di uomini e donne nell'Italia di oggi* (Rome: Presidenza del Consiglio dei Ministri, 1994), p. 58.

69. Valentini, *Le donne fanno paura*, pp. 75–6.

70. A. Treves, *Le nascite e la politica nell'Italia del Novecento* (Milan: LED, 2001), pp. 465, 467.

71. M. Barbagli and C. Saraceno, 'Introduzione', in Barbagli and Saraceno (eds), *Lo stato delle famiglie*, p. 10.

72. G. Dalla Zuanna, 'The Banquet of Aeolus: a Familistic Interpretation of Italy's Lowest Low Fertility', in *Demographic Research*, 4 (2001): 133–62, p. 147.

73. The results of this project are summarised at: www.istat.it/istat/eventi/cnel2003/sintesiperlastampa.pdf

74. D. Giovannini, 'Are Fathers Changing? Comparing some Different Images on Sharing of Childcare and Domestic Work', in Drew et al., *Women, Work and the Family*, pp. 198–9.

75. Sabbadini and Palomba, *Tempi diversi*.

76. Valentini, *Le donne fanno paura*, p. 60.

77. R. Palidda, 'Lavoro, pari opportunità e sviluppo', in Longo, *Donne e lavoro*, p. 94.

78. C. Saraceno, 'Le politiche per le famiglie', in Barbagli and Saraceno (eds), *Lo stato delle famiglie*, p. 301.

79. Blim, 'Italian Women after Development', pp. 266–7.

80. Cited in Treves, *Le nascite e la politica*, p. 493.

81. Cited in ibid., p. 496n.

82. Ginsborg, *Italy and its Discontents*, p. 71.

Conclusion

1. L. Passerini, 'Gender Relations', in D. Forgacs and R. Lumley (eds), *Italian Cultural Studies: An Introduction* (Oxford: Oxford University Press, 1996), p. 157.

2. C. Valentini, *Le donne fanno paura* (Milan: Il Saggiatore, 1997), p. 54.

Select Bibliography

J. Adler Hellman, *Journeys Among Women: Feminism in Five Italian Cities* (New York: Oxford University Press, 1987).

J. Andall, *Gender, Migration and Domestic Service: The Politics of Black Women in Italy* (Aldershot: Ashgate, 2000).

P. Bono and S. Kemp (eds), *Italian Feminist Thought: A Reader* (Oxford: Blackwell, 1991).

A. Buttafuoco, 'Motherhood as a Political Strategy: the Role of the Italian Women's Movement in the Creation of the Cassa Nazionale di Maternità', in G. Bock and P. Thane (eds), *Maternity and Gender Policies: Women and the Rise of the European Welfare States, 1880s–1950s* (London: Routledge, 1991).

L. Caldwell, *Italian Family Matters* (Basingstoke: Macmillan, 1991).

V. De Grazia, *How Fascism Ruled Women: Italy, 1922–1945* (Berkeley and Oxford: California University Press, 1992).

D. Del Boca, 'Labour Policies, Economic Flexibility and Women's Work: the Italian Experience', in E. Drew et al. (eds), *Women, Work and the Family in Europe* (London: Routledge, 1998).

D. Della Porta, 'The Women's Movement, the Left, and the State: Continuities and Changes in the Italian Case', in L. A. Banaszak et al. (eds), *Women's Movements Facing the Reconfigured State* (Cambridge: Cambridge University Press, 2003).

M. Fraddosio, 'The Fallen Hero: the Myth of Mussolini and Fascist Women in the Italian Social Republic', *Journal of Contemporary History*, 31, 1 (1996): 99–124.

M. Gibson, *Prostitution and the State in Italy, 1860–1915* (New Brunswick: Rutgers University Press, 1986).

M. Gibson, 'Women and the Left in the Shadow of Fascism in Interwar Italy', in H. Gruber and P. Graves (eds), *Women and Socialism: Socialism and Women* (New York and Oxford: Berghahn, 1998).

C. Ipsen, *Dictating Demography: The Problem of Population in Fascist Italy* (Cambridge: Cambridge University Press, 1996).

F. Lagorio, 'Italian Widows of the First World War', in F. Coetzee et al. (eds), *Authority, Identity and the Social History of the Great War* (Providence and Oxford: Berghahn, 1995).

C. La Vigna, 'The Marxist Ambivalence towards Women: Between Socialism and Feminism in the Italian Socialist Party', in M. J. Boxer and J. Quartaert (eds), *Socialist Women* (New York: Elsevier, 1978).

P. Morris (ed.), *Women in Italy, 1945–1960: An Interdisciplinary Study* (New York: Palgrave Macmillan, 2006).

L. Passerini, 'Gender Relations', in D. Forgacs and R. Lumley (eds), *Italian Cultural Studies: An Introduction* (Oxford: Oxford University Press, 1996).

A. Rossi-Doria, 'Italian Women Enter Politics', in C. Duchen and I. Bandhauer Schoffman (eds), *When the War was Over: Women, War and Peace in Europe, 1940–56* (London: Leicester University Press, 2000).

C. Saraceno, 'The Italian Family from the 1960s to the Present', *Modern Italy*, 9, 1 (2004): 47–57.

C. Saraceno, 'Women, Family, and the Law, 1750–1942', *Journal of Family History*, 15, 1 (1990): 427–42.

M. Seymour, *Debating Divorce in Italy: Marriage and the Making of Modern Italians, 1860–1974* (Basingstoke: Palgrave Macmillan, 2006).

A. Signorelli, 'Women in Italy in the 1970s', in A. Cento Bull and A. Giorgio (eds), *Speaking Out and Silencing: Culture, Society and Politics in Italy in the 1970s* (Oxford: Legenda, 2006).

J. Slaughter, *Women in the Italian Resistance, 1943–1945* (Denver, CO: Arden, 1997).

P. Willson (ed.), *Gender, Family and Sexuality: The Private Sphere in Italy, 1860–1945* (Basingstoke: Palgrave Macmillan, 2004).

P. Willson, 'Italy', in K. Passmore (ed.), *Women, Gender and Fascism in Europe, 1919–1945* (Manchester: Manchester University Press, 2003).

P. Willson, *Peasant Women and Politics in Fascist Italy: The Massaie Rurali* (London: Routledge, 2002).

P. Willson, 'Saints and Heroines: Re-writing the History of Italian Women in the Resistance', in T. Kirk and A. McElligot (eds), *Opposing Fascism: Community, Authority and Resistance in Europe* (Cambridge: Cambridge University Press, 1999).

Index